SHAFTESBURY'S PHILOSOPHY OF RELIGION AND ETHICS

SHAFTESBURY'S PHILOSOPHY of RELIGION and ETHICS

A STUDY IN ENTHUSIASM

Stanley Grean

OHIO UNIVERSITY
PRESS

1967

The Right Honorable Anthony Ashley Cooper Earl of Shaftesbury, Baron Ashley of Winbourn St. Giles, & Lord Cooper of Pawlett.

J. Closterman Pinx.   Sim: Gribelin Sculp.

ANTHONY ASHLEY COOPER, THIRD EARL OF SHAFTESBURY

FOR PAT AND NICK
All Ways

ACKNOWLEDGEMENTS

This book represents an extensive rewriting of a doctoral dissertation on the same subject completed under the Joint Committee on Graduate Instruction at Columbia University. It would be impossible for me here to adequately communicate my debt to the many teachers at Columbia University and Union Theological Seminary who contributed to my intellectual and spiritual growth. Herbert W. Schneider, Professor Emeritus of Philosophy, Columbia University, now at the Claremont Graduate School, California, started me in my investigations of eighteenth-century thought, and James Gutmann, also Professor Emeritus of Philosophy at Columbia, suggested I focus on Shaftesbury. Marjorie Hope Nicolson, Professor Emeritus of English at Columbia, gave me encouragement and valuable suggestions, and Horace L. Friess, Professor of Philosophy, Columbia, helped me greatly in the completion of my dissertation. Their keen and always humane scholarship has provided me with a model and a stimulus.

The rewriting of my earlier research in the form of this book was done during a semester off made possible by a grant from the John C. Baker Fund, endowed by Mr. and Mrs. Edwin C. Kennedy. I want to thank them for this type of assistance which has meant so much to me as well as to other scholars at Ohio University.

The third part of Chapter X, subtitled "Self-Interest and Public Interest," appeared in slightly modified form as an article entitled "Self-Interest and Public Interest in Shaftesbury's Philosophy," in the *Journal of the History of Philosophy,* II (April, 1964), pp. 37–45, and is reprinted here by permission of the editors.

Ohio University   STANLEY GREAN
Athens, Ohio

PREFACE

If the influence of Locke can be gauged by the nineteen editions that his *Essay Concerning Human Understanding* went through in the eighteenth century, the somewhat less but still great influence of Shaftesbury can be measured by the eleven editions of his *Characteristics* between 1711 and 1790. Shaftesbury's philosophy was in great vogue in England in the first half of the eighteenth century; Goldsmith wrote soon after the middle of the century that he had "more imitators in Britain than any other writer I know. . . ." [1] Herder generously styled Shaftesbury the "beloved Plato of Europe," and in 1794 the German thinker could justly write that "this virtuoso of humanity . . . has had a marked influence on the best minds of our century, on those who have striven with determination and sincerity for the true, the beautiful, and the good." [2] After reading "The Moralists," Leibniz wrote: "I found in it almost all of my *Theodicy* before it saw the light of day. . . . If I had seen this work before my *Theodicy* was published, I should have profited as I ought and should have borrowed its great passages." [3] The power of Shaftesbury's thought is not only borne out by these testimonials but is seen in the very strength and virulence of the attacks made on his philosophy in the eighteenth century, a notable example being Berkeley's *Alciphron; or, The Minute Philosopher* (1732), wherein Shaftesbury is so unfairly represented.

The roster of those who were influenced by Shaftesbury's philosophy in word and in spirit reads like a list of the literary and philosophic greats of the Enlightenment. He is most famous, of course, as the founder of the "moral sense school" in ethics. Not only did Francis Hutcheson, Bishop Butler, and Adam Smith draw heavily from him but to a remarkable extent Hume, in his ethical writings, worked Shaftesburian veins of thought. Though the Scottish philosopher made some telling criticisms of "the elegant Lord Shaftesbury," he also praised him as "a great genius." [4] Shaftesbury contributed extensively to the Deistic movement and was a friend of John Toland and Anthony Collins. In literature he influenced such men as Addison, James Thomson, Akenside, and Fielding. His ideas entered the stream of continental thought through his friendship and personal contacts with Pierre Bayle and Jean Le Clerc, among others, as well as through translations of his writings into French and German.[5] In France, Voltaire, Diderot, and Rousseau were influenced by him. Diderot may have written the penetrating comparison of Locke and Shaftesbury in the *Encyclopédie* (1751):

There are very few errors in Locke, and too few truths in milord Shaftesbury: the former is only a man of vast intellect, penetrating and exact, while the latter is a genius of the first order. Locke has seen; Shaftesbury has created, constructed, and edified. To Locke we owe some great truths coldly perceived, methodically developed, and dryly presented; and to Shaftesbury, some brilliant schemes often poorly grounded, though full of sublime truths. Even in his moments of error he pleases and persuades by the charms of his eloquence.[6]

Germany proved to be particularly receptive to Shaftesbury's philosophy, for even as his star was waning in England his concepts were affecting Lessing, Mendelssohn, Kant, Wieland, Goethe, Herder, and Schiller. The Augustan philosopher's aesthetic theory made an important contribution to the rise of Romanticism in Germany.

Many of Shaftesbury's ideas remained at the center of controversy in England through the third quarter of the eighteenth century. His defence of ridicule, his concept of the moral sense, his optimistic metaphysics, and his attack on the God of retribution, were among the aspects of his thought that continued to generate dispute. He played a key role in the development of ethics, aesthetics, and the philosophy of religion. Shaftesbury marks an important transition from the Cambridge Platonism of the seventeenth century to the ethical intuitionism and liberal theology of the eighteenth. He helped to pose some of the basic issues of ethics in the Enlightenment—the problem of the moral sense, the relation of reason and feeling and of self-interest and public interest. In aesthetics he contributed to the developing conceptions of the sublime, of creative imagination, and of genius. His doctrine of disinterested pleasure was as important in ethics as in aesthetics and philosophy of religion. Shaftesbury's religious theories laid the groundwork for later attempts to formulate a religion "within the limits of reason alone." Yet, despite all this, Shaftesbury's reputation fell into a decline in the fourth quarter of the eighteenth century in English-speaking countries from which it has only recently emerged.

His status in the nineteenth century was summarized by

Leslie Stephen in the comment that "the third Lord Shaftesbury is one of the writers whose reputation is scarcely com-
mensurate with the influence which he once exerted." [7] After
the turn of the century, new editions of his writings, including
some previously unpublished material, appeared and aroused
some flurries of interest. Yet for decades the only lengthy study
of his philosophy in English was that by Thomas Fowler, published in 1882.[8] There were, of course, occasional journal
articles and brief discussions in surveys of English thought, but
only in the last two decades have there been important signs
of a reassessment of the significance of Shaftesbury. Two books
have been published on him: R. L. Brett's *The Third Earl of
Shaftesbury: A Study in Eighteenth-Century Literary Theory*,[9] an able study which focusses on his aesthetic concepts;
and Alfred O. Aldridge's *Shaftesbury and the Deist Manifesto*,[10] a general treatment of his philosophy which unfortunately has serious failings. A milestone of some import was the
translation into English of two of Ernst Cassirer's historical
works, *The Philosophy of the Enlightenment* [11] and especially
The Platonic Renaissance in England,[12] in both of which the
depth and interest of Shaftesbury's thought is given its true
gauge. It is interesting that German scholars have often shown
a greater appreciation for Shaftesbury's importance and the
distinctive character of his thought than Anglo-American
scholars. There have also been a host of journal articles which,
while varying in quality, do give a better quantitative measure
of the breadth of interest in Shaftesbury's thought in recent
times. Two that are representative and noteworthy are Ernest
Tuveson's "The Importance of Shaftesbury," [13] and Jerome
Stolnitz's "On the Significance of Lord Shaftesbury in Modern
Aesthetic Theory." [14] Shaftesbury has also been given more

attention in several recent histories of thought. Finally, the recent reprinting of Robertson's 1900 edition of the *Characteristics* can be viewed both as a by-product of this revived interest and as the probable stimulus to further study of his ideas.[15]

*   *   *

Anthony Ashley Cooper, the third Earl of Shaftesbury, was born in February, 1671 (N.S.),[16] at the London home of his grandfather, the first Earl, who was one of the most eminent political leaders of his time. The first Earl was an advocate of parliamentary monarchy, a foe of religious intolerance, and a freethinker in religion. The philosopher John Locke was his close friend and secretary, and through the first Earl's influence Locke supervised the education of the young Lord Ashley. Locke was able to apply some of his educational theories, the end-result of which may be some evidence of their soundness. Shaftesbury was tutored at an early age in Latin and Greek and learned to read them both with ease. At eleven he was sent to a private school and the following year to Winchester, where he remained three years. In 1686 he set out on a three-year tour to the Continent, spending considerable time in Italy where, as his son expresses it, he "acquired a great knowledge in the polite arts." Returning after the Glorious Revolution in 1688, Shaftesbury devoted his time to study, concentrating particularly on classical philosophy, and apparently writing the first draft of the "Inquiry Concerning Virtue." An interest in politics, no doubt reinforced by his knowledge of the first Earl's political career, led him to seek political office, and he entered the House of Commons in 1695. Ill health forced him to withdraw from politics in 1698, at which time he traveled to

Holland for a year. There he was a member of an intellectual circle that included Jean Le Clerc, the influential editor and professor of philosophy at the Remonstrant (Arminian) Seminary at Amsterdam; Phillipus Van Limborch, professor of theology at the same institution and long-time defendant of Arminianism; and Pierre Bayle, who had published his *Dictionnaire historique et critique* the year before. In 1698 Shaftesbury's first published writing appeared, the Preface to a collection of the sermons of Benjamin Whichcote, one of the prime movers of Cambridge Platonism. While Shaftesbury was still abroad in 1699, his "Inquiry Concerning Virtue" was published by the Deist John Toland, supposedly without his permission.[17] Returning to England in 1699, Shaftesbury inherited the title upon his father's death. Once again becoming active in politics, he served in the House of Lords in 1700–01. Upon the dissolution of Parliament he returned to his studies, making another trip to Holland in 1703–04. Though the third Earl had attained a position of some importance in the Whig party, the worsening of his asthma made it necessary for him to discontinue his political activities. In general, he supported the Whig party program including such principles as the supremacy of Parliament over Crown, the Protestant succession, religious toleration for dissenters, and opposition to French totalitarianism. Though he regretted his enforced retirement from political life, it was followed by his most productive period of literary activity. He wrote and privately circulated (October, 1705) a first version of "The Moralists," entitled "The Sociable Enthusiast: a Philosophical Adventure." [18] The stir caused by the religious extravagances of the "French prophets" stimulated Shaftesbury to publish his "Letter Concerning Enthusiasm" in 1708. In the following year both "Sensus Communis; an Essay on the Freedom of Wit and Humour" and "The Moralists, A Philosophical Rhapsody" were printed, and in 1710, "Soliloquy, or Advice to an Author." These were gathered together with the revised form of "An Inquiry Concerning Virtue or Merit" [19] and a newly written "Miscellaneous Reflections on the Preceding Treatises" to make the first edition of *Characteristics of Men, Manners, Opinions, Times* in 1711.

Shaftesbury married in 1709, and an only child was born the following year. But as Locke had said, "The sword was too sharp for the scabbard," [20] and the continuing decline of the Earl's health forced him to seek respite in a milder climate. Thus, he set out for Italy in July, 1711. He spent his last fifteen months at Naples, until his death in February, 1713, busily engaged in revising the *Characteristics* for the second edition (1714). Though plagued by his physical ailments, he also found time to write two treatises on art, "A Letter Concerning Design" and "A Notion of the Historical Draught or Tablature of the Judgment of Hercules," and he prepared notes for another projected treatise to be called "Plastics or the Original Progress and Power of Designatory Art." "The Judgment of Hercules" appeared first in French, the language in which it had been written, in the *Journal des Sçavans*, November, 1712 (Vol. LII), and in English the following year. It was reprinted again at the end of the revised edition of the *Characteristics* in 1714 (3 vols.; London). "The Letter Concerning Design" was not printed until it was included in the fifth edition of *Characteristics* in 1732. These two treatises and the notes for the unfinished treatise were part of a larger projected work which Shaftesbury intended to call *Second Characters or the Language of Forms*, but they were not published together under that title until Benjamin Rand's edition of 1914. [21] Several collections of Shaftesbury's letters have been printed: *Several Letters Written by a Noble Lord to a Young Man at the University* (London, 1716); *Letters from the Right Honourable the Late Earl of Shaftesbury to Robert Molesworth, Esq.* (ed. John Toland, London, 1721); and *Original Letters of Locke, Algernon Sidney, and Anthony Lord Shaftesbury* (London, 1830). Another group of letters plus Shaftesbury's philosophical notebooks, which had not been previously published, were combined in an edition by Benjamin Rand under the title, *The Life, Unpublished Letters, and Philosophical Regimen of Anthony, Earl of Shaftesbury.*[22]

One cannot read the philosophical writings of Shaftesbury, his letters, or accounts of his life and character, without being impressed at the extent to which his life and thought were suffused by the spirit of the motto of the house of Shaftesbury, "LOVE, SERVE." In Shaftesbury we encounter that fruitful combination of the active and the contemplative life that is all too rare. Though it is not fashionable today for philosophers to be virtuous men, Shaftesbury believed that true greatness in a philosopher requires not only greatness of thought but greatness of character. However, our subject is his thought rather than his character, though it was his opinion that the two can never finally be separated.[23]

*   *   *

Since Shaftesbury's position on a number of basic philosophical issues is not difficult to grasp, it might seem that a new study of his whole thought was unnecessary. His nineteenth-century commentator, Fowler, wrote that Shaftesbury's thought was "always clear," and yet admitted to being "baffled" by some aspects of it.[24] A study of what has been written about Shaftesbury's philosophy reveals, in fact, that there are real problems in the interpretation of it. One is struck by the sharply different ways in which his thought is presented. His eighteenth-century critic John Brown complained that "the Formalist is under a double Difficulty; not only to conquer his Enemy, but to find him." [25] Another opponent, Thomas Gray, in his six satirical reasons for Shaftesbury's popularity, asserted that "he was reckoned a fine writer, and seems always to mean more than he said." [26] Yet Shaftesbury's friend and supporter, Jean Le Clerc, found the same quality a virtue: *Il a même l'art d'en faire plus entendre, qu'il n'en dit.*[27] A modern commentator, D. D. Raphael, finds "no coherent view . . . about moral theory in general" in Shaftesbury's writings,[28] an opinion that has some currency. John Laird observes that he is easy to read but not necessarily to follow, and finds the root of the difficulty in his attempt "to say half a dozen things at once," for "Shaftesbury conjoined . . . what his successors were at pain to separate." [29]

How can Shaftesbury be on the one hand clear and on the other hand rather difficult, if not incomprehensible? There are several contributing causes. One is his heavy use of irony and satire, particularly when dealing with religious issues. He found it necessary to express himself indirectly when dealing with sensitive areas of orthodox doctrine, and some interpreters have been misled by this. Another reason is that noted by Laird, that the Augustan philosopher tried to unite what others were to separate, as, for example, moral feeling and discursive reason. A third factor is Shaftesbury's method of exposition: he was no simple thinker—he rarely formulated a concept without modifying or qualifying it. Thus, the deeper one penetrates into his thought the more one appreciates its complex and subtle character. The easy turn of a phrase by this brilliant stylist of the English language may lead the reader to miss the hard thought it encloses. Of his writings, only the "Inquiry Concerning Virtue" has a systematic or logical order in the strict sense. In contrast, his other writings have a structrue which might be characterized as aesthetic or dramatic, i.e., determined by the needs of persuasion. Yet Shaftesbury's arguments are often carefully worked out and are not merely empty rhetorical devices or appeals to emotion. Not that he is free of these—he makes extensive use of them, for he consciously appeals to the heart as well as the head. Nevertheless, there is a logical structure that sustains his thought and a rigor that careful inspection discloses, but which the hasty reader may miss.

Little wonder then that interpretations differ and that one finds him variously labeled an empiricist, a precursor of Kant, a modern Stoic, or a Neoplatonist. Despite the fact that he was a defender of religion and theism, he has been charged with attacking religion and advocating atheism. Though he stressed the importance of religious feeling or "enthusiasm," he has been categorized as a rationalist and a Deist. And though Shaftesbury insisted upon the use of the intellect in moral judgment, he has been accused of assigning moral decision to mere instinct or blind feeling. Some have dismissed him as a rather unoriginal Neoclassicist, while others find him an original contributor to aesthetic theory and a precursor of the Romantics. Another important reason for these varying interpretations is the dialectical character of Shaftesbury's thought. The extent to which he was committed to a dialectical method has not been adequately recognized by commentators.[30] Yet the English philosopher speaks at length of the need for inner dialogue or "soliloquy" as a means of intellectual self-development; a dialogue like "The Moralists" is an externalized literary form of such an internal "discussion." He was aware of the inevitable polarities of human experience—reason and emotion, theory and practice, self-interest and public interest—and he tried to formulate a philosophy that would both take account of and do justice to them in a coherent whole. It is true that Shaftesbury attempted to join what others were "at pains to separate," but the result is a richly humane philosophy that comprehends a broad range of human experience. It is always better to be wise than merely consistent.

This study is an attempt to see Shaftesbury's philosophy of religion and ethics as a whole, to interpret it dialectically, and to correct exaggerations that have been made of one or another aspect of his thought to the detriment of others. I wish, in particular, to point out the centrality of love and enthusiasm in Shaftesbury's philosophy which Anglo-American scholars have for the most part failed to appreciate adequately. Only when we see Shaftesbury's vision of man and Nature and God as the product of enthusiasm do we grasp its true dynamic character.

CONTENTS

PART ONE

CHAPTER ONE

PHILOSOPHY: TRUE and FALSE

Shaftesbury compares himself to an architect who, when called upon to repair part of an old building, points out that it has fundamental defects and proceeds to design an entirely new building. This represents his attitude toward much of the philosophy that preceded him in the medieval and early modern period, with the partial exception, as will be noted, of the Cambridge Platonists. He saw his philosophy as embodying something new and different, and he shared the exhilaration felt by many thinkers in his time stemming from the belief that they were opening up new dimensions of thought. (II, 251 f.)

Philosophy itself, Shaftesbury believed, was a relatively late development, preceded by the growth of religion, government, language, and the arts, though "it was long clearing itself from the affected dress of sophists, or enthusiastic air of poets, and appeared late in its genuine, simple, and just beauty." (II, 240 f.) The Greeks brought philosophy to its perfection, but Shaftesbury considered that it had subsequently gone astray. Shaftesbury's admiration for Greek and Roman thought and his debt to it has always been recognized.[1] Yet Cassirer has overstated the case in saying that

he feels no kinship with contemporary philosophy but seeks other intellectual and historical models. It is only necessary to open Shaftesbury's philosophical diary to become aware of this aloofness toward his own time. There is scarcely an echo here of the problems affecting his era, or of the intellectual and practical decisions with which this era is confronted. Its concern lies beyond these urgent questions of the present; hence rather than to them, it looks back to the thought of the Renaissance and of antiquity. In his diary Shaftesbury communes directly with antiquity, with Plato and Aristotle, with Plotinus, with Seneca, and with Marcus Aurelius and Epictetus.[2]

There is enough truth in this to make the error all the more in need of correction. That Shaftesbury drew heavily on classical models of philosophy is amply evident, but it is quite misleading to say that he "feels no kinship with contemporary philosophy." His enormous sympathy with the Cambridge Platonists —More and Cudworth were still alive in his youth—has been fully documented by Cassirer himself, who argues that Shaftesbury was the major continuator of their tradition. The widely recognized fact that Shaftesbury was a key link in the transition of attitudes from the seventeenth to the eighteenth centuries in ethics and religion marks him as very much a man of his time. The remarkable coincidence that he and Leibniz independently worked out similar forms of metaphysical optimism suggests that both were responding to the needs and problems of their age. Moreover, the third Earl was the personal friend and correspondent of many—like Bayle, Toland, and Le Clerc —who were intimately involved in the intellectual currents of the period. As for the practical problems of his era, the *Philosophical Regimen* may have relatively little that bears on them directly, but Shaftesbury's writings as a whole reveal that he was very much concerned with them, though not with scientific or technical, but social and political, issues.

Shaftesbury's love of classical culture was no mere archaism, nor did it provide an escape from the compelling issues of his own day. Perhaps his attitude is best revealed in the advice he gave to his young protégé, the theological student Michael Ainsworth, to study either the most modern writers or the ancients, but to avoid the literature that came in between. Shaftesbury was not blind to the values of contemporary culture; he felt that considerable progress had been made, and in 1705 he wrote optimistically that if peace came there would be a great rebirth of letters and learning in the free nations of England and Holland.[3] Later, he reported in a letter from Naples that instead of purchasing paintings by the old masters for himself he was giving support to living painters, for, as he explained, "my charges turn wholly towards the raising of art and the improvement of virtue in the *living* and in posterity to come."[4] Shaftesbury dipped into the fountains of ancient learning in order to find light and guidance for the present. Like many others in his time, he believed that mankind was emerging from a long period of darkness and ignorance, and that the classics might not only provide stimuli for seeking the good life but also suggest patterns by which it might be attained.

Shaftesbury looked for inspiration to the pagan writers of Greece and Rome rather than to the Bible or the Church Fathers. The Greeks and Romans he considered "the wisest and most polished people." (I, 222) Greece was the original fount of the arts and the sciences, drawing little (he mistakenly thought) from other nations. The Greek language is "the

Fountain of all; not only of polite Learning and Philosophy, but of Divinity also. . . ." [5] Little wonder then that Shaftesbury's writings are steeped with classical references and quotations.

The *General Dictionary* reports that

among the writings which he most admired, and carried always with him, were the moral works of Xenophon, Horace, the *Commentaries* and *Enchiridion* of Epictetus as published by Arrian, and Marcus Antoninus. These authors are now extant in his library, filled throughout with marginal notes, references, and explanations, all written with his own hand.[6]

An examination of Shaftesbury's works bears this out. Horace is one of his most quoted authors,[7] and, while there are few direct references to Epictetus and Marcus Aurelius in the *Characteristics*, the *Philosophical Regimen* is virtually a running commentary on passages from all three of these writers. In the full-length portrait of Shaftesbury that is often reproduced, the two books placed at his side are appropriately by Plato, whom he refers to as the "sublime philosopher," and Xenophon, whom he praises highly. (II, 309) Socrates he rates as "the greatest of philosophers, the very founder of philosophy itself." (II, 307) Aristotle is the "great Master," but it is primarily the *Poetics* that he admired, as was common in the Augustan age. Shaftesbury often refers to Epicurus and Lucretius, though to criticize their doctrines; he speaks well of Cicero and Seneca but has some strong reservations about the latter. (II, 170) Though Cassirer implies that Shaftesbury read Plotinus, I have found no direct evidence of this. There are passages where Shaftesbury sounds very much like Plotinus, but the concepts involved may have been mediated through the Cambridge Platonists. (II, 131 f.) [8]

Shaftesbury's philosophy is a complicated fusion of Stoic and Platonic thought, plus such diverse elements as Bayle's skepticism, Cumberland's doctrine of the public good, and the humanitarianism of the Latitudinarian divines. Writers like Esther Tiffany [9] and A. O. Aldridge [10] overemphasize the Stoic element, while Cassirer sometimes does the same with the Platonic element.[11] Platonism was not a closed system for him but a living philosophic tradition capable of being applied in each new age to its special problems. He seemed to find little difficulty in combining it with Stoicism, which, as his philosophical diary reveals, Shaftesbury leaned on heavily in time of emotional stress. Shaftesbury's grouping of the ancient philosophies is described in the following revealing passage from a letter:

Nor were there, indeed, any more than two real distinct philosophies, the one derived from Socrates, and passing into the old Academic, the Peripatetic, and Stoic; the other derived in reality from Democritus, and passing into the Cyrenaic and Epicurean. For as for that mere sceptic, and new Academic, it had no certain precepts, and so was an exercise or sophistry rather than a philosophy. The first, therefore, of these two philosophies recommended action, concernment in civil affairs, religion. The second derided all, and advised inaction and retreat, and with good reason. For the first maintained that society, right and wrong was founded in Nature, and that Nature had a meaning, and was herself, that is to say in her wits, well governed and administered by one simple and perfect intelligence. The second again derided this, and made Providence and Dame Nature not so sensible as a doting old woman. The first, therefore, of these philosophies is to be called the civil, social, Theistic; the second, the contrary.[12]

It was Shaftesbury's enterprise to defend this civil, social, and theistic tradition in philosophy, and to oppose its contrary.

Shaftesbury has some very sharp criticisms to make of the

universities and philosophical schools of the Middle Ages and the early Renaissance. He charges that philosophy, separated from "the sprightly arts and sciences," has grown dull, pedantic, and impractical; it has been made a "mock-science." (I, 186)

Though Shaftesbury remarked that "the most ingenious way of becoming foolish is by a system," (I, 189) this should not be construed to mean that he opposed systematic thought as such. The "Inquiry Concerning Virtue" is ample evidence that he himself could practice what he styled the "methodic or scholastic manner." (I, 168) It is not systems as such that he opposes but rather certain kinds of systems. He doubts the worth, on the one hand, of those vast, "super-speculative" systems of thought that lose themselves in the study of abstract ideas or in the analysis of modes and substances, and on the other hand, of those scientific studies which attempt a mechanistic analysis of man and Nature. In either case, Shaftesbury argues that they are out of touch with the real needs and interests of mankind. He mocks those persons who think that "in the intellectual [world] a set frame of metaphysical phrases and distinctions can serve to solve whatever difficulties may be propounded either in logics, ethics, or any real science of whatever kind." (II, 255) In a typical argument he attacks scholasticism:

As for metaphysics, and that which in the schools is taught for logic or for ethics, I shall willingly allow it to pass for philosophy when by any real effects it is proved capable to refine our spirits, improve our understandings, or mend our manners. But if the defining material and immaterial substances, and distinguishing their properties and modes, is recommended to us as the right manner of proceeding in the discovery of our own natures, I shall be apt to suspect such a study as the more delusive and infatuating on account of its magnificent pretension. (I, 188)

Shaftesbury is in agreement with Locke in condemning much of the philosophy then current as mere logomachy, and he praises him for his contribution in clearing away "the rubbish of the schools in which most of us have been bred up." [13] "No one has done more towards the Recalling of Philosophy from Barbarity. . . . No one has opened a better or clearer way to Reasoning." [14] And yet Locke's own system comes under some of Shaftesbury's harshest criticism.[15] What is the value, he asks, of this preoccupation with the distinction between simple and complex ideas, with the agreement and disagreement of ideas, or with the analysis of our concepts of space and matter? The crux of the third Earl's argument is that by solving the problems of this kind of philosophy (to the extent that they *are* soluble) "one is neither better, nor happier, nor wiser, nor . . . of a more . . . enlarged mind or a generous heart. . . ." [16]

The same type of criticism is made of mechanistic and scientific studies. Descartes' *Treatise of the Passions*, for example, fails to teach us how to control our emotions. (I, 191) In his philosophical notebook, Shaftesbury asks, "What is it to me whether a vacuum or a plenitude? Whether matter be divisible *ad infinitum* or not divisible?" [17] Little wonder then that, as Brett observes, Shaftesbury "viewed with distaste and suspicion the activities of the members of the Royal Society." [18] Shaftesbury's dismissal of "all that pretended Study and Science of Nature called Natural Philosophy, Aristotelian, Cartesian, or whatever else it be; all those high Contemplations of Stars and Spheres and Planets . . ." [19] calls for further explanation. At its lowest level it is an indication of his own lack of interest in pursuing such studies and his own failure to comprehend their importance. On a more significant level though, he was distrustful of those who believed that the mysteries of Nature could be penetrated by the discovery of some single key which in turn would give one power over the natural world. (II, 255) Thus, his criticisms of alchemy: neither truth nor wisdom were to be found that way. Another factor influencing Shaftesbury's thought is a kind of aesthetic antipathy to the odd, the freakish, or the monstrous. This explains in part his objection to collections of natural specimens and to books on natural wonders. Shaftesbury's Neoclassical standards determine this distaste for what he considers to be disharmonious or disproportionate.

In contrast, the Cambridge Platonists had shown considerable sympathy for the new experimental research, both Cudworth and More having been members of the Royal Society. Yet they too developed a fear of the new science in so far as it seemed to give support to a narrowly mechanistic view of Nature. Henry More warned of the more "mechanical kind of genius" who goes beyond his proper sphere, i.e., "making experiments," and engages in philosophical speculations. He was troubled by the problem of the misplacement of authority, which is even more accentuated in our present age of specialization. However, the Cambridge Platonists did not distrust experiment itself but rather the narrowing conception of experience that increasingly accompanied it. They wanted a philosophy that did justice to the varieties of human experience. In the Augustan age the problem became even more acute, and Shaftesbury was by no means alone in his objections to the "mechanical" philosophy. The new science was stripping the experienced world of its variety and color, and in their place putting a series of abstractions, pointer readings, or mathematical formulae. For those who viewed Nature aesthetically, this could only be seen as an error, if not a sacrilege.

In skeptical moments, Shaftesbury doubts that one can arrive at any theoretical certainty in the sciences: "For mathematicians are divided, and mechanics proceed as well on one hypothesis as on the other." (I, 196) More often though he adopts the opposite tack, using mathematics as the archetype of cognitive certainty. The fact is that Shaftesbury knew little of mathematics or of any other science. His ideas on the subject are neither well worked out nor consistent, though his standpoint is more judicious in the *Characteristics* than in the philosophical notebooks. Perhaps his views shifted somewhat over a period of time, or, more likely, when writing for publication he was forced by his own good sense to adopt a more reasonable position. He acknowledges the practical benefits that accrue from mathematical and scientific studies. He recognizes in the mathematician the same pure, disinterested pleasure which may be found in other realms of life where truth and order are valued for themselves. His primary concern, though, is that the scientist remain within his own sphere of research and not invade the theory of value. "The study of triangles and circles interferes not with the study of minds; nor does the student in the meanwhile suppose himself advancing in wisdom or the knowledge of himself or mankind. . . . Such is the mathematician's modesty and good sense." (I, 188 f.) Philosophy provides the over-view which ". . . gives to every inferior science its just rank; leaves some to measure sounds, others to scan syllables, others to weigh vacuums, and define spaces and extensions; but reserves to herself her due authority and majesty, . . . and title of *vitae dux*. . . ." (I, 194)

Shaftesbury remained remarkably aloof from the scientific revolution of his age and failed to recognize its importance. His predominant interest was in the moral and spiritual realms of experience rather than in the physical. One has to search to find references to new scientific developments in his writings. Newton is only mentioned a few times in the letters and then not in relation to his ideas, though references to gravity and "liquid ether" (II, 113 f.) indicate that Shaftesbury had at least that degree of acquaintance with Newton's theories that one would expect in an educated gentleman of the time. Certainly one can sense in the background of his thought "the new philosophical scene of worlds unknown." (II, 12) Shaftesbury's vision of Nature as a vast but ultimately harmonious order was not wholly the product of the new science, but there is no doubt that it was reinforced by it. (I, 204) The mathematician only uncovers the "hidden numbers," the laws of harmony and proportion, that philosophic intuition always recognized were there.

True philosophy, for Shaftesbury, is not simply based on a scientific study of man, nor is it a mere summation or explanation of scientific laws. It is not just an innerly consistent logical system with occasional references to the experienced world. True philosophy is, in the classical sense, the quest for, and love of, wisdom. It cannot restrict itself to abstract theory, but in its wholeness must have practical applicability. Philosophy is "the study of happiness," and, therefore, everyone is in a sense a philosopher. (II, 150) This is not inconsistent with the previous definition, nor is it hedonistic, since Shaftesbury considers true happiness attainable only through the maximum development of man as a rational, spiritual being.[20] This requires self-knowledge and self-mastery which, therefore, become primary concerns of philosophy, the preeminent science which teaches us to assign everything its true value. It is easy to see why Shaftesbury gives so little attention to certain technical issues in metaethics, metaphysics, and epistemology that others have considered important. He concerns himself rather with those questions about the nature and destiny of man that have an immediate bearing on his activities.

There is an unresolved tension in Shaftesbury's philosophy, though, between practical and theoretical reason. While he contends that science and philosophy must have practical effectiveness, he also advocates a pure, disinterested pursuit of truth for its own sake. Whether truth always has practical value remains an open question, apart from any psychological satisfaction its possession may give. If Shaftesbury had appreciated this, he might have been willing to accede greater value to science as a theoretical inquiry. Moreover, he failed to perceive that the quest for truth can, or at least should, never be limited by our present knowledge of its practical applications.

It was Shaftesbury's conviction that philosophy must make its effects felt in the world, and that it must serve the practicing statesman and artists, and in the broadest sense, the practicing citizen. Thus, he did not direct his work primarily to other philosophers or scholars, but to the broadest circle of cultivated readers. His major writings—the "Inquiry" and "The Moralists"—are largely free of the apparatus of scholarship. By avoiding the rather heavy, scholarly style of some of the major writings of the Cambridge Platonists, Shaftesbury was able to reach a wider audience. Cassirer claims that it was "principally Shaftesbury" who saved "the Cambridge School from the fate of a learned curiosity" and made it a "philosophic force in the centuries to come." [21]

In "Advice to an Author," Shaftesbury commends the "simple manner" which is closest to Nature, and conceals the systematic thought that lies behind it under an appearance of "ease and negligence." (I, 168 f.) A good part of his own writing follows this approach. In the notes for *Second Characters,* Shaftesbury reminds himself to follow this rule:

Nothing in the text but what shall be of easy, smooth, and polite reading, without seeming difficulty, or hard study; so that the better and gentler rank of painters and artists, the ladies, beaux, courtly gentlemen, and more refined sort of country and town wits, and notable talkers may comprehend, or be persuaded that they comprehend, what is there written in the text.[22]

His success in attaining this aim is borne out by the popularity of the *Characteristics* in the eighteenth century. Yet, ironically, some of the very qualities which contributed to this success limited its appeal to later generations. Philosophers have been disappointed by Shaftesbury's failure to treat some of the more technical issues his philosophy raised, and to develop a more adequate technical vocabulary. Moreover, the façade of witty and "polite" language has made it more difficult to grasp his method and sometimes his meaning.

Shaftesbury's lack of interest in the technical issues of epistemology and metaphyiscs is to be explained in part by a strong strain of skepticism which makes him doubt that we can resolve them by sheer logical analysis. One is sometimes surprised at the casual treatment that he gives to problems that were of great concern to other philosophers of his age. Yet, though brief, his comments are often quite perceptive. In commenting on Descartes' philosophy, he accuses him of circular reasoning in his famous *"cogito, ergo sum,"* for the ego which is to be proven is already assumed in the first part of the proposition. It means no more than saying, "If I am, I am." (II, 275) However, Shaftesbury himself resorts to essentially the same reasoning when he argues that if there is "thinking," there must be a "thinker," and if there is "doubting," there must be a "doubter." Pyrrhonism, in denying the mind's existence, refutes itself, since that very denial requires the existence of mind. Elsewhere, he contends that we can be sure of the reality of thought, since it is an object of immediate consciousness. (II, 112) Yet, such attempts at a resolution of the problem by formal reasoning do not wholly satisfy him, and he admits that he must finally accept the reality of his own existence "upon trust." (II, 276) For all practical purposes, he believes that this works as well as logical proof. Actually, the problem that primarily concerns him is not the reality but the nature of the self.[23]

In the "Inquiry," he states that no matter how far we carry our skepticism, we cannot doubt the reality of our internal feelings, though we may have doubts about the reality of the objects "on which they are employed." (I, 336 f.) He suggests that for what he has been trying to demonstrate there, it does not matter whether external objects are real or illusory, whether life is a dream or not, for the emotions felt within this "dream" would still be just as "real" to us. But later, in the "Miscellaneous Reflections," he admits the inadequacy of trying "to prove morals without a world." (II, 287) Morality, and indeed the whole philosophy of Nature, require that we assume a kind of common-sense realism: "We are henceforward to trust our eyes and take for real the whole creation, and the fair forms which lie before us." (II, 287) This combination of skepticism and pragmatism is typical of Shaftesbury. He has no interest in epistemological or metaphysical questions in themselves; he doubts that we can establish one or other hypothesis by abstract reasoning, at least in a manner that will be convincing to all reasonable men. Only in so far as morality demands that we make certain epistemological or metaphysical assumptions does he enter this realm of speculation.

In one of his letters, Shaftesbury goes so far as to say that in philosophy as in politics he is "but few removes from mere scepticism, and though I may hold some principles perhaps tenaciously, they are, however, so very few, plain, and simple that they serve to little purpose towards the great speculations in fashion with the world." [24] There is little doubt that this tendency in the English philosopher's thought was reinforced by his acquaintance with the great French skeptic, Pierre Bayle. They not only visited during Shaftesbury's trips to Holland but corresponded from 1698 until the French philosopher's death in 1706.[25] Shaftesbury wrote a remarkable tribute to his late friend which I will quote from at length because it reveals so much about Shaftesbury's conception of the social role of the skeptic:

. . . whatever benefit the world in general may have received from him, I am sure no one in particular owed more to him than I, or knew his merit better. . . . [He was] a friend, who in whatever respect esteemed erroneous, had undeniably such qualities and virtues as might grace the character of the most orthodox of our age. I know very well that it is in religion and philosophy, as in most things that different opinions usually create not only dislike, but animosity and hatred. It was far otherwise between Mons. Bayle and myself, for whilst we agreed in fundamental rules of moral practice and believed ourselves true to these, the continual differences in opinions and the constant disputes that were between us, served to improve our friendship. I had the happiness to see that they lost me nothing of his; and I know my own increasing every day as my advantages increased by his improving conversation. I may well say *improving* in every respect, even as to principles in which the enemies of Mons. Bayle would least of all allow him the character of a promoter. But if to be confirmed in any good principle be by debate and argument, after thorough scrutiny, to readmit what was first implanted by prevention, I may then say, in truth, that whatever is most valuable to me of this kind has been owing in great measure to this our friend whom the world called sceptical. Whatever opinion of mine stood not the test of his piercing reason, I learned by degrees either to discard as frivolous, or not to rely on with that boldness as before; but that which bore the trial I prized as purest gold. And if that philosophy, whatever it be, which keeping in bounds of decency, examines things after this manner, be esteemed injurious to religion or mankind, and be accordingly banished from the world, I can foresee nothing but darkness and ignorance that must follow. . . . What injury such a one could do the world by such a search of truth with so much moderation, disinterestedness, integrity, and innocency of life I know not; but what good he did I in particular know and feel, and must never cease to speak and own.[26]

Perhaps Philocles, the skeptic in "The Moralists," is modeled in part on Bayle. Philocles challenges us "to dare doubt," and recommends that intellectual discipline which is "most disagreeable" since it "goes upon no established hypothesis, nor presents us with any flattering scheme, talks only of probabilities, suspense of judgement, inquiry, search, and caution." (II, 9) Shaftesbury believed that such "proving spirits" as Bayle must be given a large share of the credit for the philosophical works whose writing they provoke by their critical thought. It is a tribute to the French philosopher that his Manicheanism was a stimulus to the writing of two of the major works of the Augustan age—"The Moralists" and Leibniz's *Theodicy.*

Shaftesbury defends skepticism as an instrument of reason and as a concomitant of free inquiry. Of his own writings, he regarded the "Letter Concerning Enthusiasm," the "Essay on the Freedom of Wit and Humour," and "Advice to an Author" as exhibiting primarily the skeptical or destructive method, and therefore he grouped them as the first three treatises in the *Characteristics* to prepare the way for the more constructive and systematic "Inquiry Concerning Virtue." The men of doubt, he believed, can free men from dogma and clear away some of the obstacles to a more objective approach to truth; but doubt must be applied with thoroughness, for there is "nothing so foolish and deluding as a partial scepticism." (I, 56) "Formalities, pomps, and ceremonies must be broken through, prejudices torn off, and truth stripped as naked as ever she was born." [27] It is in this mood that Philocles sets out on his "philosophical adventures" on the "dangerous seas" of thought. Yet Shaftesbury warns that we must avoid "endless scepticism" which, by denying the possibility of any reliable knowledge, overthrows "all principles, moral and divine." (II, 19) The "bigot-sceptic" can believe in nothing, which Shaftesbury finds a neurotic symptom rather than merely an intellectual position. As Thomas Browne had observed, many prefer "doubting with ease" to "believing with difficulty." Shaftesbury understood that the activity of destruction was often easier than that of construction. But he saw his task not as that of destroying but as that of justifying faith.

CHAPTER TWO

ENTHUSIASM

In a letter to a friend, Shaftesbury once wrote, "You know me for a great enthusiast. . . ."[1] Despite this self-admission, and despite the frequent discussions of enthusiasm in his writings, one finds that Anglo-American scholars have on the whole failed to recognize the central place of love and enthusiasm in Shaftesbury's thought. This is true even of such reputable scholars as Leslie Stephen, Thomas Fowler, Basil Willey, and R. L. Brett. Basil Willey, for example, sees the importance of Shaftesbury's "enthusiasm" only as an attribute of man's response to Nature's beauties.[2] An important recent exception is Marjorie Nicolson's study of "the aesthetics of the infinite," in which she explores the concept of enthusiasm in relation to Shaftesbury's aesthetics.[3] What there has been in the standpoint of Anglo-American critics that has made them uninterested in or unaware of the importance of this concept is an interesting question. In contrast, German scholars like Cassirer and Wilhelm Windelband have recognized the centrality of enthusiasm in the English philosopher's world-view. Perhaps one reason is that a more vital tradition of philosophic idealism has survived into the twentieth century in Germany. Windelband wrote of Shaftesbury that "the centre of his doctrine and of his own nature is formed by what he himself called *enthusiasm*,—enthusiasm for all that is true, good, and beautiful, the elevation of the soul above itself to more universal values, the living out of the whole peculiar power of the individual by the devotion to something higher." [4] This is the motif that is repeated throughout Shaftesbury's writings and that gives them their characteristic tone: by giving himself to that which is greater than self, man *makes* himself and *is made*. To understand this doctrine in all its ramifications is a main goal of this study. In this chapter we will explore its background and try to define its essential significance in Shaftesbury's philosophy, with special reference to his religious concepts. In Part II of this book, its application to ethics and aesthetics will be dealt with.

Significantly, the first version of "The Moralists," as privately circulated in 1705, was entitled by Shaftesbury "The Sociable Enthusiast: a Philosophical Adventure." [5] He reports having changed this "much" before its public printing in 1709 under the final title," "The Moralists, A Philosophical Rhapsody." [6] Shaftesbury first addressed the public at length on the subject of enthusiasm in the "Letter Concerning Enthusiasm" published in 1708, though written the previous year.[7] The immediate stimulus to the writing of the "Letter" was the behavior of the Camisards, a religious group popularly known as the "French prophets," who had sought refuge in England from religious persecution in France. The Camisard movement, which first appeared in France in the Cévennes shortly after the revocation of the Edict of Nantes in 1685, proved to be short-lived, for it rapidly declined after 1715.[8] Brutally repressed in

France, the Camisards fought back with all the fury they could muster, committing massacres of Catholic priests and laymen in the name of religious truth and under the guidance of prophets who claimed supernatural inspiration. Though they had emerged from the ranks of the Huguenots, they were looked upon with dismay and disapproval by the more conservative members of that group. When some of the "prophets" arrived in London in the early years of the eighteenth century,[9] the established Huguenot community there quickly disowned them, and eventually excommunicated them.

The Camisards followed the usual pattern of evangelical pneumatism, emphasizing the necessity for direct contact with God and claiming to be "possessed" at times by the Holy Spirit. Such possession was consciously cultivated, and it manifested itself in certain extraordinary ways. An English clergyman, Nathaniel Spinckes, describes

. . . The Shakings of their Heads; Crawling on the Knees; Quakings and Tremblings; their Whistlings, Drummings, Trumpettings; their Thundrings; their Snuffling; Blowing as with a Horn; Panting, and Difficulty of Breathing, Sighing and Groaning; Hissing; Smiling; Laughing . . . Striking . . . Howling in their Assemblies like a Dog, and being in all manner of Disorder.[10]

As with other "enthusiastic" sects, the members of this one are also reported as falling into trancelike catatonic states for minutes or hours, or becoming ecstatic and speaking with tongues, or doing "violence" to themselves, though without injury. There were claims of clairvoyance and prophecy, in some cases by children. And there were the familiar predictions of the end of the world, or more modestly, of the destruction of London. In one of their most publicized pronouncements, toward the end of 1707, they predicted that a certain man, then dying, would be raised from the dead five months after his burial. A huge crowd of Londoners, waiting at the cemetery on the appointed day, were disappointed, while the prophets themselves were wisely absent. Little wonder that on some occasions the prophets were attacked by angry mobs.

Three of the prophets had been placed on trial in July, 1707, for their predictions of disaster for England, and sentenced to the pillory in November.[11] In that same year, when the literary propaganda and popular renown of this sect reached a peak, Shaftesbury wrote the "Letter Concerning Enthusiasm." The prophets had succeeded in converting "two English Gentlemen of Quality and Estates," John Lacy and Sir Richard Bulkeley, the former of whom wrote a "defence of revived prophecy" in 1707 under the title, *A Cry from the Desart: or Testimonials of the Miraculous Things lately come to pass in the Cévennes.* Shaftesbury quotes from this and reports that he saw Lacy "lately under an agitation" prophesying in a Latin style of which he was ordinarily incapable. (I, 32) Apparently the philosopher was not satisfied with second-hand reports but wanted the opportunity to observe the behavior of the prophets at first-hand; to do this, he "probably attended one of the prophet's meetings in a private bench-filled parlor." [12]

It would be a mistake to suppose that Shaftesbury's knowledge of evangelical sectarianism of this sort was restricted to the French prophets or that his doctrine of enthusiasm was shaped solely or even largely by their behavior. Shaftesbury had had ample opportunity to observe other such "enthusiastic" sects, of which England had her plentiful share.[13] Though the Camisards provided the immediate occasion for the writing of the "Letter," Shaftesbury's attitude toward "enthusiasm" had already taken shape in the first draft of "The

Moralists" (1705). Marjorie Nicolson writes that in the "Letter" Shaftesbury's "mood of wit against false enthusiasms reflected Swift," [14] whose attack on religious fanaticism, *A Tale of a Tub*, appeared in 1704. Indeed, the "Letter," which appeared anonymously like most of the treatises in the *Characteristics*, was attributed by some to Swift. Yet Shaftesbury mentions Swift disparagingly in a letter accompanying *The Sociable Enthusiast* to Lord Somers, to whom Swift had also dedicated his book. At a later time Shaftesbury attacked the *Tale* in the strongest terms as "that detestable writing of that most detestable author." [15] It is more likely that the *Tale* was a stimulus to the writing of "The Moralists" than of the "Letter." The latter concentrates on the criticism of false enthusiasm, though it gives due recognition to the nature of true enthusiasm. But "The Moralists" represents Shaftesbury's major attempt to describe the character of true enthusiasm. It is his answer to the charge, implied in the common use of the term "enthusiast" in his time, that a religious enthusiast must and could only be a fanatic.

The distinction between true and false enthusiasm is not original to Shaftesbury, for it can be found in such writers as Meric Casaubon,[16] Ralph Cudworth, Henry More, and John Dennis, though J. M. Robertson is probably right in asserting that Shaftesbury's was the main influence leading to the modern positive use of the term. In contrast, Locke and Whichcote had stressed the dangers of enthusiasm. Shaftesbury was particularly influenced by Henry More's *Enthusiasmus Triumphatus; or a Brief Discourse of the Nature, Causes, Kinds, and Cure of Enthusiasm* (1656).[17] Though More paved the way for a new understanding of the significance of enthusiasm, the emphasis in his discourse also still lay on the *triumphatus*—the conquest of false enthusiasm—and it was only at the end of it that he gave some attention to true enthusiasm, insisting that he had no intention of criticizing it. While Shaftesbury drew heavily from this work and the *Enchiridion Ethicum,* he comments that in other writings More "was perhaps as great an Enthusiast, as any of those, whom he wrote against." [18]

Enthusiasm is described by Shaftesbury as a "powerful and extensive" phenomenon of which we all have had some experience. It is the state of mind which occurs when the mind envisages the "prodigious," the "more than human," and receives or creates ideas or images too big for it to contain.[19] Enthusiasm is characterized by intense emotions, either delightful or fearful, that are felt "when the mind is taken up in vision, and fixes its view either on any real object, or mere spectre of divinity." (I, 37) It can occur when the mind is transported by some apparition, and it is associated by Shaftesbury with the apprehension of the great and awesome. "We can admire nothing profoundly without a certain religious veneration." (II, 177) The fact that such emotions border on fear has led some to regard them as products solely of that emotion, but Shaftesbury rejects this explanation, finding the real basis of enthusiasm not in fear but in man's natural passion for the sublime and the beautiful.

Whether Shaftesbury was familiar with John Dennis's early critical writings I do not know, but there are some interesting parallels in their views.[20] According to Dennis, "enthusiasms" in contrast with ordinary emotions are strong passions such as "Admiration, Terror or Joy" whose cause is "not clearly comprehended by him who feels them," [21] though "Poetical Enthusiasm is a Passion guided by Judgment . . . ," [22] for otherwise it would be madness. The greatest enthusiasms are stimulated by religious subjects, "for all which is great in Religion is most

exalted and amazing, all that is joyful is transporting, all that
is sad is dismal, and all that is terrible is astonishing." [23]

Dennis distinguished between beauty and the sublime, finding the true source of the latter "in God and in the manifestations of His greatness and power in Nature." [24] Marjorie Nicolson further interprets Dennis as believing that beauty and
sublimity were antithetical, and Shaftesbury as considering the
sublime a "higher beauty." This seems correct of Shaftesbury,
but I think Professor Nicolson errs in stating that "the word
sublime was so seldom on Shaftesbury's lips that it surprises.
When he used it at all, it was usually with disparagement." [25]
The word "sublime" is not that rare in Shaftesbury, and by my
tabulation it is used considerably more often in an approving
than in a disapproving sense. A breakdown of the way in which
he uses the term reveals two basic usages: first, as a stylistic
concept referring to various of the arts; and second, as char-
acterizing the higher types of human behavior, thought, or
character. He rarely uses the term to refer directly to Nature's
grandeur.[26] In the stylistic context it is true that Shaftesbury
is often critical of the "false sublime." (I, 157 ff.) For just as
there are true and false forms of enthusiasm, so there are of the
sublime, in both art and life. The sublime, on the one hand,
may be linked with the truly lofty, noble, and inspired, and on
the other, with the pompous, bombastic, and vulgarly sensa-
tional. Shaftesbury understood that the enthusiastic and the
sublime by only a slight transformation can be falsified and
perverted. The true sublime is not mere rhetoric but grounded
on a true idea of Nature and of God. We experience the
sublime when the mind is taken hold of by that which is infinitely greater than itself, by that which can only be grasped
by intuitive vision in an act of enthusiasm.

Shaftesbury writes in the "Letter" that "inspiration is a real

feeling of the Divine Presence, and enthusiasm a false one."
(I, 37) But he means to say that true inspiration or enthusiasm
is based upon the actual apprehension of the Divine, while false
enthusiasm is produced by a mistaken sense of the Deity's presence. Henry More agreed, and both writers considered false
enthusiasm to be a product of an unregulated imagination.
True enthusiasm, in contrast, employs the powers of the
imagination as controlled by reason in order to attain a higher,
intuitive grasp of truth. But More's language in describing
true inspiration differs significantly from Shaftesbury's, for
More writes that "to be inspired is to be moved in an extraordinary manner by the power or Spirit of God to act, speak, or
think what is holy, just and true." [27] The Cambridge Platonist
is still using the language of traditional religion which implies
a God who is personal and transcendent, though immanent in
certain respects. But in Shaftesbury's philosophy God is largely
impersonal, and His immanence is given greater stress. More
still believes in the effectiveness of supernatural grace, while for
Shaftesbury this doctrine has in large part been either elimi-
nated or naturalized. For More, a special divine act of revelation is still possible; for Shaftesbury, revelation is general in
the sense that the individual makes himself capable of receiving
what is always given or being given to all men. This is one of
the points at which we can see rather clearly how Shaftesbury contributed to the growing process of secularizing and
"demythologizing" the religion of his time.

Ronald Knox interprets Shaftesbury to mean that those who
are taken with false enthusiasm are really conscious frauds.[28]
Actually, Shaftesbury's position was that they may be entirely
sincere though deceiving themselves as well as others. Shaftesbury's attitude seems a good deal more judicious than that of

some of his contemporaries—the so-called "men of wit"—who regarded all religion as the product of conscious fraud. The third Earl points out that the Bible itself discriminates between a good and evil spirit of prophecy. But he notes ironically the difficulty in distinguishing the two since their outward symptoms are so much the same in all religions. His description of their characteristic "ecstasies . . . quakings, tremblings, . . . convulsions" (I, 35) sounds much like the reports of the behavior of the French prophets. Shaftesbury's approach to this problem was more complex than that taken by some of his contemporaries who denied that any higher, divine power could affect the human mind. In examining the symptoms of enthusiasm, Shaftesbury reports that some thinkers "endeavour to solve the appearances of this kind by the natural operation of our passions and the common course of outward things." (II, 173) While attempting on the one hand to deny a crude supernaturalism, Shaftesbury sought to formulate a genuine doctrine of inspiration. Thus, he suggests that there is "a kind of enchantment or magic" in enthusiasm. The harmonious and the beautiful grasp us, "inspires us with something more than ordinary, and raises us above ourselves." (II, 174) Yet this is an ecstasy of reason, not an abandonment of it. Shaftesbury characterizes his "Philosophical Rhapsody," "The Moralists," as comprising a "variety of styles . . . even the poetic or sublime, such as is the aptest to run into enthusiasm and extravagance." (II, 334) Yet, significantly, he insists that it is at bottom just as "systematical" and rational as the more formal "Inquiry." Indeed, he goes even further, contending that "The Moralists" is his "principal performance" because it stirs the imagination and excites the mind as the more "scholastic manner" cannot do. (II, 334) [29]

To discriminate between true and false enthusiasm required careful and objective reasoning, according to Shaftesbury. The claims of religious enthusiasts must be assessed and checked by impartial observers. He agreed with Henry More that enthusiasm could be tested by whether or not it issued in moral behavior and reasonable beliefs. However, Shaftesbury would not have agreed to More's third condition for true enthusiasms—that it be based on belief in the Bible, rightly interpreted, and in Jesus Christ, Son of God and Saviour. But both men warned that if we were to avoid the contagion of powerful delusions we had to have self-understanding as well as self-control.

Since the doctrine of enthusiasm provides an important link between Shaftesbury's religious, moral, and aesthetic doctrines, it is not surprising that he considered poetry to be characterized by enthusiasm. To be great, a poet must imagine a "divine presence" and be inspired by a vision of that which is greater than himself and greater than mankind. "Poets are fanatics too," though "poetic madness" must be subject to the control of the mind if it is to be genuinely creative. (I, 36) Shaftesbury approvingly quotes More's statement that "a poet is an enthusiast in jest, and an enthusiast is a poet in good earnest," (II, 197) [30] though he adapts More's thought to a more positive conception of poetic inspiration.

Shaftesbury follows More and Cudworth in finding an affinity between atheism and enthusiasm also. He recognizes that the atheist, like other men, has his ultimate concerns for which he may even sacrifice his life. Shaftesbury quotes Cudworth's delightful explanation:

All atheists being that blind Goddess Nature's fanatics . . . are possessed with a certain kind of Madness, that may be called Pneu-

matophobia, that makes them have an irrational but desperate Abhorrence from Spirits or Incorporeal Substances, they being acted
also, at the same time, with an Hylomania, whereby they madly
dote upon Matter, and devoutly worship it, as the only Numen.
(II, 196 f.)[31]

Even the "cold Lucretius," disciple of "this unpolite philosophy," is forced despite himself to give way "to admiration and
rapturous views of Nature" while at the same time he "arraigns
the order of it. . . ." (II, 175) In Shaftesbury's model of
human nature this capacity for enthusiasm or ultimate commitment is a necessary trait of man. Yet it is a paradox of
Shaftesbury's dialectic that the same psychological phenomenon can in one context lead to the highest forms of creativity
and self-affirmation, and in another to the greatest delusion and
self-deception. It is in part explained by Shaftesbury's belief
that extremes tend to generate their opposites, as "the extreme
passion for religious objects" can turn into an extreme aversion
for them.

   Unless it is properly regulated and directed toward the
appropriate objects, enthusiasm is likely to be perverted either
into fanaticism through excess of love or into superstitution
through excess of fear. Shaftesbury notes a similarity between
the emotions of lovers and the ecstasies of "quietists" and
"pietists." This "amorous" type of enthusiasm he finds cultivated particularly by female saints. (II, 179) Superstition, on
the other hand, results when the religious objects on which we
focus are terrifying to us. However, religious zeal is seldom
without a mixture of both these tendencies, as love and fear
alternate with the changes in an individual's mood. Shaftesbury
writes that "in religions, therefore, which hold most of love,
there is generally room left for terrors of the deepest kind,"

(II, 180) and the converse is also true. But in Shaftesbury's own religious philosophy fear is transmuted into awe, and terror into love. Despite the similarities between his and John Dennis's concept of enthusiasm, Dennis's God is a God of infinite power who arouses "Enthusiastic Terrour"; Shaftesbury's is a God of infinite benevolence who inspires love.[32]

Like Henry More, Shaftesbury considers melancholy or "ill-humour" to be a basic source of false enthusiasm, and, in fact, he even wonders "whether anything beside ill-humour can be the cause of atheism." (I, 17) This makes more sense when we remember that for Shaftesbury atheism means the denial of all natural order. Shaftesbury quotes More to the effect that the religious fanatic who thinks he is moved by the Spirit of God is actually subject to "the power of Melancholy, . . . a kind of natural inebriation," which works in a way deceptively similar to divine grace. (II, 198) [33] It can produce "ecstatic" states which are completely convincing to the individual in its grasp, since all power of free judgment has been temporarily destroyed. Shaftesbury had observed how easily such ecstatic states are communicated to others by a kind of mass hysteria, or in his terms, "panic." Any emotion, he comments, is stronger when it is "social and communicative." (I, 13) Melancholy and ill-humor distort our vision of God, for we project our own ill-temper upon Him, which prevents us from approaching Him freely and joyfully. In a state of dread or anxiety we cannot have a true conception of God: "We can never be fit to contemplate anything above us, when we are in no condition to look into ourselves, and calmly examine the temper of our own mind and passions." (I, 24) If Shaftesbury's analysis here seems superficial in the light of modern Crisis Theology, there is, nevertheless, an important element of truth in it. Religion, like all fundamental human institutions, is subject to the distortions of neurosis and mental derangement.

Actually, Shaftesbury's philosophy is part of a broad movement—not always connected—which manifested itself in seventeenth- and eighteenth-century Europe in such diverse quarters as Spinozism, Hasidism, and Cambridge Platonism, a movement to recover the joy in religion. Shaftesbury himself was, of course, primarily influenced by the Cambridge men as well as by the English Latitudinarian divines. Good humor, he writes, is "not only the best security against enthusiasm, but the best foundation of piety and true religion." (I, 17) And Christianity itself, "notwithstanding the dark complexion and sour humour of religious teachers . . . [is] in the main a witty and good-humoured religion." (II, 217) Shaftesbury believed that there was a close correlation between one's emotional mood and one's beliefs, and he thought, moreover, that a good-humored and joyful state of mind made possible a more objective and better-rounded conception of God.

We have seen then that for Shaftesbury true enthusiasm was a state of being in which man was inspired by the Divine and raised beyond his ordinary capacities. Henry More eloquently described it as "the triumph of the Soul of man inebriated, as it were, with the delicious sense of the divine life. . . ."[34] All true greatness, according to Shaftesbury, whether in "heroes, statesmen, poets, . . . even philosophers," is the product of some "noble enthusiasm." (I, 38 f.) Yet enthusiasm is not restricted to great men or to special occasions; it belongs to common experience. It is whatever makes men seek something beyond mere animal satisfactions. The joys of "the lover, [and] the ambitious man," would be much less if in that "which they admire and passionately pursue there were no reference or regard to any higher majesty or grandeur than what simply results from the particular objects of their pursuit." (II, 175)

All sound love and admiration is enthusiasm: "The transports of poets, the sublime of orators, the rapture of musicians, the high strains of the virtuosi—all mere enthusiasm! Even learning itself, the love of arts and curiosities, the spirit of travellers and adventurers, gallantry, war, heroism—all, all enthusiasm!" (II, 129)

But if enthusiasm has its roots in the common pursuits of man, it has its flower in "whatever is sublime in human passions." (I, 38)

Yet Shaftesbury sharply differentiates his concept of enthusiasm from supernatural revelation. Enthusiasm has a natural basis in the structure of the human mind: "There is a power in numbers, harmony, proportion, and beauty of every kind, which naturally captivates the heart, and raises the imagination to an opinion or conceit of something majestic and divine." (II, 174) Shaftesbury draws an analogy between our grasping of a particular harmonious whole, as in a work of art, and our apprehension of Deity.

For is there a fair and plausible enthusiasm, a reasonable ecstasy and transport allowed to other subjects, such as architecture, painting, music; and shall it be exploded here? Are there senses by which all those other graces and perfections are perceived, and none by which this higher perfection and grace is comprehended? (II, 129)

But just as in aesthetic experience man must develop and train his taste, so in the sphere of religious experience the affections must be ordered and the capacities of the mind exercised.

The concepts of enthusiasm and of love are inextricably connected in Shaftesbury's thought. The Platonic doctrine of *eros*, as developed by Plotinus and reformulated by the Renaissance and Cambridge Platonists, is given new life in his philosophy.[35] In Plotinus, *eros* was the bond between the highest and the lowest forms of being, as the lower reaches for the higher, and the higher for the lower. The Cambridge men, fusing Neoplatonic and Christian doctrine, made a fundamental part of their philosophy what Pope was to describe as

> . . . *the chain of Love*
> *Combining all below and all above.*[36]

For Shaftesbury too, love is the energy that unites all things.

Just as enthusiasm has its highest object in God, so does love; and just as enthusiasm appears at different levels of human experience, so does love. There is a hierarchy of love—similar to that found in other idealistic philosophies—extending from self-love to familial love, to love of friends, of country, of mankind, and finally of the cosmos itself. Each level involves higher and wider spheres of affection; each entails a further possibility of self-transcendence.[37] Though man has an obligation to expand the objects of his affection, Shaftesbury does not place emphasis on that but rather on the point that only by so doing can man realize his own true being. There is a natural movement, he contends, from the more restricted to the more comprehensive loves. One notes the ease with which Shaftesbury can use the same term, "natural affection," to mean either love within the family, or the social affections in general, or finally the love of Nature as a whole. He is aware though that there are counterforces and that the lesser loves can be an obstacle to the higher. But man alone of all creatures is capable of grasping his relationship to the Whole of Being; and man alone is under an obligation to strive for the good of the Whole, which takes priority over all partial goods. Shaftesbury was convinced, as we will see in the following chapters, that all things in the universe worked for the good of the Whole. In his notebook he wrote that, if this be true, "it follows that I must in a certain manner be reconciled to all things, love all things, and absolutely hate or abhor nothing whatsoever that has being in the world." [38] Only when this supreme affection is dominant can we properly regulate our lesser affections.

In "The Moralists" Theocles seeks to convince the skeptical Philocles of the importance of the love of humanity and of Nature. But Philocles finds it hard to grasp such "universal friendship," or "mystical love." While he can understand love of the individual, affection for humanity is "too mysterious, too metaphysical"; affection ordinarily requires a "sensible, material image." (II, 39) Theocles (who is Shaftesbury's spokesman) responds that a mental image may be an object of affection. One may, for example, become fond of an individual even before meeting him in person, or may love a particular nation before having any direct contact with it. Philocles concedes this possibility but he wonders if he could love a mental image of mankind or Nature very deeply unless "it could be sensible of my love and capable of a return." (*Ibid.*) Theocles dares to meet even this challenge, saying: "I will endeavor to show you that beauty which I count the perfectest, and most deserving of love, and which will not fail of a return." However, Philocles must first attain "at least some faint and distant view of the sovereign genius and first beauty." (II, 40) Nowhere is it clearer that Shaftesbury conceived the relationship of God and man as being dialectical and dynamic in character. While he sought to preserve the nonpersonal character of

Deity, he also had a sufficiently deep understanding of religious experience to know that when man loves God, he is in turn "loved."

In developing his philosophy of love, Shaftesbury, like the Cambridge Platonists, tried to steer a path between the extremes of the mystics and the Deists. The mystics' "high-raised love" went beyond reason (II, 55); the Deists, on the other hand, had stripped their "rational religion" of all genuine religious feeling and imaginative vision.[39] Henry More had remarked that they "ill deserve the name of Christians, who so indulge a sort of dry and hungry Reason, as wholly to exclude all manner of Enthusiasm." [40] Shaftesbury further charges the advocates of rational religion with grounding religion on the fear of punishment and the hope of reward, rather than on disinterested love of God for His own sake. By so doing, they debase religion, "for how shall one deny that to serve God by compulsion, or for interest merely, is servile and mercenary?" (II, 55) True affection for Deity is distinct "from everything worldly, sensual, or meanly interested. [It is] a love which is simple, pure, and unmixed, which has no other object than merely the excellency of that being itself, nor admits of any other thought of happiness than in its single fruition." (II, 54)

Shaftesbury admits that he is propounding a "paradox of faith," (II, 56) for in his system God is the symbol of man's true good or true interest. To love God is to love one's own true good; yet at the same time it must be a disinterested love. Only in relation to the dialectic of enthusiasm can this be understood. In religious, moral, and aesthetic experience, Shaftesbury pictures man as involved in a continual process of self-transcendence. By giving himself to that which is more than self, man both *makes* himself and *is made*. Self-giving is a necessary condition of self-discovery and self-realization; without it we cannot comprehend either Nature or God. The process itself is not only the means *to* Deity, but *is* Deity. Love is the energy that impels man beyond himself to seek the good, to seek that which has intrinsic value. Love of others—the giving of self to others—means participation in wider and deeper communities of meaning. Enthusiasm is the rapturous state in which the mind is "taken up in vision," and possessed by the highest— the state in which man experiences his own true fullness of being.

In Shaftesbury's system, the highest point of man's inner development is the "free and voluntary love" of God, in which all enthusiasms have their consummation:

Shall I be ashamed of this diviner love and of an object of love so far excelling all those objects in dignity, majesty, grace, beauty, and amiableness? Is this enthusiasm? Be it: and so may I be ever an enthusiast. Happy me, if I can grow on this enthusiasm, so as to lose all those enthusiasms of every other kind and be whole towards this. . . . Is the beatific vision enthusiasm? Or suppose it enthusiasm, is it not justifiable and of a right kind? What can be more highly reasonable? [41]

CHAPTER THREE

KNOWLEDGE and INTUITION: REASON and REVELATION

One looks in vain for any well-worked-out or even explicit theory of knowledge in Shaftesbury's writings. Epistemological issues that many philosophers of the Renaissance and the Enlightenment gave extended treatment to, he either ignores or, more often, merely touches upon in passing. Yet from such scattered remarks, and from the few passages where he does confront the issues, we must attempt to sketch at least the broad outlines of the epistemology that undergirds his philosophy of man and Nature.[1]

Shaftesbury clearly rejects any appeal to authority per se as a criterion of truth. As for sense-knowledge, he agrees with Henry More that "the strength of perception is no sure ground of truth." (II, 199)[2] Though More is quoted in the context of a discussion of ecstatic visions, it is Shaftesbury's position in general that sensations cannot be taken in themselves; they must be analyzed and evaluated in relation to the total situation of the perceiving mind. (I, 209)

The dictates of authority and the reports of the senses need, for one thing, to be checked against common sense, which

Shaftesbury often appeals to in the assessment of truth. Yet he recognizes that common sense cannot simply be taken to mean the opinions held by all or the majority of mankind, not only because it is difficult to determine what the majority-opinion is, but also because majority-opinion is likely to change from time to time, leaving us in doubt as to the truth. In religion he observes that "*common* sense . . . [is] as hard still to determine as *catholic* or *orthodox*" (I, 55); the situation is even worse in morals. Later, however, Shaftesbury suggests a different interpretation of common sense, understanding it to mean a "sense of public weal, and of the common interest; love of the community or society, natural affection, humanity, obligingness, or that sort of civility which rises from a just sense of the common rights of mankind, and the natural equality there is amongst those of the same species." (I, 70) Thus, he shifts our attention to the sources of what men can and do hold in common. Common sense is a guide to truth when it is rooted in common affection and in commitment to common interests. It is in this context that we must understand his recommendation that the ordinary man does "best to stick to common sense" in morals, for "men's first thoughts in this matter are generally better than their second: their natural notions better than those refined by study or consultation with casuists." (I, 88) Yet, Shaftesbury, as we shall have ample opportunity to see, was no primitivist. He stressed the need for cultivating and exercising one's mental capacities, but he did not restrict these to the intellectual dimension. Man's emotional commitments play a vital role in determining his grasp of "truth"; the intellect divorced from natural affection will only mislead us.

Cassirer interprets Shaftesbury's *sensus communis* as meaning a "certainty which reveals itself only to the nobler and finer

nature, which for this reason does not possess less, but rather
the very highest evidence and true universality." [3] While it is
true that common sense in its highest forms can only be found
in those who have cultivated their mental and spiritual capabilities, it must be pointed out that Shaftesbury believed that
it exists in some degree in all men in so far as they share in a
communal life made possible by natural affection and a common commitment to the public good. Shaftesbury combines an
aristocratic philosophy with a democratic sympathy for the
"common honest man." He is well aware that "speculative
men" have too often perverted "the original plain principles of
humanity." (I, 88) In formulating his concept of "common
sense" as a source of insight into universal truths, Shaftesbury
drew from the Stoics, the Cambridge Platonists, and no doubt
in part from Lord Herbert of Cherbury's theory of "common
notions." While seeking to avoid an appeal to mere consensus
of opinion, Shaftesbury argues that there are some moral and
philosophical ideas that are universally true and self-evident.
Indeed, he finds it easier to imagine half of mankind mad than
to suppose they would reject these basic ideas grounded in
"natural knowledge, fundamental reason, and common sense."
(I, 97) He refers to them sometimes as "innate ideas," a concept we will return to shortly. For Shaftesbury, then, common
sense has its ground in these commitments of the total self—
involving the intellect, the emotions, and the will—which underlie civilized society. The meaning is subtly shifted away
from what men *do* in fact hold in common to what they *ought*
to hold in common—to the ideal possibilities of universal
knowledge.

Shaftesbury objects to any limitation of the quest for truth
to formal and discursive reason. As against those "moon-blind

wits" who will allow us "to know nothing beside what we can prove by strict and formal demonstration," (II, 287) he makes an appeal to common sense and intuition. As Cassirer states, for Shaftesbury " 'truth' signifies rather the inner intellectual structure of the universe, which cannot be known in terms of concepts alone or grasped inductively by means of an accumulation of individual experiences, but which can only be immediately experienced and intuitively understood." [4] Aesthetic experience provides him with the model of such intuitive comprehension, for in it the separation of inner and outer, subjective and objective, is overcome in the act of apprehending the "inner form" of an aesthetic totality. True understanding is grasping the "whole" of a particular system of things—its characteristic form—and from this moving to its parts. "Reason and good sense . . . ," he writes, "must be *caught*, not learnt in the common way of instruction," as a painter is said to "catch a likeness." [5] Such intuitive awareness of the truth cannot be attained merely by constructing a system of logical concepts, nor by merely adding one fact to another. It is an immediate creative insight which gives coherent meaning to a structure of being. This doctrine of intuition is essential to any understanding of Shaftesbury's philosophy even though he himself never, to my knowledge, uses the term "intuition" as such.

In arriving at his position Shaftesbury turned from Locke, in whose philosophy he could not find an adequate doctrine of creative imagination, to the Cambridge Platonists. Locke significantly had little interest in the arts, a lack of which Shaftesbury deplored. In his discussion of the difference between "wit" and "judgment" Locke defines the former as a facility in putting together ideas that have some similarity, and "thereby to make up pleasant pictures and agreeable visions in the fancy." [6] Judgment, which consists in the ability to distinguish carefully between ideas even though they may appear congruous, is the superior faculty since clear thought depends on it. Wit proceeds by way of

metaphor and allusion, wherein for the most part lies that entertainment and pleasantry of wit which strikes so lively on the fancy, and therefore so acceptable to all people; because its beauty appears at first sight, and there is required no labour of thought to examine what truth or reason there is in it.[7]

Locke concludes with the warning that these "agreeable visions" of wit fail to measure up to the "severe rules of reason."

Shaftesbury sought to go beyond such a distinction. While no less critical of "mere fancy," he attempted to formulate a concept of intuition which was something more than Locke's "wit" or "judgment," or Hobbes's concept of "fancy" as an associative process of secondary value. He found a clue to this in the Cambridge Platonists, particularly Cudworth, who conceived of the understanding as an active, creative process. Unfortunately, because of Shaftesbury's lack of interest in the technical formulation of his epistemology, we have to reconstruct it on the basis of hints or what is implied in his writings, rather than on the basis of any explicit formulation of it. But it is clear that he conceived of intuition as a spontaneous, creative, mental process sharply distinct from mere passive sensation or reflex response, as well as from discursive reason.

Since Shaftesbury's interest in the arts evidently was an important factor in the shaping of his thought, it is not surprising that many of the clues that we have to follow here come from his aesthetic theory. In his analysis of "poetic truth" Shaftesbury follows Aristotle's distinction in the *Poetics* that "poetry is something more philosophic and of graver import than history, since its statements are of the nature rather of universals, whereas those of history are singulars." [8] Poetry may teach us more about human nature than history even though the latter is more correct in reporting individual matters of fact. The poet, the "moral artist," does not convey truth merely by copying Nature, or by describing what has been or is, but rather by enabling us to envision the possible, the probable, and the necessary. According to Shaftesbury, the creative mind grasps a pattern, a coherent "whole" which gives meaning to the particular facts. Facts have no "meaning" in isolation, only in relation; in the same way, the individual person has no meaning in isolation, only in relation. "Facts unably related, though with the greatest sincerity and good faith, may prove the worst sort of deceit; and mere lies judiciously composed, can teach us the truth of things beyond any other manner." (I, 222 f.) The particular "lies" of a poet like Homer may be part of the fabric of a larger vision which communicates the highest moral truth. This idea, familiar enough in Neoclassical aesthetics, was carried over by Shaftesbury into the sphere of moral theology. Moral and religious truths, like poetic fictions, belong to the realm of the unseen—the realm of the imagination—and they convey not merely a collection of particulars, but a pattern of meaningful possibilities. They are intended not merely to describe but to transform reality as experienced. Theocles must take flight on "wings of fancy" to travel through these "invisible ideal worlds." Moral and religious truths are ideal projections which conform, not to the external world of appearance, but to the inner form of Being itself, to Nature's "pure *self.*" [9] The discovery of these truths is dependent on a creative act of the imagination in which the mind grasps a "whole" of things, if not "the Whole." In Shaftesbury's philosophy, God and Nature are known only through such synthetic intuition.

Shaftesbury's rejection of a simplistic empiricism or a reductionistic naturalism is, of course, not a defense of supernaturalism. Intuition for him is always a rational process of mind. Moreover, both moral and religious knowledge have their foundations in our own inner nature: man is "not only born to virtue . . . but to religion." (II, 294) [10] Religion is natural to man; it is, as John Smith had expressed it, "no Art, but an inward Nature." [11] Despite Locke's powerful attack on "innate ideas," Shaftesbury dared to argue that the idea of God was "in a manner innate, or such as men were really born to and could hardly by any means avoid." (II, 178) But he does not mean by an "innate idea" one that is present in consciousness at birth or even in childhood; such a theory could hardly be defended. Rather it is an idea that germinates almost inevitably in the natural process of human development, because of the way the human mind is structured. It is a natural capacity which is developed as the power of our thought matures. In Shaftesbury's philosophy, such innate ideas as those of beauty, good, and God are essential aspects of his model of man. To be a man means, by definition, to have the capacity for such ideas and to have realized that capacity in some degree. Through his reason man becomes conscious of participating in successively larger communities which give meaning to his individual life. Ultimately, this develops into an awareness of belonging to a cosmic community.

Yet as we saw in the discussion of enthusiasm, Shaftesbury was well aware that man's natural religiosity can express itself in a variety of forms, some of which are distortions of true religion. It was to guard against this possibility that the Augustan philosopher stressed the need for reason in religion. His view of the relation of reason and revelation represents the culmination of a line of development in seventeenth-century philosophy that extended through Herbert of Cherbury, the Cambridge Platonists, Locke, and Bayle. In general the Cambridge men held the position that the truths of revelation must and indeed would harmonize with those of natural reason. Locke admitted the existence of revealed truths that were above reason, but denied that they could be contrary to reason. A divinely revealed truth could not be questioned, but one could ask whether a purported revelation was in fact from God or not. While Locke grants reason a key role as a judge of revelation, his position remains more traditional than that of Shaftesbury. Whereas Locke and the Cambridge Platonists aimed to demonstrate on broad grounds the reasonableness of Christianity, the third Earl and the Deists gave more attention to exposing the irrationality of many of the teachings of positive religion and aimed only to establish the rationality of natural religion. Whereas the former continued to hold to doctrines of supernatural grace and revelation, the latter rejected both of these in formulating a religion, in Kant's phrase, "within the limits of reason alone."

It is Shaftesbury's belief that God has endowed man with reason: "Nor could God witness for himself or assert his being any other way to men, than by revealing himself to their reason, appealing to their judgment, and submitting his ways to their censure and cool deliberation." (II, 91) When men are asked to believe what is "above" reason or contrary to it, they are only alienated from religion. Shaftesbury has Philocles define the two erroneous extremes: "You who are rationalists, and walk by reason in everything, pretend to know all things, whilst you believe little or nothing. We, for our parts, know nothing and believe all." (II, 18) The kind of rationalism that makes it impossible to have faith in anything is just as destructive as the kind of skepticism that allows us to accept religious doctrines on faith even though they are clearly unreasonable.

Shaftesbury argues that those who hold to orthodox Christian beliefs actually don't have as much certainty as they may think. Anyone who has not himself received a revelation or a miraculous sign can have no more than a conditional faith. "And the best Christian in the world, who being destitute of the means of certainty depends only on history and tradition for his belief in these particulars, is at best but a sceptic Christian." (II, 201) His must be a "critical historical faith" dependent on doctrinal speculation and biblical criticism. He either has to undertake an independent study of the original documents of his religion or accept the interpretation of some other person whom he considers a competent authority. In the former case, he has to rely on his own critical judgment; in the latter, on that of others, so that his faith is actually not in the ancient Scriptures but in contemporary interpreters of them. In either case interpretation is required and an element of skepticism will inevitably enter his mind, no matter how hard he tries to exclude it. Shaftesbury points out that Paul himself, though said to have had an original revelation, exhibited such skepticism, for he often spoke with hesitation and reserve, distinguishing carefully between his own opinion and what he believed to be divinely revealed. The founders of our religion evidently didn't require as absolute an assent to their writings as later, less inspired, teachers have for their *interpretations* of those writings. On the other hand, the Gnostics, who claimed to have certain knowledge of the mysteries of faith, are considered the "worst of heretics." Shaftesbury concludes that "if the most dangerous state of opinion was this dogmatical and presumptuous sort, the safest, in all likelihood, must be the sceptical and modest." (II, 203)

Shaftesbury is anxious to convince his reader that no book in human language should be placed in the privileged category of being above criticism, since language itself is a creation of men, and the meaning of the written word is, therefore, necessarily a matter of interpretation. "Mere enthusiasts" may claim that they can understand the Bible solely through the inspiration of the Holy Spirit, and without the aid of objective scholarship, but in fact they rely on a text which is itself a translation and the product of a textual tradition in which scholarship and criticism played an important part. More "judicious divines" have recognized this fact, and have acknowledged the necessity for critical scholarship and the free examination of texts. Since, according to Shaftesbury, there is "at present no immediate testimony of miracle or sign in behalf of Holy Writ, and there being in its own particular composition or style nothing miraculous or self-convincing," there is all the more need for the "collateral testimony" of other ancient, pagan writings to support its sanctity. (II, 301) At the same time, Shaftesbury seeks to assure the orthodox that where divine sanction has been given to a document it would be immoral to dispute "the least line." [12] However, he adds with irony, if the Scripture, instead of being short and consistent, is "multifarious, voluminous, and of the most difficult interpretation," it would be impossible to suppress differing interpretations of it. (II, 298) Thus, Shaftesbury argues that even religions which appeal to an original revelation cannot escape the exercise of critical reason. A religious document is subject to the same criteria as a philosophical writing or a work of art. It too must conform to the eternal rules of beauty and goodness, and such conformity can only be determined by rational analysis.

One of Shaftesbury's basic arguments is that no one can believe in God and His goodness without first having a clear conception of the concept of God and of goodness itself. "By goodness alone trust is created." (II, 92) Thus, reason precedes faith, and ethics precedes theology. Shaftesbury places great weight on the teleological argument, as we will see in the next chapter. The order of Nature leads us to conclude that there is a Divine Orderer. With such a well-founded faith the individual

can then hearken to historical revelation, and is then fitted (and not till then) for the reception of any message or miraculous notice from above, where he knows beforehand all is just and true. But this no power of miracles, nor any power besides his reason, can make him know or apprehend. (II, 92)

If, as the skeptics say, theology cannot be grounded on philosophy apart from revelation, then "theology must have no foundation at all. For revelation itself, we know, is founded on the acknowledgement of a divine existence; and 'tis the province of philosophy alone to prove what revelation only supposes." (II, 53 f.)

True religion is, then, dependent on philosophy, but is philosophy in turn dependent on religion? Taking Shaftesbury's thought as a whole, the answer to this must be affirmative. We must remember that for Shaftesbury "reason" and "philosophy" are broadly conceived. Philosophy is not a narrow empiricism or a strict rationalism, but a discipline so comprehensive that it can take in the realm of enthusiasm too. True philosophy needs the guidance and inspiration of religious commitments; without this, philosophy would lack an inner dynamic. Reason and faith are neither inconsistent nor opposed. Faith is a commitment of the whole person, intellectually, emotionally, and volitionally. Though Shaftesbury can write in his philosophical notebook, "All is faith, and without faith all must be Atheism," [13] faith is understood to mean substantially "the reserved powers of reason" itself.[14]

Shaftesbury's treatment of this problem implies a recognition of the need for a continuing dialogue between philosophy and religion. However, he is also interested in keeping each in its proper sphere (I, 232), and is especially concerned with protecting philosophy from the interference of ecclesiastical hierarchies or narrowly conceived religious orthodoxies. The "unnatural union" of philosophy and religion in the Middle Ages, he believes, wrecked philosophy, producing "a thousand monsters of a scholastic brood." (II, 206) To prevent this, philosophy must retain its autonomy. Shaftesbury moves beyond the position of the Cambridge Platonists though in asserting the primacy of reason over revelation. And it is philosophy rather than theology that is made the final judge of all sciences and all knowledge, for by it "religion itself is judged, spirits are searched, prophecies proved, miracles distinguished. . . ." (I, 193)

It is also philosophy rather than theology that is given the job of refuting atheism, because its method, Shaftesbury thinks, is more appropriate. In trying to convince atheists of their error, he warns against relying on an emotional appeal alone. The best strategy is to approach the subject with objectivity, even an air of "indifference," and to indicate a willingness to follow the argument to its logical conclusion, whatever it may be. This method has the best chance of removing the obstacles to religious faith.

The knowledge of God cannot be attained solely through a scientific study of physical realities, or through a process of logical deduction or induction. True, there is evidence for believing, but evidence is insufficient apart from a framework of interpretation. This "framework" is what Shaftesbury means by "innate ideas," the *a priori* categories of the mind. But along with this, Shaftesbury's theory, like all genuine theories of religious experience, postulates an immediate consciousness of Deity itself. Such knowledge is possible because we share in His Being as He shares in ours. This knowledge of God has an immediacy and certainty comparable to that of our own self-consciousness. Nothing, Shaftesbury writes, is more real or more certain to us than "thought," and

thus are we in a manner conscious of that original and eternally existent thought whence we derive our own. And thus the assurance we have of the existence of beings above our sense and of thee (the great exemplar of thy works) comes from thee, the all true and perfect, who hast thus communicated thyself more immediately to us, so as in some manner to inhabit within our souls, thou who art original soul, diffusive, vital in all, inspiriting the whole. (II, 112)

Not only do all things "sympathize" in the natural world, as the Stoics taught, but by a natural sympathetic attraction we are drawn to the "centre of souls." But it is only through the power of creative intuition that we can transcend the limitations of our finitude and comprehend the Infinite, however imperfectly.

CHAPTER FOUR

NATURE and GOD

Shaftesbury's doctrine of enthusiasm provides the dynamic context in which he approaches Nature. As is said of Theocles, " 'Twas Nature he was in love with; 'twas Nature he sung." (II, 25) The rhapsodic hymn to Nature in "The Moralists" is the poetic expression of this attitude. Unlike the Baconian empiricists who sought to comprehend the structure of Nature in order to control it, Shaftesbury follows the Platonic tradition, seeking to understand the order of Nature for its own sake, and believing that this understanding could be achieved only by an act of sympathy. The Platonists, as Cassirer writes, "do not seek dominion; they seek a knowledge of that which holds the world together at its core. And they find this substantial bond, not in power, but in love. . . ." [1] Shaftesbury, as we have seen, scorns the scientist who seeks some simple but marvelous formula by which to use Nature for his own ends. Our ultimate aim must not be power over Nature, but communion *with* Nature—a communion which makes it possible for the power of Nature to work in and through us. The inner reality of Nature will not be disclosed by mechanistic analysis, but only by aesthetic intuition. Love not only provides the dynamic means by which we grasp this truth, it is also the innermost bond of Nature itself.

Although the distinction between God and Nature is not always clearly drawn in Shaftesbury's writings, he generally speaks of God as the more ultimate concept. God has created Nature and has endowed her with creative powers so that she might carry on the work of providence. The "restless and fighting elements" have been composed into the harmony of Nature, ". . . supremely fair and sovereignly good! all-loving and all-lovely, all-divine!" (II, 98) It is significant that Shaftesbury more often pictures the order of Nature as analogous to living organisms than to machines. Nature is conceived in terms of change and purposive process; he goes so far as to speak of it as animate and intelligent. Nothing could be farther from the Lockian view of Nature as "a dull affair, soundless, scentless, colourless; merely the hurrying of material, endlessly, meaninglessly." [2] For Shaftesbury, Nature is the bountiful "creatress" overflowing with all the possibilities of being. And if it is true, as Basil Willey says, that Nature and reason are generally associated in the early part of the eighteenth century, and Nature and feeling in the latter part, it must be said that Shaftesbury united both emphases in his world-view. While Nature always signifies for him the rational structure of reality, it is a structure that cannot be grasped except through enthusiasm. Like his contemporaries, Shaftesbury is none too consistent in his uses of the term "Nature." At times it is used to denote the created universe as it appears to us, but its more fundamental meaning is the rational laws governing the cosmos —the ideal possibilities of form.

According to Shaftesbury, "whatsoever is superior in any degree over the world, or rules in Nature with discernment

and a mind, is what by universal agreement, men call God."
(I, 240) Intelligence is the supreme attribute of Deity, and
true theism is defined as believing that "everything is governed, ordered, or regulated for the best, by a designing principle or mind, necessarily good and permanent." (*Ibid.*) The
strict theist can admit no element of chance in his ordered universe, while, in contrast, the atheist attributes all events to
chance, denying that there is any "designing principle or mind
. . . so that in Nature neither the interest of the whole nor of
any particulars can be said to be in the least designed. . . ."
(*Ibid.*) Demonism is defined as the belief that a Deity is "not
absolutely and necessarily good, nor confined to what is best,
but capable of acting according to mere will or fancy." (I, 241)
Shaftesbury comments that since men are usually not too consistent in their religious philosophies, one usually finds the
above theories (along with polytheism) mixed together. (I,
241 f.) These definitions are important for they already imply
much of Shaftesbury's concept of Nature and God.

Arguments for God

Since Shaftesbury contended that the existence of God could
be demonstrated rationally, our first concern must be with his
treatment of the various traditional arguments for God, and
his own particular formulation of some of them. First of all,
there is the famous "wager" argument which was much in
vogue at the end of the seventeenth century, and which is
remembered today mainly for the rather subtle form that
Pascal gave it.[3] Whether Shaftesbury was familiar with Pascal's
statement of it, I do not know, but it is to Archbishop Tillot-

son's version that he refers in the "Letter Concerning Enthusiasm." (I, 26) Tillotson argued that it is the better part of wisdom to believe in God since, if God exists, you will be rewarded for your faith, and if He does not exist, you will have lost nothing. Furthermore, if there is a Deity, and you have not believed in Him, you will be punished. Tillotson, of course, is assuming a God who rewards and punishes, and it is just this aspect of the argument that Shaftesbury chooses to attack. If God is indeed such a retributive Being, perhaps the wager has a certain cogency. But Shaftesbury rejects the concept of a God who punishes men for lack of faith. A benevolent God of truth would want men to use their minds freely and with integrity. It is inconceivable that He would want anyone to pretend to "believe" in order to be rewarded. Furthermore, the idea that God would approve of immorality—in this case, dishonesty—would damage rather than support belief in Deity. In a later chapter we shall see that Shaftesbury had still a further objection: even if one honestly believed in a God of retribution, if one's motives were self-centered, it would not be the truest and highest form of faith.

Shaftesbury's conception of the order of Nature and his definition of true theism make it impossible for him to accept the argument for the existence of God based on miracles, at least if miracles are understood as violations of natural law or products of sheer chance. True theism is based on our conviction that Nature is governed by law, but belief in miracles in the above sense would only tend to undermine this conviction. Since I will discuss Shaftesbury's ideas about miracles more at length later, here I will restrict myself to the remarks he directly aimed at this traditional argument, which was still very popular in his time and remained so until Hume's brilliant critique largely shattered its force for modern man. The third Earl took the position that the occurrence of miracles was not required to establish the validity of religion. However, even if we admitted that they occurred at times, how could we know whether they were the work of benevolent or malevolent powers? Bayle had raised the same question about the comet of 1680, and since the church traditionally acknowledged this problem, this was an effective line of attack. Shaftesbury writes:

What powers, whether one or more, whether superior or subaltern, mortal or immortal, wise or foolish, just or unjust, good or bad; this would still remain a mystery, as would the true intention, the infallibility or certainty of whatever those powers asserted. Their word could not be taken in their own case. They might silence men indeed, but not convince them; since "Power can never serve as proof for goodness, and goodness is the only pledge of truth." By goodness alone trust is created. By goodness superior powers may win belief . . . and . . . be confided in; "When by repeated marks their benevolence is proved, and their character of sincerity and truth established." (II, 92)

To this Shaftesbury adds the crucial point that miracles cannot establish the existence of God, for to attribute miracles to God we must already have presupposed His existence.

Shaftesbury believed, as did Locke, that the existence of God could be demonstrated by reason, but instead of stressing a proof based on causation, he rested his case almost entirely on the teleological argument. In "The Moralists," Philocles says to Theocles, "I expected to have heard from you, in customary form, of a first cause, a first being, and a beginning of motion. How clear the idea was of an immaterial substance, and how plainly it appeared that at some time or other matter must have been created." (II, 69) But instead, Theocles has attempted to prove from present experience that a Deity exists *now*, and to show that the order and design evident in the world necessarily point to a supreme, designing Mind. This was, in fact, the prevailing conviction of the Augustan age.

"All Nature's wonders," Shaftesbury writes, "serve to excite and perfect this idea of their author. 'Tis here he suffers us to see, and even converse with him in a manner suitable to our frailty." (II, 112) Shaftesbury gives considerable attention to detailing the evidence for harmony in Nature. In general, he argues along the following lines: Knowledge of the functions and purposes of the parts of living organisms—the ingenious adaptation of means to ends—leads us to recognize the same relationship of parts in Nature as a Whole. The carefully organized coordination of the parts of particular things reveals an inward order or coherence which must also be an attribute of the Whole. Microcosm reveals macrocosm. Each "whole" or "entire system" of things is a composite of proportioned parts, revealing inward order or unity of design. Each particular existing thing is dependent on all other parts of the system of which it is a member; and each particular system is dependent on, and a member of, a larger system or systems, until all things are at last seen as united in one Universal System, the parts of which are proportionate and consistent. (II, 64) [4]

Resorting to analogy, Shaftesbury argues that a man who comes across a strange construction in the desert, even though not knowing its purpose or its maker, would still reasonably assume it to be a product of design rather than of mere chance. In the same way, a person entirely ignorant of sailing, who was taken aboard a ship, would quickly recognize that a designing intelligence had arranged the various parts of the vessel, even though he might be unaware of the exact purpose of each item.

Thus, the overwhelming evidence of design in Nature should be sufficiently convincing to us even though we do not know the purpose of each individual thing.

Shaftesbury found purposeful order no less in the nature of man than in the realm of things outside of man. A central aspect of his teleological argument was his theory of the natural harmony of the human affections, and his contention that the moral order is a further extension of the purposeful continuity of Nature. Man is not only capable of true virtue, but in virtue lies his only true happiness; the cosmic order guarantees this moral law.[5]

It is easy to see then why Shaftesbury particularly attacked those religious writers who thought that the concept of Nature governed by law and order would play into the hands of the deterministic atheists, and who, therefore, stressed the miraculous and the extraordinary. As we have seen, Shaftesbury rejected the argument from miracles on grounds that it, rather than the teleological argument, would lead men to doubt the Divine. Furthermore, the order of Nature could not be proven by first establishing Deity; to the contrary, "the contemplation of the universe, its laws and government, was . . . the only means which could establish the sound belief of a Deity." (II, 91)

However, the skeptical Philocles doubts the validity of Theocles's statement of the teleological argument, contending that he has failed to provide demonstrative proof of a Supreme Intelligence, but has, at best, suggested a probability. If a finite mind cannot comprehend all, he cogently argues, how can one assert that there is an infinite cosmic order? He continues:

For grant that this all, which lies within our view or knowledge, is orderly and united, as you suppose; this mighty all is a mere point still, a very nothing compared to what remains. " 'Tis only a separate by-world (we'll say) of which perhaps there are, in the wide waste, millions besides, as horrid and deformed as this of ours is regular and proportioned. In length of time, amidst the infinite hurry and shock of beings, this single odd world, by accident, might have been struck out, and cast into some form (as among infinite chances what is there which may not happen?). But for the rest of matter, 'tis of a different hue. Old Father Chaos (as the poets call him) in these wild spaces reigns absolute, and upholds his realms of darkness. He presses hard upon our frontier, and one day, belike, shall by a furious inroad recover his lost right, conquer his rebel state, and reunite us to primitive discord and confusion." (II, 71)

But despite such objections Shaftesbury remains convinced that it is reasonable to infer that if natural law rules in the realm of our present experience it must extend throughout the cosmos. This conviction, which reflects the prevailing temper of mind in the Enlightenment, had been strongly reinforced by scientific discoveries, such as the law of gravity, which provided evidence that the physical laws operative on earth functioned throughout the universe. Yet in the strict sense Shaftesbury cannot overcome Philocles's objection without appealing to enthusiasm, or indeed, faith.

In all his writings, Shaftesbury repeatedly attacks the ancient materialists, Epicurus and Democritus, and their modern followers. It is unreasonable to suppose that the universe and thinking beings emerged by pure chance from a chaos of atoms. Order could not arise from mere disorder; the continuity of Nature could not originate by sheer accident. The "modern hypothesis" that the universe is an eternal system of self-regulating matter cannot stand up under analysis. For one thing, Shaftesbury shares the popular opinion of his age that mechanistic materialism could not account for the marvelous

adaptation to environment by plant and animal organisms.[6]
And had not the great Newton even conceded that the organization of the solar system could not be explained entirely in
terms of mechanical causation? The universe may be analogous
to a machine but, if so, Shaftesbury argues that it is intelligible
only as a "God-governed machine." (II, 93)

Shaftesbury has Philocles agree with "the spiritual men" that
a material, unthinking substance could never produce an immaterial, thinking substance. But he goes on to say that

> their argument will hold good against a Democritus, an Epicurus,
> or any of the elder or latter atomists. But it will be turned on them
> by an examining Academist, and when the two substances are fairly
> set asunder, and considered apart as different kinds, 'twill be as
> strong sense, and as good argument, to say as well of the immaterial
> kind: "That do with it as you please, modify it a thousand ways,
> purify it, exalt it, sublime it, torture it ever so much or rack it, as
> they say, with thinking, you will never be able to produce or force
> the contrary substance out of it." (II, 70)

Philocles is convinced that he has posed an insoluble dilemma—
indeed, Descartes had struggled over the same issue. Yet the
dualistic terms in which he poses the problem are really alien to
Shaftesbury's thought, which is essentially monistic. It is significant that in "The Moralists" he consciously turns away
from an attempt to solve this problem on the level of abstract
metaphysics, but focusses instead on the teleological argument
and the experiential evidence of a natural order.

Yet Shaftesbury, no less than the Cambridge Platonists, is
certain that "what is intelligent cannot be produced out of
what is not intelligent," [7] that the higher, i.e., the mental, cannot evolve from the lower—the nonmental—but only the lower
from the higher. More cannot come from less, or something
from nothing. Mechanistic materialism not only cannot explain

how atoms became "wise," but it falls into the error of reductionism, blotting out all distinction between the higher and the
lower. Mind must have preceded matter, for otherwise there
would have been an everlasting chaos. "Thought" is indeed
"pre-eminent . . . the realest of beings." (II, 112)

Since the universe not only produces intelligent beings but
exhibits rational organization and structure, it must be the
product of a Supreme Mind. Nature is comparable to a "self"
that is governed by a principle that unites its parts, and thinks
and acts for the Whole. Thus, Shaftesbury argues that our
experience of purposeful order in the structure of Nature
leads the mind inevitably to the hypothesis that all things are
infused by an eternal, active, governing principle of intelligence. The contemplation of the rational structure of Nature
and true theism are inseparably joined. Yet, however much he
may have been convinced of the reasonableness of his argument, he recognized that apart from religious experience his
vision of Nature could not convince the human mind. Significantly, the "cold, indifferent" Philocles only overcomes his
doubts after the highly emotional and romantic rhapsody on
Nature in Part III of "The Moralists" enables him to share in
Theocles's divine enthusiasm.

Deism

Though Shaftesbury is commonly classified as a Deist, it should
be evident in what has preceded that he was a Deist with a difference. In a letter of 1701 Shaftesbury writes that he has "a
general acquaintance with most of our modern authors and
free writers, several of whom I have a particular influence

over." [8] He identifies himself there with this group of "free-thinkers." Among his Deistic friends were John Toland and Anthony Collins. The former received an annual stipend from the third Earl, and was responsible for the unauthorized publication of the "Inquiry Concerning Virtue" in 1699.[9] Shaftesbury wrote that he had the "highest respect and friendship" for Anthony Collins, and that he admired his "virtue . . . and public spirit." [10] Shaftesbury's grandfather, incidentally, was reputed to be a Deist, and the third Earl himself was charged with promoting "Deism and Atheism" as early as 1709,[11] while "The Moralists" was called by some "the Deist's bible."

Shaftesbury was, of course, sympathetic with the Deistic attempt to found religion on reason. Through Palemon in "The Moralists" Shaftesbury defends Deism:

For as averse as I am to the cause of theism, or name of Deist, when taken in a sense exclusive of revelation, I consider still that in strictness the root of all is theism, and that to be a settled Christian, it is necessary to be first of all a good theist; for theism can only be opposed to polytheism or atheism. Nor have I patience to hear the name of Deist (the highest of all names) decried, and set in opposition to Christianity. "As if our religion was a kind of magic, which depended not on the belief of a single supreme Being. Or as if the firm and rational belief of such a Being on philosophical grounds was an improper qualification for believing anything further." Excellent presumption for those who naturally incline to the disbelief of revelation, or who through vanity affect a freedom of this kind! (II, 19)

Shaftesbury would also have agreed with the Deists in rejecting the idea of a God who favors one group of people with a special revelation that is not given to others, or who damns those denied special grace. God's relations with man cannot be governed by mere arbitrary will or power, but must conform to the universal laws of reason. Both Shaftesbury and the Deists wanted to preserve theology while freeing it from supernaturalism; both denied the occurrence of miracles; both called for free criticism of the Bible and questioned the absoluteness of its authority; both shared a distrust of sacramental and priestly religion; and both stressed the importance of morality in religion.

However, despite this broad area of agreement, Shaftesbury did not identify himself unreservedly with the developing Deistic movement, and he expressed some serious doubts about certain aspects of it. In 1709 he commended Matthew Tindal's theories on church and state but stated that Tindal's philosophy and theology differed widely from his own.[12] He went on to express his regret that the "free writers" of his time were in general following in the footsteps of Hobbes and, in some respects, of Locke. In "The Moralists" Theocles wonders whether all of the Deists are really true *theists:*

All affectation, but chiefly in philosophy, I must own, I think unpardonable. And you, Philocles, who can give no quarter to ill reasoning, nor endure any unsound or inconsistent hypothesis; you will be so ingenuous, I dare say, as to reject our modern Deism, and challenge those who assume a name to which their philosophy can never in the least entitle them.

Commend me to honest Epicurus, who raises his deities aloft in the imaginary spaces, and setting them apart out of the universe and nature of things, makes nothing of them beyond a word. This is ingenuous and plain dealing; for this every one who philosophises may easily understand. (II, 53)

Shaftesbury was bothered by an element of evasion and subterfuge in some of the Deistic writings. He expected Deism to meet the same standards required of theism. To deny the reality of providence or the order of Nature, to limit the benevolence or the rational potency of the Divine, is to fall short of Deism in its true sense. The Deists were wrong if they relegated God to the status of a Prime Mover without subsequent contact with the universe; Deity must be conceived as being in constant and living interaction with the creation; otherwise the concept is "dry and barren." (II, 54) Along the same lines, Cudworth had attacked both Hobbes and Descartes for making God an "idle spectator" of the universe, and for conceiving of the world as having "nothing neither vital nor magical at all in it." Thus, Shaftesbury emphasized the immanence of God, while the Deists placed greater stress on His transcendence. Their God was too cold and abstract; their rational religion lacked devotion and warmth. But for Shaftesbury a true conception of God would both stir us to action and arouse our deepest affections. God cannot be approached exclusively by way of reason and logic but, as the doctrine of enthusiasm requires, by way of feeling and love also.

While Shaftesbury, like the Deists, rejects the idea of supernatural revelation, he provides a central place for religious experience in his concept of enthusiasm which sets him apart from them and marks him once again as a true continuer of the tradition of the Cambridge Platonists. The latter, Basil Willey writes, "seem always to have grasped, what their deistic and scientific successors lost sight of, that religious belief is founded not upon 'evidence' but upon 'experience.' "[13] The religious dimension of the human spirit requires a movement of the total self. Religion, as John Smith expressed it, is "a divine life, rather than a divine science. . . ."[14] For Shaftesbury the living experience of Deity has its consummation in a mystical sense of identity with Him. Thus, the Augustan philosopher carried the vital religion of Cambridge Platonism as far as one could in the direction of rationalism without cutting off the emotional and intuitive sources of the religious life. The Deists went further, providing no significant place for religious experience. Thus, Shaftesbury stands somewhere in between the Cambridge men and his Deistic contemporaries: he was a Deist with a difference. Diderot aptly remarked that it is unfair to include Shaftesbury *"au nombre des Asgil, des Tindal, et des Toland, gens aussi décriés dans leur Église en qualité de chrétiens, que dans la république des lettres en qualité d'auteurs: mauvais protestans et misérables ecrivains."* [15] The Deists performed an important service, nevertheless, in preparing the way for later studies of religion, contributing, for example, to the development of biblical criticism, even though their biblical studies have been rendered archaic by the scholarship of the last one hundred years. As for the rest of the Deists' work, in contrast to Shaftesbury's writings, which have retained much of their verve and excitement, theirs seem strangely dry and dusty. They have fallen into an obscurity from which it is doubtful they will ever emerge.

The Nature of God

Shaftesbury's arguments for God and his differences with the Deists already tell us much about his conception of the nature of God. It is evident that he considers the most important attributes of Deity to be goodness and rationality. We will have more to say about the first of these in the next chapter. Shaftesbury argues for the unitary nature of God on grounds that if there were two or more conflicting principles in the universe, chaos would prevail—but this is patently false. On the other hand, if there were two or more principles that *did* agree, it would imply a single higher ruling intelligence which coordinated them. He also appeals to the Law of Parsimony to support his conclusion.

The traditional attributes of eternity and infinity are also assigned to Deity by Shaftesbury, who writes:

In vain . . . we pursue that phantom time, too small, yet too mighty for our grasp, when, shrinking to a narrow point, it escapes our hold, or mocks our scanty thought by swelling to eternity, an object unproportioned to our capacity, as is thy being, O thou ancient cause! older than time, yet young with fresh eternity.

In vain we try to fathom the abyss of space, the seat of thy extensive being, of which no place is empty, no void which is not full. (II, 111)

Shaftesbury rejects the possibility that God might be limited in power: "God" by definition means omnipotence. However, he makes it quite clear that divine omnipotence does not mean arbitrary or willful power. Both Shaftesbury and the Cambridge Platonists directed much of their attack against the Calvinists on grounds that they glorified sheer power in God at the expense of the divine reason and goodness. The power of God does not transcend the laws of moral reason: God cannot do what is unjust. Thus, for Shaftesbury God is "limited" but only in the sense that His activity is controlled necessarily by the laws of His own moral nature. "For 'twas impossible, you thought, that Heaven should have acted otherwise than for the best." (II, 16) But God could not successfully carry out His purposes without being omniscient. Since God thinks and acts for the sake of the totality of being, he must be aware of whatever is felt or done in the universe.

Shaftesbury's conception of the immanent creativity of God is derived ultimately from the Stoics and the Cambridge Platonists. The Stoic conception of Nature, or *Phusis*, implies a "soul" or vital force pervading matter as well as living organisms. It is a conscious, teleological principle governing natural causation. The Cambridge Platonists developed the doctrine of "plastic natures" as intermediaries between God and Nature. Cudworth conceived of them as immanent, creative principles which were unconscious though rational instruments of God's will, operating in the created universe. Thus, they provided a teleological explanation for what otherwise were assumed to be fortuitous mechanisms of Nature. The concept of "plastic powers" marks a transition from the older doctrine of Christian Platonism, that in the creation the divine Ideas were directly stamped on unformed matter, to Shaftesbury's conception of an immanent, creative Mind. "Shaftesbury," Cassirer writes, "looks upon the world as a work of art, and he wants to go back from the work of art to the artist who formed it and who is immediately present in all its manifestations of form." [16] The world-artist, or "sovereign Genius," is not conceived as copying an external model, but rather as a force which works from within and which realizes its purposes in its very activity. Deity "*is* only in so far as it is active." [17] Thus, Shaftesbury abandons the idea of "plastic powers" as separate agents of transcendent purpose, and assigns their functions directly to the creative Mind. (II, 105 f.) R. L. Brett suggests that for Shaftesbury the mind in Nature is a subordinate principle working for God rather than identical with God. [18] I fail to find this distinction though. The intelligibility of Nature—the very structure of natural law itself—is a direct manifestation of Deity. As Theocles rhapsodizes:

O mighty Genius! sole animating and inspiring power! author and subject of these thoughts! thy influence is universal, and in all things thou art inmost. From thee depend their secret springs of action. Thou movest them with an irresistible unwearied force, by sacred and inviolable laws, framed for the good of each particular being, as best may suit with the perfection, life, and vigour of the whole. The vital principle is widely shared and infinitely varied, dispersed throughout, nowhere extinct. . . . Munificent and great, she imparts herself to most and makes the subjects of her bounty infinite. (II, 110)

Because of this stress on the divine immanence, Shaftesbury does not always distinguish clearly between "God" and "Nature." He seems to use the terms interchangeably at times, particularly in the *Philosophical Regimen*, which most directly reflects Stoic influence. But though Leslie Stephen writes that "the school of Shaftesbury . . . made a God out of Nature . . . ," [19] in the *Characteristics* Shaftesbury usually makes a distinction between them. As we saw earlier in this chapter, God is defined as what is "*superior . . .* or *rules in* Nature." (I, 240) [20] Though God is found *in* Nature, He is always *more than* Nature. This is "panentheism" rather than "pantheism." It may be formulated as "God is *in* all, and all is *in* God," rather than simply as "God is All." Generally, Shaftesbury holds to this distinction.

While Shaftesbury places great emphasis on the immanence of God, perhaps in reaction to Calvinism, he also conceives of Deity as transcendent, for God is always *more than* Nature and man. He transcends Nature in power, and He transcends man's knowledge. The human mind cannot penetrate the immensity of Being itself, nor fathom the "abyss of Deity." (II, 98) God is manifest but also hidden—appearing "to our weak eyes . . . under a veil." (II, 124) Divine transcendence is not destroyed by divine immanence. Deity remains both a symbol of man's capacity for self-transcendence and the vital force that makes that transcendence possible.

Shaftesbury stresses the impersonal nature of God, yet such traits as consciousness, purpose, and intelligence, which he ascribes to Deity, are clearly "personal." For the English philosopher God cannot be *less than* personal, while at the same time He is also *more than* personal. Thus, while Shaftesbury wages a war against a crude, literalistic anthropomorphism, he cannot avoid using anthropomorphic language himself. God is our "friend," "father," or even "tender mother," though, of course, these terms are used figuratively. His quarrel with anthropomorphism is not directed against such metaphorical language—which, in fact, the doctrine of enthusiasm requires—but against the assumption that it is to be interpreted literally. He also warns repeatedly against ascribing to Deity traits such as anger or jealousy that are characteristically human but which are not appropriate to the moral nature of the Divine. God is "loving" in the sense that He is an impersonal force working for the good of all, but not in the sense that He acts like a human being and intervenes in behalf of particular individuals that He favors. God is "loving," but He cannot suffer—Shaftesbury's optimism, as we shall see, precludes that possibility.

The problem of drawing a line between these polar principles of immanence and transcendence, personality and impersonality, has always been a central one in "pantheistic" philosophies. As Mario Rossi has expressed it, "the solution lies somewhere in a balance between pantheism and personal theism, and in the great pantheists of the history of philosophy one should search for their particular attempts at maintaining this balance, at giving both aspects their due." [21] Shaftesbury could not avoid this polarity either, but found it necessary to use both sets of concepts dialectically to symbolize the nature of God's being and His relationship to man.

According to Shaftesbury, the concept of Deity must be the product of the highest reach of the imagination. God is both the source and the goal of our ideal aspirations: every perfect possibility is united coherently in His being. God is either not good at all, or absolutely good. Shaftesbury insists that there can be no malice in His nature, for a universal Being can have no interest other than the good of the Whole. So conceived, Deity arouses love instead of fear. In the creative activity of God Shaftesbury finds "the source and principle of all beauty and perfection," (II, 98) for "as beings partake of this, they are fair, and flourishing, and happy; as they are lost to this, they are deformed, perished, and lost." (II, 69) The infinite variety and beauty of forms in Nature—the Great Chain of Being—reveals the limitless activity of a bountiful Deity.

Miracles

If a miracle is defined as the intervention by the supernatural in the natural order causing the interruption or suspension of natural law, the occurrence of miracles is precluded by Shaftesbury's conception of Nature and God. We have already described his criticisms of the argument for the existence of God based on miracles. His strategy there was to demonstrate that even *if* miracles did happen they did not provide grounds for believing in a Deity, particularly a benevolent one. But Shaftesbury goes further than this in attempting to establish the impossibility of miracles, though he masks his real opinion with transparent irony.

He finds the source of the belief in miracles in a taste for the irrational and the disorderly, coupled with a delight in novelty. "You will own 'tis no small pleasure with mankind to make their dreams pass for realities, and that the love of truth is, in earnest, not half so prevalent as this passion for novelty and surprise, joined with a desire of making impression and being admired." (II, 86) This it is that leads some on a "visionary chase . . . in ghostly company of spirit-hunters, witch-finders, and layers-out for hellish stories and diabolical transactions." (II, 89) Shaftesbury may have had Henry More, among others, in mind when he wrote this for, in his later years, More relied more and more on proofs of the reality of Spirit based on apparitions and "witchcraft." Shaftesbury also found a type of atheist, of a variety one still encounters, who, while questioning the verity of Christian miracles, was completely taken in by any account of marvelous happenings in non-Christian cultures.

Shaftesbury's strategy is to purport to believe in the truth of those ancient miracles supported by the authority of Scripture, while questioning the occurrence of modern miracles. By proceeding in this way, he protects himself from charges of heresy, and he utilizes a common Protestant doctrine to cast doubt indirectly on the possibility of all miracles. Many clergymen at that time, including such well-known figures as Archbishop Tillotson and Robert South, accepted the doctrine that "miracles had ceased." Tillotson argued that after the Gospel was once established, miracles were no longer necessary, for its truth could be spread by reason alone. Scripture itself, Shaftesbury observes, warns against false prophets and false claims of the miraculous. How can we best protect ourselves, he asks, against such false claims, or against pious frauds perpetrated in support of some belief? His answer is to propose that we disbelieve in any present or future miracles. "For being satisfied of the truth of our religion by past miracles, so as to need no other to confirm us, the belief of new may often do us harm, but can never do us good." (II, 88) Pious Christians should be "miracle-proof," for a miracle that supports faith is unnecessary, and one that conflicts with faith must be rejected.

Shaftesbury appeals to supporters of the Established Church by contending that admitting the possibility of present-day miracles would only weaken its influence and reinforce the claims of the radical sects. With patent irony, he writes of himself:

He speaks indeed with contempt of the mockery of modern miracles and inspiration. And as to all pretences to things of this kind in our present age, he seems inclined to look upon them as no better than mere imposture or delusion. But for what is recorded of ages heretofore, he seems to resign his judgment, with entire condescension, to his superiors. He pretends not to frame any certain or positive opinion of his own, notwithstanding his best searches into antiquity and the nature of religious records and traditions; but on all occasions submits most willingly, and with full confidence and trust, to the opinions by law established. (II, 200 f.)

With tongue in cheek, he admits that his position might lend support to those who doubt that miracles *ever* occurred, but he professes to be convinced that, on the whole, Christianity would benefit by adopting it. He presses his point even further when he suggests that certain oracles and prodigies may have been allowed "as an imperfect kind of revelation" to the pagans, since they lacked Scripture, and to the Jews, because of the hardness of their hearts. "But Christians, for their parts, had a far better and truer revelation; they had their plainer oracles, a more rational law and clearer Scripture, carrying its own force, and withal so well attested as to admit of no dispute." (II, 90) Not content with arguing that miracles stopped after the completion of the Bible, Shaftesbury implies that the New Testament miracles themselves were unnecessary if the Christian revelation was indeed reasonable, as is claimed. Shaftesbury's heavy use of irony may suggest insincerity, but any criticism of his method of indirection must be tempered by our recognition of the legal limits placed on free discussion of religious topics in his time. This, as well as Shaftesbury's attitude toward the Established Church, will be discussed at length in Chapters VII and VIII.

The change in attitude toward miracles in the seventeenth century is illustrated by the transition of ideas from Herbert of Cherbury to Shaftesbury. The former still recognized the possibility of miracles, but the scientific achievements of the seventeenth century so impressed educated men with a sense of natural order that it became increasingly difficult to believe in interruptions of that order. Shaftesbury notes that some religious apologists were attacking this concept of natural order on grounds that it led to atheism. However, he contends that the opposite is true: the conception of a universe governed by law is the only foundation of true theism. If Nature is a chaos, if natural laws can be violated, then atheism or polytheism are the logical hypotheses—atheism preaching the rule of chance, and polytheism the rule of conflicting powers. But the continuity of Nature and the uniformity of natural law make miracles impossible. We should not expect the laws of Nature, which necessarily operate for the good of the Whole, to be set aside for the *supposed* benefit of a particular person. Such inconsistency would be a mark of cosmic chaos. While denying the possibility of interruptions of the natural order by a personal providence, at the same time Shaftesbury affirms the benevolent activity of the Supreme Mind throughout the fabric of the intelligible universe.

CHAPTER FIVE

OPTIMISM and EVIL

Shaftesbury's enthusiastic vision of Nature is the source of his metaphysical optimism. His defense of theism required that he demonstrate not only the order of Nature but also its ultimate goodness. He attempts to establish the rule of providence in Nature on the basis of our present experience rather than by an appeal to a hypothetical future existence in which all wrongs are righted and all evils made good: "A providence must be proved from what we see of order in things present." (II, 58) But he must face the problem of evil which Philocles states in these terms: "Through what contingency, what chance, by what fatal necessity, what will, or what permission it [evil] came upon the world, or being come once, should still subsist." (II, 14) In his solution, Shaftesbury rejects the way taken by "our divines in general," who, he says, are quite willing to admit evils in Nature, and yet do not consider the Deity accountable for them. This would require that we postulate an opposing evil force or that we place limits on divine power. These are inacceptable to Shaftesbury since he takes "God" to mean in the true sense One who is all-powerful and perfectly good. Thus, he parts company with theologians who postulate a personal Devil, as well as with philosophers like Bayle who propose a Manichean approach to evil. "The Moralists," like Leibniz's *Theodicy* (1710) and Le Clerc's *Parrhasiana ou Pensées Diverses* (1699), was written in part as an answer to the questions raised by Bayle in his *Dictionnaire historique et critique* (1697). Bayle had formulated the objections that a Manichean might raise against a system grounded on belief in a good, all-powerful Deity, arguing that the existence of such a Being could not be reconciled with our experience of physical and moral evils.

The myth of Prometheus is used by Shaftesbury to attack indirectly the Christian doctrine of original sin and the concept of Satan. These purported explanations of evil simply provide a scapegoat who can be blamed for evil on the supposition that the Deity is then cleared of any responsibility. "They reckoned it a fair game if they could gain a single remove and put the evil cause farther off." (II, 15) But a philosopher can see the fallacy in this, for

the Gods either could have hindered Prometheus's creation or they could not. If they could, they were answerable for the consequences; if they could not, they were no longer Gods, being thus limited and controlled. And whether Prometheus were a name for chance, destiny, a plastic nature, or an evil daemon, whatever was designed by it, 'twas still the same breach of omnipotence. (II, 16)

The reference to a "plastic nature" may be aimed at the Cambridge Platonists or possibly even at John Ray's book, *Wisdom of God Manifested in the Works of the Creation* (1691). Ray postulates a "vegetative soul" or "plastick Nature" which functions as an agent of Deity and to which any imperfections in the creation could be attributed. Shaftesbury rejects any such intermediate principle.

Fowler suggests that Shaftesbury may have meant that the source of evil was in matter conceived as a coexistent, coeternal, though blind, force which limited God's power.[1] The Cambridge Platonists held that the Logos is not found in its purity in the natural world because it is limited by matter. It is true that Shaftesbury regarded material forms as being only imperfect shadows of the ultimate, perfect beauty, but this is in part an aesthetic conception, and if its metaphysical implications are pressed too far it threatens Shaftesbury's doctrine of divine immanence. It is evident that there are conflicting currents in his system. While matter is frequently spoken of as inferior to mind, his approach is fundamentally monistic and he generally avoids falling into a simple dualism which attributes evil to matter, and good to mind. He rejects the idea that there are any limitations on the power of God other than those stemming from the Logos of His own Being. Thus, Fowler's suggestion must be rejected. Matter in itself is inferior because it does not represent the wholeness of Being, but matter given form reveals the Divine. Only in a figurative sense could it be said to limit God's activity.

Shaftesbury's philosophy reflects the change in attitude toward Nature and evil that occurred in the transition from the seventeenth to the eighteenth century. In his *Sacred Theory of the Earth* (1681–89), Thomas Burnet argued that though there was sufficient evidence of the existence of God in Nature, it was a mistake to attempt to ground belief in the supposed perfection of Nature. This was *not* the best of all possible worlds, since both human nature and the natural world itself had been corrupted in the fall of man. As we move from Burnet and John Ray to Shaftesbury and William Derham (*Physico-Theology*, 1713), we note the emergence of a very different point of view. As Basil Willey expresses it: "The Fall is no longer a haunting obsession, and whatever may be true of Man, Nature is now to be contemplated as the finished and unimprovable product of divine wisdom, omnipotence, and benevolence." [2]

A parallel change occurred in the attitude toward the Devil. In his discourse entitled *A Christian's Conflicts and Conquests, or a Discourse Concerning the Devil's Active Enmity and Continual Hostility Against Man,* John Smith accepted the traditional mythology of the Devil but subtly modified it. [3] While not actually denying that Satan was a particular, personal spirit, he suggested that he symbolized "the spirit of apostasie" present in all men. Along with this tendency to depersonalize the concept of Satan went a decline in belief in witchcraft. Satan was driven first from the natural world at large, and then from human nature; there is no Devil in Shaftesbury's universe. His optimistic philosophy was to play a major role in the process of transforming Nature from a fallen world into a revelation of divine goodness and beauty. Nature was God's good creation to be utilized and enjoyed by man as best he could.

Shaftesbury's vision of Nature demands that the Creative Intelligence have perfect foresight and control. The creation is not an error or a product of miscalculation.

'Twas better still that the project should be executed, whatever might become of mankind, or how hard soever such a creation was like to fall on the generality of this miserable race. For 'twas impossible, you thought, that Heaven should have acted otherwise than for the best. So that even from this misery and ill of man there was undoubtedly some good arising, something which overbalanced all, and made full amends. (II, 16)

The skeptical Philocles wonders though whether one can approve in Deity what one disapproves in man, i.e., using evil means to produce good ends. It reminds him of one of those "mountebanks" who produce disease in order to cure it. Moreover, "had she [Nature] been originally healthy, or created sound at first, she had still continued so. 'Twas no credit to the Gods to leave her destitute, or with a flaw which would cost dear the mending. . . ." (II, 17)

But Shaftesbury will allow no real flaws in his perfect universe. The goodness or evilness of each system of things has to be judged in terms of the functioning of that system as a totality. Philocles himself suggests the line along which this argument is to be pursued: "pleasure and pain, beauty and deformity, good and ill, seemed to me everywhere interwoven, . . ." and yet, like a tapestry made of many contrasting colors, it produces a harmonious over-all effect. (II, 14) Though a detail might not be attractive or pleasing in itself, when seen as an organic part of a coherent Whole, it is. This aesthetic analogy seems to be the central argument in Shaftesbury's metaphysical optimism. What we consider "evil" is comparable to the details of a tapestry, the shading in a picture, or the dissonances in a symphony. Just as the artist makes harmony out of contrasting or opposing elements, so does Nature, the sovereign Artist.

It had been a long-standing principle of literary criticism that if a work of art was on the whole successful, imperfections in it might be forgiven. This was gradually transmuted into the doctrine that in a successful work the apparent imperfections were really necessary to the aesthetic whole. John Dennis, for example, contended that just as certain "irregularities" contribute to the harmony of the universe, so certain elements of a poem which "at first sight" appear to be "against reason" are, nevertheless, "at the bottom . . . perfectly regular . . ." and necessary to the total design.[4] This is Shaftesbury's position

too. Even Newton had allowed that there were some irregularities in the world order, but he resolved this difficulty by
providing for the periodic intervention of God to set things
right. This is alien to Shaftesbury's thought, however, for he
would consider this to be evidence of a limit to divine knowledge or power. There are no *real* irregularities in his cosmos,
only apparent flaws or "seeming blemishes" which result from
our limited perspectives. Nature does not err, and "when she
seems most ignorant or perverse in her productions, I assert
her even then as wise and provident as in her goodliest works."
(II, 22)

Shaftesbury views Nature as an arena of conflicting forces
and interests in which the lower species must always yield to
the higher, the lesser to the greater. Ecology reveals the mutual
interdependence of living organisms in their natural setting.
Terrestrial forms are maintained by mutual sacrifice and yield-
ing, as one species preys upon another in the cycle of Nature.
If in the hierarchy of organisms the sacrifice of one species to
another is considered appropriate or even "just" at the lower
levels, it must be so at all levels including that of man himself.
Each system of organisms is contained in some larger system to
which its own interest or good is subordinate. Ultimately, all
species are subject to "the superior nature of the world." (II,
22) We must not expect exceptions to be made to preserve
individual creatures or even species that are necessarily transient. Not only is it justifiable for one species to prey upon another; but physical evils, such as earthquakes or floods, which
harm individual creatures or destroy whole species, are justified on grounds that all lesser systems of beings must submit to
the necessary order of Nature as a Whole. " 'Tis good which is
predominant; and every corruptible and mortal nature by its

mortality and corruption yields only to some better, and all in common to that best and highest nature which is incorruptible and immortal." (II, 23)

Nature is pictured by Shaftesbury as a scene of continuing change:

All lives, and by succession still revives. The temporary beings quit their borrowed forms and yield their elementary substance to new-comers. Called in their several turns to life, they view the light, and viewing pass, that others too may be spectators of the goodly scene, and greater numbers still enjoy the privilege of Nature. . . . No time nor substance is lost or unimproved. New forms arise, and when the old dissolve, the matter whence they were composed is not left useless, but wrought with equal management and art, even in corruption, Nature's seeming waste and vile abhorrence. The abject state appears merely as the way or passage to some better. But could we nearly view it, and with indifference, remote from the antipathy of sense, we then perhaps should highest raise our admiration, convinced that even the way itself was equal to the end. (II, 110 f.)

Nature, as in Stoic doctrine, manifests a perfect adjustment of matter to form, and of form to environment. Later we shall see that Shaftesbury finds the same perfection *within* man in the harmony of the affections.[5]

Shaftesbury contends that each particular organism in Nature "certainly and constantly produces what is good to itself, unless something foreign disturbs or hinders it, either by over-powering and corrupting it within, or by violence from without. . . . All weaknesses, distortions, sicknesses, imperfect births, and the seeming contradictions and perversities of nature . . ." result from the influence of some alien element. (II, 106) There is a built-in tendency in all organisms to correct their own ailments or imperfections. Shaftesbury's argument seems particularly weak at this point. Granted that all organisms have some self-correcting functions, they also have within themselves inherent possibilities of decay and self-destruction, as Shaftesbury's own cyclical theory of natural change implies. At its weakest, his contention is tautologous—"alien" being taken to mean "whatever works against a creature's good or survival." At any rate, he argues that if it is true that each particular organism works constantly for its own good, we must then deduce that Nature—the organic Whole—works for its own good, which is "the good of all in general." (II, 107) And there can be nothing to corrupt this process, for by definition there is no entity existing outside of or "foreign" to Nature.

It follows from the above that any knowledge we can obtain of the uses or purposes of various species, and of natural processes in general, would prepare us for an understanding of the harmony of the Whole. But Shaftesbury did not claim that we could understand the purpose of every element in the created universe:

We need not wonder to find ourselves at a loss in many things relating to the constitution and frame of Nature herself. For to what end in Nature many things, even whole species of creatures, refer, or to what purpose they serve, will be hard for any one justly to determine; but to what end the many proportions and various shapes of parts in many creatures actually serve, we are able, by the help of study and observation, to demonstrate with great exactness. (I, 243)

He is at least more restrained than some eighteenth-century writers who confidently outlined the purpose of everything in the natural world from moths to meteors.

It is interesting that Shaftesbury accepts the older cyclical theory of history rather than the newly developing progressive theory. The natural world is characterized by periodic "revolutions" such as we see in plant and animal life. Generation, growth, decay, follow each other in an endless cycle. In human history, nations rise, prosper, and die in the successive ages of the world. Barbarism and civilization fluctuate; even manners and "wit" have their periods. Shaftesbury is more explicit in his commitment to this cyclical theory in the *Philosophical Regimen* than he is in the *Characteristics*. "All is but of a moment, all must again decline. . . . Must not there be again an age of darkness? . . . and after many revolutions, the same over again. Nothing is new or strange. That, that now is, after it has ceased, shall one time or another be again; and that, that is not now, shall in time be as it was before." [6] Such a theory seems to offer only limited room for hope. In fact, Shaftesbury warns that we must realize that what "we strive about . . . can never be accomplished, never brought to perfection, never kept at a stay. . . ." [7] Yet we must know "how to acquiesce and be contented," rather than trying to "correct the order of Providence." [8] This acquiescence is possible if we learn to see the necessity and the beauty of these cycles at every stage of their development, whether of growth or decay.

In "The Moralists" Shaftesbury follows the Stoics in applying this cyclical theory to the cosmos itself, but he does so hesitantly. Theocles expresses the fear that in such "high flights" he might, like Icarus, burn his wings. Yet he indicates at least conditional acceptance of a cyclical theory of cosmic creation and destruction. In the intervals between creations nothing would exist but the divine Mind; all would be ONE, self-contained, and "subsisting (as they imagined) rather in a more simple and perfect manner, than when multiplied in more ways; and becoming productive, it unfolded itself in the various map of Nature and this fair visible world." (II, 118) It seems inconsistent with Shaftesbury's concept of the perfection of the universe to say that Being is "more perfect" when self-contained in the One than when manifest in the multiplicity of the natural world. Yet Shaftesbury does not wish to rest his case on such metaphysical sallies; instead, as we have seen, he attempts to prove the perfection of Nature by appeal to the experienced universe.

Even if conditional, this acceptance of a cyclical theory of history makes Shaftesbury's philosophy closer to the teachings of earlier seventeenth-century thinkers (for example, George Hakewill) than to theories of historical progress developing in his own time.[9] And from the perspective of post-Enlightenment philosophies which tend to exalt a view of human destiny in which Nature and history offer infinite possibilities for self-transcendence, Shaftesbury's cyclical theory seems too constricting and pessimistic. It marks one of the limits of his optimism. While he conceives of progress as possible for the individual and for mankind, it is always limited by the larger cycles of Nature, turning like wheels within wheels. Lovejoy has pointed out that the Great Chain of Being, as usually formulated, was a "perfect example of an absolutely rigid and static scheme of things."[10] This is in general, though not wholly, true of Shaftesbury's philosophy, for in his exaltation of the ever-working creative energy of Deity, he prepares the way for the temporalizing of the Chain of Being, though he takes no more than hesitant steps in that direction himself. There is an unresolved tension in his thought between the dynamic elements in his concept of God and his rather static view of reality as a present manifestation of the ideal.

The Cartesian form of the ontological argument is reflected

in Shaftesbury's contention that man's ability to conceive of
perfection is in itself evidence of the perfection of Nature. It
is unreasonable to suppose that man is capable of conceiving a
perfection which Nature herself lacks. The cosmic system does
indeed exclude "all real ill." (II, 57) He further argues that if
it is possible that there is no real evil, it follows that there *is*
no real evil. "For whatever is possible in the whole, the nature
or mind of the whole will put in execution for the whole's
good; and if it be possible to exclude ill, it will exclude it. . . .
For nothing merely passive can oppose this universally active
principle." (II, 109)

Evil is, therefore, relegated to the status of appearance, and
is denied ultimate reality. In writing that "whatever is void of
mind, is void and darkness to the mind's eye," (II, 144) Shaftesbury suggests the Neoplatonic doctrine that evil is negative—
the absence of good or of mind. However, there is no systematic exposition of this, though it is implied that evil cannot
exist by itself: it has no metaphysical status. Nothing that is
wholly evil could exist since it would be entirely self-negating.
Evil is "real" only as a part of the structure of our experience,
not as an absolute entity. The same doctrine was given classic
expression by Pope:

> *All Nature is but Art, unknown to thee;*
> *All Chance, Direction, which thou canst not see;*
> *All Discord, Harmony not understood;*
> *All partial Evil, universal Good.*[11]

This is the "magical glass" which, according to Shaftesbury,
turns evil into good, and good into best, and enables us to see
what ordinary vision may not—that this is the best of all possible worlds.

Whatsoever then is so as that it could not really have been better, or any way better ordered, is perfectly good; whatsoever in the order of the world can be called ill, must imply a possibility in the nature of the thing to have been better contrived or ordered. For if it could not, it is perfect, and as it should be. (I, 239)

According to Shaftesbury, the common error that men make is to evaluate the natural order in relation to the satisfaction of their individual needs and desires. But it is the species as a whole that must be considered, and ultimately the universal scheme of things. Nature is "not for man, but man for Nature . . . ," and it is man who must "submit to the elements of Nature, and not the elements to him. Few of these are at all fitted to him, and none perfectly." (II, 73) Yet Shaftesbury also contends that providence works in and through all events, even the smallest: no part of the universe could be logically exempt from the purposive control of the Supreme Mind. "Providence is in all. . . ." [12] This line of reasoning leads him to make some of the extreme statements that appear in the *Philosophical Regimen*. For example: "Persuade them that to be affronted, to be despised, to be poor or to smart, is not to suffer; that the sack or ruin of cities and destruction of mankind are not in themselves ill; and that with respect to the whole, these things are orderly, good and beautiful." [13] One should learn not only to accept whatever happens in the course of events, one should love it, whether it be "hardship, poverty, sickness, death. . . ." And in a chilling passage, he writes: "Can He [God] kill otherwise than kindly, fatherly; for the good of everything, and as the preserver of the whole?" [14] It was optimism in this form that Voltaire so mercilessly lampooned in *Candide*. It is significant that Shaftesbury uses more carefully guarded language in the *Characteristics*, though the underlying thought is the same. The paradox in Shaftesbury's philosophy is that providence is both universal and particular, but only when we see it as universal can we understand it as particular.

However, Shaftesbury is in no sense proposing that we eliminate the term "evil" from our vocabulary as though it had no meaning or reference. For one thing, "evil" and the related words, "vice" and "wrong," are fundamental moral concepts. We will see in a later chapter though that the existence of moral evil or vice is not allowed by Shaftesbury as evidence against the ultimate teleological order.[15] "Evil" also has significance as designating those happenings judged to be unfortunate in relation to a finite individual or even a nation. Shaftesbury does not try to deny that evils are an *actual* part of the structure of our experience; it is absolute, not proximate, evil that he rejects on grounds that it has no ontological status. His treatment of the *actual* evils of experience is remarkably rigorous, and his optimism is by no means as naïve and unrealistic as caricatures and lampoons would suggest. He does not seek to gloss over or deny the depth or extent of moral and social evils. When compared with the exaggerated optimism of Soame Jenyns' *Free Enquiry into the Nature and Origin of Evil* (1757), Shaftesbury's seems cautious and realistic. The third Earl was keenly aware of the power of irrational impulse —the "unnatural affections"—in human nature, so much so that Leslie Stephen thought it inconsistent with his optimism. On the other hand, the nineteenth-century critic wrote that Shaftesbury "ignores the very existence of vice and misery . . . ,"[16] a statement which not only contradicts the above criticism but demonstrates that he had not read the *Characteristics* very carefully. Shaftesbury's letters reveal even more clearly that he viewed life as a continual struggle against evil forces and corrupt interest. He never taught the doctrine of inevitable progress, and he denied the moral perfectibility of man. Readers overly impressed by Shaftesbury's optimism are prone to forget that in comparing man with other species he wrote: "For as the highest improvements of temper are made in human kind, so the greatest corruption and degeneracies are discoverable in this race. . . . 'Tis hard to find in any region a human society which has human laws." (I, 291 f.) Elsewhere he cries out: "Oh! what treacheries! what disorders! and how corrupt is all!" (II, 13) Unlike Soame Jenyns, Shaftesbury did not try to demonstrate that the existing social and political order was perfect. Nor did he ignore the fact of suffering or seek to blind us to the tragic facts of our finite experience.

That Shaftesbury's metaphysical optimism functioned for him as a personal faith that enabled him to face "corruption and rottenness" without being destroyed by them is revealed in such passages as this from his philosophical notebook:

Everything wastes and is perishing; everything hastens to its dissolution; already thou thyself art come to a perfect growth; and now thy body is in decline, and faster and faster must corrupt. Mortalities must every day be expected—friends dropping off, accidents and calamities impending, diseases, lamenesses, deafness, loss of sight, of memory, of parts. Few persons in the world grow better, and many grow worse every day, so as to lose the natural good dispositions they once had. All is misery, disappointment, and regret. . . . He and he only is in any degree happy, who can confront these things; who can steadily look on them without turning away his sight; and who, knowing the sum and conclusion of all, waits for the finishing of his part, his only care in the meanwhile being to act that part as becomes him and to preserve his mind entire and sound, unshaken and uncorrupt; in friendship with mankind, and in unity with that original mind with respect to which nothing either does or can happen but what is most agreeable and conducing, and what is of universal good.[17]

In Shaftesbury's universe there is finite but not infinite tragedy.

Basically, Shaftesbury argues for his optimistic metaphysics in two ways: on the one hand, he contends that the evidence of benevolent design to be found in the natural world establishes the existence of a ruling Mind that is benevolent and all powerful; on the other hand, he reasons that given such a directing Intelligence it necessarily follows that the cosmic order is good. However, he admits that to know with certainty that all things work for the best would require that we comprehend the universe as a Whole, which seems impossible for a finite mind. "In an infinity of things, mutually relative, a mind which sees not infinitely can see nothing fully, and must therefore frequently see that imperfect which in itself is really perfect. . . . For nothing beside what is infinite can see infinite connections." (II, 108) If this is the case, it would seem that Shaftesbury would have to retreat from his position, and concede that we *cannot* know that everything "demonstrates order and perfection." (II, 67) But it is just at this point that the doctrine of enthusiasm is relevant. Man is able, according to Shaftesbury, to surmount the limitations of his finitude and, at least at moments, to intuit the harmony of the Whole. These are the ecstatic moments of faith—of enthusiasm—in which the mind is "caught up in vision." Again, Shaftesbury's final appeal is not to evidence or logic alone, but to enthusiasm, though it must be remembered that he considers enthusiasm a rational process which is not contradictory to logic or evidence, but a higher vantage point from which they derive their meaning. Only from this standpoint can one be reconciled to his view of the paradoxical relationship of universal and particular providence, and to the concept of particular evils that are swallowed up in universal Good.

Judged as a purely rational system which attempts to justify

God's ways to man, Shaftesbury's philosophy fails. The evidence he presents can at least be matched by an equal amount of counterevidence. Much of what he thought clearly implied a designing Mind, we see today as a product of natural mechanisms of adjustment operating according to the patterns of statistical probability. As a philosophy of life, it will fall short for many in the contemporary world because, despite Shaftesbury's realism, his effort to see the necessity of all things prevents him from doing full justice to the inexplicably tragic dimensions of human experience. Yet, as a religious faith, his philosophy finally stands or falls just to the extent that it makes the tragic and the absurd endurable by including them in an ultimately meaningful universe.

CHAPTER SIX

FREEDOM and DESTINY

In criticizing Locke for his treatment of the problem of freedom of will, Shaftesbury wrote that "he made great alterations on these points where, though a *divine* may often waver, a *philosopher*, I think, never can." [1] This problem, he adds, is "the test and touchstone of a genius in philosophy." [2] If Shaftesbury means by this remark that the test is not merely in the position taken but in the arguments advanced for it, then he himself fails the test. Though he is clearly committed to a form of indeterminism or self-determinism, he never explains exactly what his position is and he never faces the problems relating to human freedom inherent in his metaphysical system. We have seen that Shaftesbury opposes atheism—belief in the rule of chance in Nature—to theism, and if the postulates of true theism are correct, then it follows that all things are interrelated and interdependent, and "everything is necessary to everything." [3] Nothing that happens, therefore, is unnecessary, and the removal of a single cause in the Great Chain of Being would throw the Whole into disarray.

At the same time that Shaftesbury commits himself to this

concept of an ultimate necessity, he also assumes that man has the freedom to choose between alternative actions or modes of life. Like the Cambridge Platonists, he clearly rejects the Calvinistic doctrine of predestination in favor of a form of Pelagianism. He argues that providence has granted us the power to know and obtain what is good, and to know and avoid what is evil. It is up to us to make use of these powers, to be *men* in the true sense—autonomous agents of Deity itself. But if we fail to do so, we sink to the level of animals, and are used by Nature for her ends, whether we will or not. Shaftesbury assumes that man can rebel against God and resist His will, even though Deity is all-knowing and all-powerful. But since God wills the good of man, to do so is to act contrary to one's own interests. Rebellion is unreasonable, but how it is even possible in Shaftesbury's universe is a puzzle. If all that happens must happen as it does, then even the rebel is doing God's will; nor could he do otherwise. And regardless of what choices men make, right or wrong, the will of God inevitably prevails. Shaftesbury never faces the question of how necessity and freedom are to be reconciled.[4]

According to Shaftesbury, it is God who sets the goals of life, and we who must submit. The ends of human life are predetermined, even if our choices are not, so we had better concentrate on changing ourselves, which is possible, rather than attempting to change the order of Nature, which is not possible. *True* freedom, for Shaftesbury as for the idealists in general, is realized only through the harmony of the individual will and the divine will. True freedom is not license—it is not the ability to think or do *anything* you please. It is a life *of* principle, not *without* principle. Restraint and self-mastery are not contradictions of freedom but the very conditions of it.

Thus, Shaftesbury finds the same conception of freedom "in true moral philosophy as in painting, viz. 'That the truly austere, severe, and . . . regular, restraintive, character . . . corresponds (not fights or thwarts) with the free, the easy, the secure, the bold.' " [5] Shaftesbury's theory of art and morals cannot be understood apart from this concept of freedom. It underlies his attempted reconciliation of Neoclassical and "Romantic" principles in art as well as his combination of moral intuitionism with a commitment to moral law. It explains his attack on "libertinism" in philosophy and life, and his defense of the "free-thinker" as the "noblest of characters." Only the mind able to move freely over the whole range of human possibilities is able to decide wisely and to live authentically. Freedom is a necessary condition of knowledge, virtue, and happiness. "Liberty of mind," he wrote Lord Somers, "is the highest good a philosophical friend can wish you." [6]

Immortality

Since Shaftesbury attempts to establish the intelligibility of the world as presently experienced, the whole emphasis of his philosophy is on the present rather than on the future: "If the now do not belie thee, the hereafter cannot. . . . The *now* . . . mind this: in this is all." [7] Either we live in the present or we do not *live* at all, for "life is this present moment." [8] Following in the path of the Cambridge Platonists, Shaftesbury conceives of the task of religious faith and philosophical wisdom, not as preparing us for an unknown future life, but as enabling us to live in the present. Deity—the Eternal—is known in the present moment. Even if this bodily existence is "the trial and exercise of inferior minds," as he suggests in his note-book,[9] the test must be met *now* and without fear, for whatever the future may bring, we can be assured that the cosmic order will guarantee that it will be good and just. "If more life after this, will it not be the better still for what I am doing?" [10]

Shaftesbury notes the logical connection between belief in immortality and belief in God and the cosmic order. Theism allows for the possibility of a future life; atheism makes it highly improbable, if not impossible. Here as elsewhere Shaftesbury puts the emphasis on belief in God and the natural order rather than on any subsidiary doctrine. A theist *may* believe in a future life, but he is not impelled by logical necessity to do so. Those who attempt to establish the providential order of things by deducing it from a future existence with rewards and punishments are reasoning poorly, since they are assuming exactly what is in question. The only reasonable procedure, Shaftesbury thinks, is to demonstrate the reality of providence in our *present* experience—to show that virtue is rewarded and vice punished here and now. Then we may reasonably "apprehend a larger scheme, and easily resolve ourselves why things were not completed in this state, but their accomplishment reserved rather to some further period." (II, 58) If there is such a providential order, Theocles reasons, is it not probable that "this providential care is extended yet further to a succeeding life, and perfected hereafter? This is what . . . may be said in behalf of a future state to those who question revelation. 'Tis this must render revelation probable, and secure that first step to it, the belief of a Deity and Providence." (*Ibid.*)

These and other references by Shaftesbury to immortality are conditional in nature, and do no more than suggest the logical possibility of personal survival. Thus, it does not seem correct to say, as Fowler does, that Shaftesbury regarded the future life as making up for the evils of this life. Rather he believed that the justice we observe in the world of our present experience continues to operate in any and all forms of existence. Since Nature is a continuing process, the completion of any particular line of purpose may not always be seen in the limited range of our experience. But that Nature inevitably realizes her purposes is the faith that underlies the doctrine of immortality. Much of Shaftesbury's polemic against the religion of his time was directed against those who denied that there was a moral order evident in the present life because they thought this would make belief in future retribution all the more necessary in a supposedly just universe. This procedure, which Shaftesbury describes as "building a future state on the ruins of virtue," can only succeed in undermining our faith in Deity itself. (II, 59)

Shaftesbury's agnosticism on the question of personal immortality reflects another change in the religious temper of the times, for there was growing skepticism about this doctrine. Herbert of Cherbury had considered belief in retribution in a future life as one of the five basic principles of natural religion. Locke, however, did not find this belief demonstrable by reason alone, and argued that our acceptance of it required the support of revelation. Shaftesbury, also unconvinced by the rational arguments for it, and not ready to accept it on grounds of revelation, remains in doubt.

Shaftesbury's commitment to a cyclical theory of history and Nature opens up the possibility for him of accepting some form of immortality even though it be impersonal. Man, as all creatures and things, is involved in a continuing cycle of change in which old forms perish, and new arise. We neither know what form we existed in before this life or what form we will have after death. Some argued that the doctrine of pre-existence must be false since we have no memory of a previous life. Shaftesbury rejects this argument but at the same time does not explicitly accept the doctrine either, at least in the sense of the pre-existence of a particular individual soul which retains its identity in two or more lives.[11] He goes on to comment that "we may happen to be again and again to perpetuity, for any reason we can show to the contrary. All is revolution in us. We are no more the self-same matter or system of matter from one day to another. What succession there may be hereafter we know not, only perish and are renewed." (II, 35) At any rate, we can be sure that this "assemblage of fleeting particles" will pass. But the imagination that seeks to penetrate further into the past or future loses itself in the "vastness of time, . . . the abyss before and after." [12]

In their cyclical theory, the Stoics, whom Shaftesbury follows closely here, had postulated that the world would end in a divine conflagration in which all souls would be united with God.[13] In "The Moralists," Shaftesbury writes mysteriously and poetically of light, that "invisible ethereal substance . . . diffused throughout the universe," which like a "vital flame . . . frames, animates, and nurses all the various forms." (II, 117) But when the cosmic cycle turns from construction to destruction, this creative power destroys all that it had once formed, for "their noblest end was to be here wrapt up, consumed and lost." (II, 118) Thus, in the giant pulsations of infinite Being, all would issue from the One, and all would return to the One. This would be, of course, impersonal immortality, and elsewhere Shaftesbury describes death as like the merging of a river with the sea. However, it is typical of

Shaftesbury that he does not rest his case on such metaphysical speculations about the cosmic cycle. He was no doubt aware of the defense of pre-existence made by Joseph Glanvill and Henry More, and the arguments for metempsychosis presented by Lady Conway and Francis M. Van Helmont.[14] But Shaftesbury is more skeptical than they about our ability to answer the questions they raised. His acceptance of a cyclical theory and his belief in the possibilities of self-transcendence for the individual combine to suggest that a theory of reincarnation would have been more acceptable to him than the traditional Christian doctrine of a future life. But to live with a "right mind," and, when the time comes, to die with a right mind, is, according to Shaftesbury, to realize one's true being. This is the only "consummation" to be hoped for, when "all the numbers are full; the measures perfect; the harmony complete." [15]

Thus, Shaftesbury is less concerned with the theoretical question of whether there is a life after death than with the relation of that belief to our present attitudes. In a later chapter we will discuss his criticism of the doctrine of retribution in its connection with his ethical theory.[16] To desire a future life solely because we fear death is no mark of wisdom. What we should fear is the death of the spirit in this life, not the death of the body which is a mere transient form. "It is in life, therefore, or nowhere, that death is. It is death indeed to fear death." [17] The excessive fear of death destroys our sense of values, and makes it impossible to enjoy the present moment. Reflecting Stoic influence, Shaftesbury writes that it is in the power of man to raise himself

from this sink, these dregs, this guise of a world, to manliness, to reason and a natural life; to come again on the stage as an actor, not as a machine;—as knowing the author of the piece, as conscious of the design, to join in the performance, the disposition, the government; to be a spectator, a guest, a friend, and with the same friendship to retire and thank the inviter.[18]

There is no fear in Shaftesbury's universe: "To die any death is natural, for one door is the same as another." [19]

Despite the fundamental optimism of Shaftesbury's thought, he saw himself as taking an intermediate path between the extremes of optimism and pessimism with respect to the value of this earthly life. Not everything about this life is good—at least in the proximate sense—and not everything about it is bad. The wise man neither overvalues nor undervalues his present existence. Shaftesbury's attitude is best revealed in his reaction to a letter written by Locke, shortly before his death, to Anthony Collins. Locke wrote:

All the use to be made of it is that this life is a scene of vanity, that soon passes away, and affords no solid satisfaction but in the consciousness of doing well, and in hopes of another life. This is what I can say upon experience, and what you will find when you come to make up the account.[20]

Locke was only repeating a view widely held among pious Christians in the seventeenth century. Sir Thomas Browne had expressed it in observing that the world was "not an Inne, but an Hospitall, and a place, not to live, but to die in." [21] In response to Locke, Shaftesbury writes:

The piece of a letter you sent me savours of the good and Christian. It puts me in mind of one of those dying speeches which come out under the title of a Christian warning piece. I should never have guessed it to have been of a dying philosopher. . . . Our life, thank heaven, has been a scene of friendship of long duration, with much and solid satisfaction founded on the consciousness of doing good for good's sake, without any farther regards, nothing being truly pleasing or satisfactory but what is thus acted disinterestedly, generously, and freely. This is what I can say upon experience, and this you will find sufficient at the last to make all reckoning clear, leaving no terrible account to be made up, nor terrible idea of those who are to account with. . . . *Life is vain* ('tis true) to those who make it so. And let those cry *vanity*, for they have reason. For my own part, who never could be in love with riches of the world, nor ever made any great matter of life, so as to love it for its own sake, I have therefore no falling out with it, now at last when I can no longer keep it; so without calling names or giving hard words, I can part freely with and give it a good testimony. No harm in it all that I know; *no vanity*. But (if one wills oneself) a fair, honest sensible thing it is, and not so uncomfortable as it is made. No, nor so over-comfortable as to make one melancholy at the thoughts of parting with it, or as to make one think the time exceeding *short* and *passing*. For why so short if not sound and sweet? Why complain both ways? Is vanity, mere vanity, a happiness? or can misery pass away too soon? But the sweet is living (it seems), mere *living* and doing just the ordinary animal offices of life, which good manners will not allow one to call by plain names . . . [and] other offices more immediately human, and of the rational kind, such as friendship, justice, generosity, acts of love, and such like, the exposing of life, health, or fortune, spending of it, throwing it away, laying it readily down for others. . . . I ask no reward from heaven for that which is reward itself. Let my being be continued or discontinued, as in the main is best. The author of it best knows, and I trust Him with it.[22]

CHAPTER SEVEN

CHRISTIANITY
and the CHURCH

Our discussion of Shaftesbury's philosophy of religion has already revealed in broad outline his attitude toward traditional Christianity. However, there are other aspects of his attack upon Christendom that need yet to be reviewed, including his ideas on the Bible and the place of the church in society. Countering Shaftesbury's claim that many churchmen were attempting to build "a future state on the ruins of virtue," (II, 59) Mandeville made the accusation that "under Pretence of lashing Priestcraft and Superstition, [Shaftesbury] attacked the Bible it self; and . . . by ridiculing many Passages of Holy Writ, he seems to have endeavored to sap the Foundation of all revealed Religion, with Design of establishing Heathen Virtue on the Ruins of Christianity." [1] If there is some justice in this charge, there is little in Bishop Berkeley's claim that Shaftesbury not only did not believe in providence but was "without one grain of religion." [2] Fairness to an intellectual opponent was an often violated principle in that age, as is amply evident in Berkeley's caricature of Shaftesbury as Alciphron in *The Minute Philosopher* (1732). Lessing later called Shaftesbury the "most dangerous enemy of Christianity," but paying tribute to him in the same breath, added, "because the finest." [3] Yet Shaftesbury's attitude toward Christianity is complex.

In his Preface to Whichcote's sermons, Shaftesbury distinguishes between his position and that of some of his contemporaries who thought "even the Gospel itself, and our holy religion to be a fraud." [4] He asks that we approach Christianity with objectivity and make a fair appraisal of it, recognizing its good qualities where they are found. He is just as much opposed to those who find *no* truth in traditional Christianity as to those who consider it to be the sole possessor of truth. Yet there is ambiguity in his reference in the *Characteristics* to the skeptical opinion that "the holy records themselves were no other than the pure invention or artificial compilement of an interested party in behalf of the richest corporation and most profitable monopoly which could be erected in the world." (II, 301) Shaftesbury evidently rejects the charge that the Christian religion was based on fraud because this would suggest there was no truth in it, and perhaps because it might be extended to all religion. On the other hand, it is clear that he did feel that there was an element of fraud and insincerity present in the rise of priestly religion. And there is little doubt that he considered the church—particularly the Roman Catholic Church—to be the "most profitable monopoly in the world."

Modern historical studies have made Shaftesbury's theories about the rise of religion in the Western world largely archaic, though, of course, they reflect his attitude toward Christianity. He considered the "ancient model" of religion—the liberal and tolerant religion of cultivated Greeks and Romans—far superior to the "modern model." Unfortunately, this liberal religion was swept aside by the "unsociable" religion of Egypt—that "motherland of superstition" (II, 181)—which was passed on to Judaism and thus to Christianity. The spread of tyranny in the Roman Empire and its cultural decline is seen by Shaftesbury as closely connected with the rise of Christianity. When to the power of the church was added the power of the empire, a host of evils followed. In his analysis Shaftesbury accepts the principle that the greater the number and the power of the priesthood, the greater the amount of superstition and the greater the corruption of religion. This distrust of priestly religion was characteristic of liberal religious writers.

According to Shaftesbury, the decay of the ancient schools of philosophy and the absorption of their intellectual function by the church resulted in that "contentious learning" which produced senseless and bitter religious disputes. (II, 195) The merely "defensive zeal" of the pagan sects was replaced by the "offensive zeal" or persecuting spirit of the Christian churches. With the sound of the religious wars of the seventeenth century still ringing in his ears, Shaftesbury wrote that even in his time the nations "in religion's cause forget humanity: whilst savage zeal, with meek and pious semblance, works dreadful massacre; and for heaven's sake (horrid pretence!) makes desolate the earth. . . ." (II, 122) Christianity had betrayed its greatest principle—love: "Who would dream that out of abundant charity and brotherly love should come steel, fire, gibbets . . . ?" (II, 227) Shaftesbury's attitude hardly seems to be "the supercilious contempt of an indifferent spectator," as Leslie Stephen described it.[5] He was "indifferent" only in the sense that he regarded many of the religious controversies as being based on false problems, but he was certainly not indifferent to their social consequences.

As one would expect in a defender of liberal religion, Shaftesbury was violently opposed to the Roman Catholic form of Christianity. Having no need to conceal his true sentiments, which reflected the prevailing opinion in Protestant England, he spoke of Roman Catholicism as "the horridest of all religions." [6] Yet there is a mixture of dismay and admiration in his attitude toward this "ancient hierarchy which . . . cannot but appear in some respect august and venerable. . . ." It "may even persecute with tolerable grace," unlike its High Church imitators for whom Shaftesbury has nothing but contempt. (II, 214 f.) The Roman Church has succeeded in appealing to the broadest range of human needs by combining the grossest superstition with the loftiest philosophic speculation. When comparing it with the religious fanaticism of the sects, Shaftesbury commends the Vatican for encouraging scholarship and the arts. His strong feelings against Roman Catholicism have to be assessed in the light of the fiercely partisan religio-political conflicts of the seventeenth century in which his own family had been so deeply involved.

Shaftesbury belongs to the liberal or "leftwing" of Protestantism, and he supports the Reformation primarily because it enabled Western Europeans to break the hold of the Roman Church upon them. In one of his few direct references to "our first reformers," he suggests that they were "little better than enthusiasts," (I, 22) but in a subsequent letter he claims that he had no intention of "bringing any contempt on our good Reformers of early times." [7] Nevertheless, Shaftesbury was particularly concerned with criticizing Calvinism, as were the Cambridge Platonists and his Arminian friends on the Continent, and his philosophy of religion, as we have seen, was in large part directed against the Calvinistic concepts of predestination, original sin, and election by supernatural grace.

Shaftesbury's son claims that his father read the Scriptures diligently, making notes in almost every chapter.[8] This is probably intended to counter charges that Shaftesbury was anti-Christian. While there are numerous references to the Bible in Shaftesbury's writings, there are far more to classical literature, and the biblical references are often out of context, and designed to support Shaftesbury's own ideas rather than to present the biblical point of view. In fact, Shaftesbury had little use for the Scriptures, and clearly regarded the Judeo-Christian tradition as inferior in wisdom to the classical tradition. Taking cognizance of the fact that many Protestants considered their religion to be based on the Bible, he tries to suggest that the grounds are none too solid. Chillingworth, whom Shaftesbury quotes, had formulated the Protestant doctrine as being that "the Scripture was the religion of Protestants." (II, 354)[9] Speaking through the mouth of a "gentleman of rank," described as having moderate opinions and "an apparent deference" to religion and the Established Church, Shaftesbury asks *which* Scripture is to be accepted as authoritative—which canon, which texts, or which translations? He points to the great variation in the interpretation of certain passages, to the difficulty of deciding whether they were to be interpreted literally or figuratively, and to variant readings in the texts themselves. He quotes at length from Bishop Taylor's *Polemical and Moral Discourses* (1657) and Archbishop Tillotson's *Rule of Faith* (1666) since both had raised similar questions in arguing that there can be no infallible interpreter or interpretation of Scripture. Shaftesbury uses the prestige and authority of these liberal churchmen in asserting the necessity for free interpretation and rational scrutiny of the Bible. Yet he formulates an argument which goes considerably beyond their aims, for he questions, even though indirectly, the supernatural authority of Scripture and casts doubt upon its intrinsic worth as literature.

Having made the point that a work in human language must be subject to human judgment, Shaftesbury remarks that it is impossible "that a celestial hand, submitting itself to the rudiments of a human art, should sin against the art itself, and express falsehood and error instead of justness and proportion." (II, 298) In the context this is clearly aimed at the Bible though it encompasses all supposedly revealed scriptures. Subsequently, he adds that intelligent churchmen do not claim either that the Bible is a "masterpiece," or that it is "absolutely perfect in the purity and justness" of its style and composition. (II, 302) Another example of his ironic attack is found in his reasons for opposing the use of biblical material in contemporary literature. Since the sacred book was "divinely dictated and inspired," the rules of "human wit" do not apply to its contents. (I, 229) It follows then, he reasons, that a modern author should not employ scriptural characters and stories in his writings, for if he does, he can expect little success. It is just too difficult to present these figures in a manner that accords with our ideas of "heroism and generosity." Moreover, divine justice is not always too clearly evident in the biblical account. Indeed, "the manners, actions, and characters of sacred writ are . . . matters incomprehensible in philosophy," and above the grasp of the mere historian, moralist, or poet. (I, 230) And so, Shaftesbury concludes, "it becomes not those who are uninspired from heaven and uncommissioned from earth, to search with curiosity into the original of those holy rites and records by law established." (I, 231) If one should attempt such an inquiry, it would probably have little success, particularly if we have "no better warrant left us for the authority of our sacred symbols than the integrity . . . of their compilers." (I, 231) He notes that unfortunately there is a lack of independent sources against which to check the biblical record. Obviously, Shaftesbury did not consider the Bible "divinely dictated," but he was quite willing to make a pretense of accepting this premise in order to mount his biting attack on the inspiration of the biblical writers. The meaning of Shaftesbury's sustained irony ought to have been clear to contemporary churchmen, and yet in the midst of it he seeks to reassure them that the sacred mysteries of the established religion will not be attacked. To the significance of this we will have to return later in this chapter.

Like many of the Deists, Shaftesbury reveals a strong aversion for the Jews. He writes that this "stubborn" and "stupid" people, had "in religion, as in everything else, the least good-humour of any people in the world. . . ." (II, 227) This bias seems surprising in men who were otherwise advocates of toleration and objectivity. However, this anti-Semitism was doctrinal rather than racial. It reflects, for one thing, a special hostility to Old Testament religion, but it has deeper implications than that. It was not possible to attack Christianity directly and openly in that age, but attacks upon the Jews were an accepted tradition. Anti-Semitism was here, as it has been throughout history, a covert attack upon Christianity itself.

One of the recurring arguments that Shaftesbury and the Deists used against institutional Christianity was the failure of professing Christians to live up to the moral precepts of their religion. Shaftesbury never tires of pointing to this disparity between profession and practice: Christians hardly seem better and are too often worse than non-Christians. The clergy, expectedly, come under particularly heavy attack. Shaftesbury warns a young theological student to avoid "above all . . . the Conceit and Pride, which is almost naturally inherent . . ." in the priesthood.[10] He further charges that "our holy religion" is for the most part "adapted to the very meanest capacities" of mankind, and the piety of some sects seems to be "founded in Moroseness, Selfishness, and Ill-will to Mankind; things not easily reconcilable with a Christian spirit." [11] Yet Shaftesbury concedes that, for all its failings, without the institution of the church not only Christianity but, more important, morality itself would suffer a decline. This implies, of course, that no other institution took over the functions of the church.

Whether one labels Shaftesbury a "Christian" or not depends, of course, on one's definition of that term. In any strict use of the term, Shaftesbury was certainly not a Christian, since he did not believe in the unique divinity of Jesus as the Christ, or in such characteristic doctrines as the atonement or the resurrection. His references to Jesus as "our Savior" or "Divine Master" represent merely conventional usage. He regarded Jesus as only one among the ethical teachers of mankind and, evidently, of less authority than a Socrates or Epictetus. He refers to Jesus infrequently, and, when describing his own belief, Shaftesbury clearly prefers the more general term "religion" to "Christianity." His professions of orthodoxy are all clearly ironic. With tongue in cheek, he "professes to believe as far as is possible, for any one who himself had never experienced any divine communication, whether by dream, vision, . . . or other supernatural operation, . . ." or witnessed any miracle. (II, 200) Yet, as our previous discussions made clear, Shaftesbury was deeply religious, if by "religious" one means believing in a reality which is the ultimate source of value, which is greater than man or Nature, and in which man may participate and attain the true good. Shaftesbury's piety is more akin to the natural or rational piety of the ancient Stoics, or, in twentieth-century philosophy, to that of Frederick Woodbridge or Samuel Alexander, than it is to orthodox Christian forms. It seems misleading to refer to him as a "Christian Platonist," as Marjorie Nicolson does, unless "Christian" is clearly intended in the broad sense that would include a modern theistic Unitarian. Of course, we must not forget that Shaftesbury was writing within the context of a "Christian" culture. A comparison of his approach to certain problems with that of a Buddhist or Hindu philosopher, for example, would demonstrate how much Shaftesbury was a part of the Christian civilization from within which he wrote. However, to attempt this would go far beyond the scope of this study. Suffice it to say that Shaftesbury's doctrine of enthusiasm and his emphasis on love have their sources not only in Platonism but in Christian tradition itself.

Shaftesbury's position marks another step in the gradual process then occurring in Western religious thought of simplifying religion and stripping it of traditional theological symbols. Locke had felt that the essential faith of Christians could be reduced to two articles: (1) that Jesus is the Messiah; and (2) that God exists. The ethical implications of Christianity could be summarized in the commandment to love thy neighbor. Shaftesbury follows Locke but takes the further, critical step of dropping, in effect, the first article, in formulating his natural religion. Not only Locke, but the Cambridge Platonists and the Latitudinarian divines shared the conviction that Christians should concentrate on the essentials of religion rather than on secondary or nonessential dogmas. The Gospel was not merely a set of doctrines to be subscribed to but a living force within the soul of man. But while Shaftesbury jettisoned much of the structure of traditional Christian theology, the Cambridge men were devout Christians who tried to rediscover the meaning of the traditional symbols and concepts of Christianity. That is why they were widely regarded in the Enlightenment as religious reactionaries, and Shaftesbury, on the other hand, was seen as the champion of truly liberal religion.

Shaftesbury saw himself as following a path of moderation that fell somewhere in between the dogmatic orthodox and the skeptical "men of wit." On the publication of "The Moralists," he wrote: "The fear is that the men of wit will rather think the author retained on the priest's side, and will despise him as much for an enthusiast in this piece as the priests have reviled him for an atheist in another." [12] The third Earl associated himself with the "men of latitude" in his effort to find a moderate position that would avoid what he considered the extreme and unreasonable positions of the Roman Catholics, the High Churchmen, the Calvinists, Puritans, and evangelical sects. "Unhappy bigots," he writes, "breaking out of the common road of religion, are entangled in bypaths and deeper in the briars than before." [13] Despite this, Shaftesbury was regarded by many contemporaries, as well as later in the century, as a skeptic and an enemy not only of revealed religion but of all religion. The publication of the "Letter Concerning Enthusiasm" in 1708 aroused a violent reaction against its anonymous author, and during the Sacheverell trial in 1710, the "Letter" was listed by the defense as one of those publications containing "Blasphemies and impious Doctrines and Tenets." There is the famous remark attributed to Pope by Warburton: "Mr. Pope told me, that to his knowledge, the *Characteristicks* had done more harm to Revealed Religion in England than all the works of Infidelity put together." [14] Shaftesbury *was* an "enemy" of revealed religion, if that term is taken to mean orthodox or creedal Christianity, and if an enemy is anyone who rejects such characteristic doctrines as the Trinity, the Christ, the Atonement, or the Resurrection. But there is little sense in the charge sometimes made that he ridiculed "all religion, natural as well as revealed." [15] Because of his essential religiosity, and because Shaftesbury's criticisms of certain aspects of Christianity were shared by many liberal churchmen, his philosophy continued to exercise an influence within church circles, particularly on philosophically minded clergymen like his follower, the Presbyterian Hutcheson, and the brilliant Bishop Butler. However, Shaftesbury's sarcasm and his evident lack of commitment to basic Christian doctrines was a source of concern even for moderate churchmen. This is reflected in John Leland's comments on his philosophy in *A View of the Principal Deistical Writers* (1754). While praising Shaftesbury for his genius, imagination, and taste, Leland notes that "it cannot be denied, that there are many things in his books, which seem to be evidently calculated to cast contempt upon Christianity and the holy Scriptures." [16] Butler was troubled by the same fact, though there seems little justification for the remark he is reported to have made that "if Shaftesbury . . . had lived to see the candor and moderation of the present times, in discussing religious subjects, he would have been a good Christian." [17]

Shaftesbury's exact views on traditional Christian doctrines are often difficult to determine since he says little or nothing of some, and others he treats indirectly or with irony. Furthermore, he felt no obligation to make all his private views public.

He shared the opinion held by many intellectuals in the Renaissance and Enlightenment that it was not only entirely proper but often necessary to draw a distinction between one's private religion and one's public religion, and that it was not wrong to conform in public while not in private. Shaftesbury confesses that "what one writes freely to a friend in private is very different from what one writes for public view." [18] This may seem to reveal a lack of integrity, but we must remember that we approach this from the vantage point of a society wherein freedom of expression of religious ideas is an accepted principle. In the Augustan age nonconformity still brought with it severe penalties. The odor of the Clarendon Code was still in the air, and many of its provisions were yet in force. During the "Indian Summer" of exclusive Anglicanism, made possible by the accession to power of the Tories in 1710, the High Church party attempted to enforce existing legislation against the Nonconformists, and to add new laws such as the Act Against Occasional Conformity (1711). In 1731, even after the situation had eased somewhat, the dissenter James Foster wrote that the Deists should not be blamed for disguising their views as long as the expression of unorthodox opinions was punishable by law.[19]

Shaftesbury published his own writings anonymously though the identity of their author soon became known. He points out that lack of religious freedom forces writers to use irony and "redouble their disguise." (I, 50) "It may be necessary, as well now as heretofore, for wise men to speak in parables, and with a double meaning, that the enemy be amused, and they only who have ears to hear may hear." (I, 45) Nevertheless, he insists that a writer with integrity *will* communicate his essential meaning even though indirectly. It is in this context that we can interpret the comment made in one of his letters that "I . . . can neither write nor speak but as I think. . . ." [20] Given the limitations imposed upon him by his age, Shaftesbury did convey his basic religious views to the perceptive reader; even his silences could be revealing.

Shaftesbury avoids a frontal attack upon the "mysteries of revelation" not only for the reasons already noted, but out of a sincere desire to avoid giving offense.[21] " 'Tis real humanity and kindness to hide strong truths from tender eyes." (I, 45) He seeks to allay the fears of churchmen by professions of orthodoxy, claiming that "we" have never "in practice acquitted ourselves otherwise than as just conformists to the lawful church; so we may, in a proper sense, be said faithfully and dutifully to embrace those holy mysteries, even in their minutest particulars, and without the least exception on account of their amazing depth." (II, 352) The irony cannot be missed. Moreover, he could hardly have believed seriously that such practical conformity was really equivalent to a faithful acceptance of revealed truths. When he adds that "we" are "fully assured of our own steady orthodoxy, resignation, and entire submission to the truly Christian and catholic doctrines of our holy church as by law established," (II, 352) we recall his comment that churchmen themselves have great difficulty in deciding what the definition of true orthodoxy is. By these professions of "orthodoxy," Shaftesbury was not merely attempting to divert criticism, he was also trying to free himself of theological issues that he considered of little value in order to concentrate on more fundamental philosophical questions.

Though it may seem surprising in the light of his bias against orthodox Christianity, Shaftesbury was a sincere supporter of the Church of England from a Broad or Low Church position, though for his own reasons and with his own reservations. The fourth Earl wrote of his father that "whenever his health permitted, he was constant in attending the services of the Church of England, and received the Holy Communion regularly three or four times a year." [22] However, since the fourth Earl was only three at his father's death, this is obviously not first-hand information. It is no doubt intended as an answer to the charges of atheism that were being made against his father. What may be a more accurate and objective account is given in a letter by Henry Needler, dated 1711:

I find, though his lordship is reported not to frequent the church, he does not altogether neglect religion. He seems to be of the opinion of the Quietists who believe that the most acceptable worship of the Deity, and that which suits best with his spiritual nature, consists in silent contemplation and inward adoration of his infinite perfections.[23]

The fourth Earl quotes from an unpublished discourse on religion which Shaftesbury wrote to his brother "some years before the *Letter of Enthusiasm.*" In it he expresses gratitude that England had an Established Church that on the whole had avoided the "wild fanaticisms of blasphemous visionaries," and which had "such established rites of worship as were so decent, . . . a church where in respect of the moderate party and far greater part the principle of charity was really more extensive than in any Christian or Protestant church besides in the world." [24] Paralleling this, in the Preface to Whichcote's sermons, Shaftesbury remarks that his criticisms of the Christian churches apply least to the Anglican Church which "shows Herself, above all others, most worthily and nobly Christian." [25]

Shaftesbury is strongly critical of the High Church party

throughout his writings, and he was very disturbed by the Sacheverell affair (1709) and by the rise to power of the High Church clergy in the following year through their alliance with the Tory party. Shaftesbury's later writings, e.g., the "Miscellaneous Reflections," and his letters from 1709 on, attack the church and clergy in sharper terms, reflecting his dismay at this turn of events. Of course, the close interconnection of religious and political movements at that time played an important part in his judgments. In 1711 he wrote to the young theological student who was his protégé, and who was about to be ordained, that

true Christianity [is] now set at nought and at defiance by the far greater part and numbers of that body of clergy called the Church of England, who no more esteem themselves a Protestant church. . . . You have been brought into the world, and come into orders, in the worst time for insolence, riot, pride, and presumption of clergymen that I ever knew or have read of. . . .[26]

On the other hand, the leaders of the Latitudinarian movement in the Church of England are singled out for praise by Shaftesbury. Of the earlier generation, he speaks highly of "the pious and learned Bishop [Jeremy] Taylor," whose religious writings put him "in the front of this order of authors." (II, 358 f.) William Chillingworth is commended, particularly for his *Reasons Against Popery*, and "our excellent Archbishop" Tillotson is described as "a great author." (II, 360) We have already amply documented in this study Shaftesbury's admiration for the Cambridge Platonists and their influence upon him. The fact that he was instrumental in bringing Whichcote's sermons to publication is significant in itself. In the Preface Shaftesbury lauds this pioneer of liberal religion for his "happy Temper and God-like disposition," and for the

"Excellency of his Life . . . even in the worst of Times. . . ."[27] And in specific references to More and Cudworth, Shaftesbury praises the former as "a learned and good man,"[28] and the latter for his acknowledged "capacity and learning." (II, 50) Among church leaders in the early years of the eighteenth century, Shaftesbury particularly respected Gilbert Burnet, the Bishop of Salisbury, an advocate of Broad Church views. He describes Burnet as "the truest Example of Laborious, Primitive, Pious, and Learned Episcopacy," and recommends his *Exposition of the Thirty-nine Articles* (1699).[29] It is not surprising that Shaftesbury also took sides with the young and aggressive Reverend Benjamin Hoadly, a leader of the extreme Latitudinarian party, in his controversies with High Churchmen.[30] Shaftesbury's connection with parallel religious movements on the Continent is seen in his close friendship and association with Jean Le Clerc and Phillipus Van Limborch, both of whom taught at the Remonstrant Seminary at Amsterdam. As an editor and writer, Le Clerc played an important part in liberal religious intellectual circles, and Shaftesbury refers to him as a "most learned defender of religion." (II, 305) Van Limborch was the leading Arminian theologian.

Like many intellectuals in the eighteenth century, Shaftesbury took the aristocratic view that the institutional church was necessary and desirable for the masses even though acceptance of its dogmas should not be obligatory for more cultivated minds. As Leslie Stephen expresses it, "the Church . . . was useful in so far as it tied the hands of the priests and fanatics, and acted as a gag instead of a trumpet. . . ."[31] The church could serve as an instrument of social control as well as of moral and religious education. Thus, Shaftesbury accepted the common Deistic position that the public rites of the established religion should be respected and that on appropriate occasions one should join in them. In his philosophical notebook, he wrote: "Remember therefore to respect these rites, whatever they be, which others have within their own minds erected to the Deity, as well as those other rites which they have publicly erected and in other outward temples. If modern superstition disturb thee be thankful it is not Indian and barbarian, that they are not human sacrifices. . . ." [32] To attack the religious beliefs and public rites of "the vulgar" directly might, instead of leading them to a more enlightened religion, undermine their belief in God and in virtue. A weakening of the social authority of the church could also open the door to religious fanaticism and the consequent social disorder. Shaftesbury seems to have recognized that ritual could function as a social symbol of our belief in a moral order, and as such could have emotional and educational value. This explains in part his support of liberal Anglicanism and his belief in the desirability of having an established national church.

Church and State

It is a temptation to the modern reader to apply the norms of present-day Western liberalism to Shaftesbury's language, and suppose that all of his references in the *Characteristics* to "religion by law established" are intended to be ironic and to discredit the idea of a national church. But actually he did believe —in terms of his era and its peculiar problems—in the advisability of having an established religion, and he believed this for eminently practical reasons, as suggested above. In a letter, Shaftesbury expressed agreement with the theory of the nature and authority of the church set forth by Matthew Tindal in *The Rights of the Christian Church Asserted* (1706), an attack on the nonjurors and the High Churchmen.[33] Like most of the Deists, Shaftesbury wanted to keep the clergy under the control of Parliament. Following Tindal closely, he argues that the original apostles had "proper testimonials in their lives, their manners, and behaviour, as well as in powerful works, miracles, and signs from heaven," but it is doubtful that the present-day, self-styled "ambassadors" from heaven come with the same credentials. (II, 365) Rejecting the doctrine of apostolic succession, he contends that the authority of the clergy does not, in fact, come from God, but from the magistrate or sovereign, who appoints them as agents. They have, it is true, "legal charter and character, legal titles and precedencies, legal habits, . . ." but these are not equivalent to the "immediate testimony and miraculous signs of power from above." (*Ibid.*) But since Shaftesbury obviously does not believe that such supernatural signs are *ever* given, he is, in effect, using this conventional belief as a lever to weaken the present authority of the clergy. His ultimate aim is, of course, to cast doubt on all claims of supernatural commissions. Thus, he goes on to say that pretended commissions from heaven have been claimed by so many different sects that we don't know which to believe. He sardonically asks if we must wait for "fire and sword, execution, massacre, and a kind of depopulation of this earth . . ." to determine finally which is true. (II, 368)

Tindal had attacked the High Church theory of the supernatural rights of the church according to which ecclesiastical authority was independent of the state. Taking a similar tack, Shaftesbury insists that ministerial authority is "from the public." Despite his frequent differences with Hobbes, their views converge on the point that the sovereign has the right and authority to determine what the national form of public worship should be. However, Shaftesbury criticizes Hobbes as one of "those writers who have been forward in making this unprosperous alliance, and building a Political Christianity. . . ." [34] Their difference seems to be on the character of the relationship of church and state. Shaftesbury observes that in some countries the church has entered political affairs, but just to the extent that it has, and concerned itself with "any other Interest than that of Christ's Kingdom," it has been less able to bring about the desired "Revolution in Manners." [35] The union of politics and religion has benefited neither. Shaftesbury wants to place control of the church in the hands of the sovereign but does not want an organic union of church and state; the church is to be a subsidiary institution restricting itself to spiritual matters, while the state should concentrate on political affairs.

Shaftesbury praises James Harrington, the political theorist, as "a notable author of our nation," (I, 14) and adopts his concept of "a public leading" in the sphere of religion. Harrington wrote that

there is nothing more certain or demonstrable to common Sense, than that the far greater part of Mankind, in matters of Religion, give themselves up to the public leading. Now a National Religion, rightly established, or not coercive, is not any public driving, but only the public leading.[36]

Shaftesbury agrees that " 'tis necessary a people should have a *public leading* in religion. For to deny the magistrate a worship, or take away a national church, is as mere enthusiasm as the notion which sets up persecution. For why should there not be public walks as well as private gardens?" (I, 14) Elsewhere he notes that many who defend religious tolerance do not recognize this need for a publicly recognized religion; but they are making a grave error since religion needs "the Care and Countenance of the Magistrate." [37]

As noted previously, Shaftesbury favors an Established Church because he believes it can serve as an instrument of social control by which the passions of the mob might be kept in check. He certainly did not intend that the ecclesiastical authority should control the state, or that political leaders should go into the business of saving souls. He distinguishes between "a public leading" and "leading by the nose," which he opposes, for he is against any effort to enforce uniformity of opinion, knowing that individual religious belief cannot be imposed by law. He does not advocate the use of force in behalf of the national religion; it has all the advantages it needs if it is in any way consonant with reason. Yet an Established Church, governed by the principles of moderate Anglicanism, can serve as a barrier against the rise of fanaticism, provide a peaceful forum for the mediation of religious differences, and thus serve to forestall the types of religious conflict that previous centuries had suffered from—conflicts that issued in violence, and even the "shock and ruin of empires." Just as he thought that political leadership was responsible to the public and should be changed if it failed in this responsibility, so it is implied that the church was responsible to the public, and should be reformed if it likewise failed.

With biting irony, Shaftesbury argues that religion, "as by law established," ought to be granted the same ceremonial rights and privileges as heraldry. While individuals may make designs as they please in private, "they must blazon only as the public directs. . . . Naturalists may, in their separate and distinct capacity, inquire as they think fit into the real existence and natural truth of things; but they must by no means dispute the authorised forms." (I, 233) Shaftesbury continues with the hope that the College of Heralds (meaning, of course, the church), their power now reduced by law, will not try again to "set us to tilt and tournament, and raise again those defiances and moral frays of which their Order were once the chief managers and promoters." (*Ibid.*) Yet he is willing to allow that "the Christian theology, the birth, procedure, generation, and personal distinction of the Divinity, are mysteries only to be determined by the initiated or ordained, to whom the State has assigned the guardianship and promulgation of the divine oracles." (I, 231) But since such matters are largely mythology in Shaftesbury's opinion, it is no great loss to philosophy to leave their discussion to the clergy. The important thing is to keep the provinces of philosophy and religion distinct and separate. For this and for the other reasons previously mentioned, Shaftesbury recommends that we accept the guidance of our "lawful superiors" in matters of public worship. Though in philosophy, he wryly adds, there is no justification for "being such earnest recognisers of a controverted title." (II, 102)

There is an apparent contradiction in Shaftesbury's position for he argues on the one hand for freedom in the interpretation of the Scriptures on grounds that no one can claim infallibility in this task; on the other hand, he seeks to assure the orthodox that the "mysteries of revelation" will not be questioned. The inconsistency arises out of conflicting motives in his thought. His fear of unregulated sectarianism and of the conflicts it generates leads him to support an Established Church, and he realizes that such an institution, to function effectively, must have its own prerogatives and rights, even though ultimately deriving its authority from the state. But, as an advocate of freedom of thought and of the principle that all ideas must meet the test of reason, he cannot consistently exempt any area of thought from examination. Shaftesbury's position, though, leads logically to modern religious liberalism which, under different social conditions, has been able to formulate a point of view which escapes these difficulties. Given the separation of religion and politics, and the general acceptance of the principle of freedom of religious conscience in the Western world, liberals holding presuppositions similar to Shaftesbury's no longer believe for the most part in the need for an Established Church or in the necessity for any limitation on the examination of religious claims or beliefs. There is every reason to think that under present conditions Shaftesbury would have modified his views along the same lines.

CHAPTER EIGHT

HUMOR and LIBERTY

The concept of humor plays an important part throughout Shaftesbury's discussion of religion. Humor is not only a method of attack upon all forms of narrow-mindedness, intolerance, and bigotry, but in a more fundamental sense it characterizes the state of mind in which truth is best apprehended. Humor is a means of liberation from patterns of action or thought that are life-destroying rather than life-giving. In Shaftesbury's philosophy it denotes a fundamental capacity of the soul which prepares man for the apprehension of the true, the beautiful, and the good. Humor relaxes the mind, allowing it to view problems freely and objectively from various perspectives, and thus, it is the enemy of all pretense and falsity. If we fear humor, Shaftesbury writes,

we may be charged perhaps with wilful ignorance and blind idolatry for having taken opinions upon trust, and consecrated in ourselves certain idol-notions, which we will never suffer to be unveiled or seen in open light. They may perhaps be monsters, and not divinities, or sacred truths, which are kept thus choicely in some dark corner of our minds. The spectres may impose on us whilst we refuse to turn them every way and view their shapes and complexions in every light. For that which can be shown only in a certain light is questionable. Truth, 'tis supposed, may bear all lights; and one of those principal lights, or natural mediums, by which things are to be viewed, in order to a thorough recognition, is ridicule itself, or that manner of proof by which we discern whatever is liable to just raillery in any subject. (I, 43 f.)

Shaftesbury argues that though some persons object to having serious matters treated humorously, the only way that we can distinguish between true and false gravity is to apply humor, and observe which is able to hold up under this treatment. "Gravity is of the very essence of imposture" (I, 10), and we can only avoid being deceived by it by subjecting it to the *proving* power of ridicule. Satire functions by comparing the actual with the ideal, or the theory of what a thing is supposed to be with its existing form, and thus exposing the discrepancy between the two. In Shaftesbury's philosophy, the humorous state of mind, which is closely akin to the skeptical and questioning temper, is seen as opposed to the dogmatic mentality, and it is dogmatism which has the most to fear from the free exercise of wit. What Shaftesbury was talking about has been succinctly stated recently by Kingsley Amis: "A culture without satire is a culture without self-criticism and thus, ultimately, without humanity." [1]

Shaftesbury's defense of humor, as expressed particularly in the *Letter Concerning Enthusiasm* and the *Essay on the Freedom of Wit and Humour*, provided a rationale for the flowering of satire in the Augustan age, which the third Earl viewed as a sign of national health. The temper of the times made Shaftesbury's doctrine immensely popular but, at the same time, as one would expect, there was a strong reaction against it in some quarters, and probably no concept of Shaftesbury's generated as much continuing controversy for so long as did his defense of ridicule. There was nothing new in the idea that comedy was to be used to expose the follies of mankind and to encourage men thereby to think and act in new ways. But Shaftesbury went further than other writers in recommending that wit be given larger scope and greater freedom. It was easy enough to agree that humor should be used to expose acknowledged evils; but it was hitting dangerously close to home when Shaftesbury urged that wit be directed even against those elements in society which were generally considered respectable, virtuous, and orthodox. Satire, as one of the greatest weapons we have in the cause of truth, must be used against *every* form of tyranny whether political, moral, or religious.

It was this latter recommendation that religion itself be subjected to the proving power of ridicule which disturbed many of Shaftesbury's ecclesiastical contemporaries most. Not that the idea was new—Dryden, for example, considered the "satirical poet . . . the check of the laymen on bad priests," [2] and poking fun at clerics was at least as old as Chaucer—but Shaftesbury gave it more pungent expression. Not only enthusiasm, but all religious practices and beliefs should be able to vindicate themselves in the light of humor. He commends those "reverend authors" who make use of humor to answer heresy and doubt, suggesting that they may laugh some men *into* religion who had previously been laughed *out*! In our discussion of enthusiasm earlier, we saw that Shaftesbury found a deep underlying connection between true religion and "goodhumour." Thus, he believes that only false religion has anything to fear from humorous treatment, for "wit and humour are corroborative of religion, and promotive of true faith," and ". . . are used as proper means of this kind by the holy founders of religion." (II, 217) The mental attitudes associated with humor open rather than close the mind to true faith.

Throughout the eighteenth century Shaftesbury's doctrine of humor was compressed into the words, "ridicule, the test of truth," a phrase attributed to him not only by adversaries like Berkeley, but by his defenders as well. This phrasing, as careful readers have noted, never appears in exactly that form in the *Characteristics,* though Shaftesbury comes close to it in several places. For example, he asks why we are "such cowards in reasoning, and are so afraid to stand the test of ridicule?" (I, 10) Or again, he writes that "without wit and humour, reason can hardly have its proof or be distinguished." (I, 52) An even closer approximation is found in some of the entries in the index which Shaftesbury himself composed as it appears in the 1714 edition of *Characteristics:*

> RIDICULE, its Rule, Measure, Test.
> TEST of Ridicule.
> TRUTH bears all Lights.—Ridicule a Light, Criterion to Truth.[3]

Unfortunately, the phrase "ridicule, the test of truth," tends to misrepresent Shaftesbury's views, although he himself is certainly responsible in part for contributing to this misunderstanding. Certainly Shaftesbury never even implied, as one preacher claims, that "Ridicule is the only infallible test of Truth," [4] nor did he ever contend, as John Brown charges, that ridicule "may be successfully applied to the investigation of unknown Truth." [5] For Shaftesbury ridicule is not a means for the discovery of new truth in the positive sense, nor is it a logical proof of the truth or falsity of a proposition. But as we have been suggesting here, it has two aspects: first, humor is a means—whether by satire, irony, or farce—of examining the various aspects of a subject; and second, it denotes the free and objective state of mind with which we approach a subject and evaluate it. It is doubtful that Shaftesbury ever thought of humor as being a mode of cognition: it is an instrument of reason, and it is reason ultimately which must distinguish between the true and false. Shaftesbury undoubtedly produces a false impression by using such logical terminology as "test" and "criterion." However, they have at least a figurative application: ridicule does have a kind of *proving* power in that what cannot stand up under free and humorous examination, in Shaftesbury's opinion, is not well-grounded in reason and Nature.

Even if wit exceeds its proper limits, which Shaftesbury concedes it may, the solution is not an appeal to the magistrate for its repression by force. If men don't have the good sense to correct erroneous impressions in their own minds, governmental interference is not likely to help, and, in fact, may make the situation worse, for political repression only tends to stimulate the "bantering" spirit. Shaftesbury is convinced that wit tends to correct itself, and thus, "freedom of wit" is the best protection that we have against false wit or "scurrilous buffoonery." Wit and humor tend to refine themselves when allowed to operate freely: "All politeness is owing to liberty. We polish one another, and rub off our corners and rough sides by a sort of amicable collision." (I, 46) Indeed, the satirical "wars" of the eighteenth century, however crude and bitter they may seem, were a more civilized and civilizing alternative to the fratricidal bloodshed of the previous century. And R. L. Brett contends that they were accompanied, as Shaftesbury himself had said that they would be, by "an increasing regard for the rules of fair debate and impartial argument." [6] Satire and wit became important instruments of social progress, and, as Brett continues:

The irony of Swift and Hogarth produced a real improvement in both private and public morality, while the *Spectator* and *Tatler*, followed by such periodicals as Fielding's *Covent Garden Journal*, were a mighty social force. . . . Satire, indeed, could penetrate where sentiment could not; it could reach the more sophisticated classes who were impervious to the sentimental appeal and religious fervour of the Methodist revival.[7]

Shaftesbury never seems to doubt that where there is a truly free interplay of ideas the best will come out on top; only bad ideas suffer from free and humorous treatment.

I can very well suppose men may be frighted out of their wits, but I have no apprehension they should be laughed out of them. I can hardly imagine that in a pleasant way they should ever be talked out of their love for society, or reasoned out of humanity and common sense. A mannerly wit can hurt no cause or interest for which I am in the least concerned; and philosophical speculations, politely managed, can never surely render mankind more unsociable or uncivilised. (I, 65)

And in the *Letter* he asks: "What ridicule can lie against reason?" (I, 10) Indeed, he suggests ironically that virtue has less to fear from its "witty antagonists" than from some of its ardent defenders! And yet, one cannot help asking, "What of wit that is not 'mannerly,' and philosophy that is not 'politely managed'?" Leibniz, though he approved of the use of wit against fanaticism, had the same apprehensions, fearing the consequences of its application to the truly sacred and good. Like others in the eighteenth century, he believed that the widespread employment of ridicule might hurt the truth itself since "men love less to reason than to laugh."[8] Leibniz pointed out that anything, regardless of its merit, could be made to appear ridiculous. Shaftesbury is particularly open to this criticism, for at times he seems to forget the diabolical ends to which humor (and for that matter, intellect itself) may be put.

Nevertheless, there are two answers to these charges suggested in the *Characteristics*. One is Shaftesbury's contention that he advocates controlled or regulated humor; the other is his assumption that truth is congruous or harmonious. Acknowledging the excesses to which wit may be carried, he writes:

'Tis in reality a serious study to learn to temper and regulate that humour which nature has given us as a more lenitive remedy against vice, and a kind of specific against superstition and melancholy delusion. There is a great difference between seeking how to raise a laugh from everything, and seeking in everything what justly may be laughed at. (I, 85)

There is a difference between "genteel wit" or "true raillery," on the one hand, and mere "buffoonery" or "banter," on the other. The former is an instrument of reason; it is premised upon self-control and the regulation of the passions. True mirth has in it the proper mixture of gravity, as true gravity has an element of mirth. Defending Shaftesbury's conception of humor, Le Clerc described it as *"la joie intérieure, qui nait de l'amour de la Vérité. . . ."* [9] For Shaftesbury, *true* wit is always appropriate to its objects. The measured irony of Socrates or Horace embodies his ideal, but he has harsh words to say of his contemporary, Swift:

Witness the prevalency and first success of that detestable writing of that most detestable author of the *Tale of a Tub*, whose manners, life, and prostitute pen and tongue are indeed exactly answerable to the irregularity, obscenity, profaneness, and fulsomeness of his false wit and scurrilous style and humour. Yet you know how this extraordinary work pleased even our great philosophers themselves, and how few of those who disliked it dared declare against it.[10]

The other, and more fundamental, answer that Shaftesbury offers to his critics is based upon his conviction that truth and virtue are ultimately congruous and harmonious, while error and vice are incongruous and inharmonious. It follows that error and vice are inherently ridiculous, for the essence of the comic is incongruity and inconsistency. On the other hand, truth and virtue do not lend themselves properly to comic treatment. That is why Shaftesbury can affirm with such confidence that "nothing is ridiculous except what is deformed; nor is anything proof against raillery except what is handsome and just. . . . A man must be soundly ridiculous who, with all the wit imaginable, would go about to ridicule wisdom, or laugh at honesty, or good manners." (I, 85 f.) He is well aware that humor may be directed against good causes and against truth itself, but he is willing that we run the risk entailed because of his deep conviction that in a free society true wit will in the long run prevail because it applies to its objects while false wit does not. Shaftesbury's conception of laughter goes far beyond such narrow definitions as that proposed by Hobbes, who described laughter as "a sudden glory arising from some sudden conception of some eminency in ourselves, by comparison with the infirmity of others, or with our own formerly. . . ."[11] Hobbes typically tries to find the meaning of humor in a reflex response of immediate self-interest. Shaftesbury's concept is both more fundamental and broader in scope: we laugh at incongruity, at the contrast of the ideal and the actual—of what is and what ought to be. And we can laugh at our own expense too, a point Hobbes's theory would not let him see. In sum, there is no better description of the function of humor in Shaftesbury's philosophy than that which Cassirer gives of Shakespearean humor:

> In the moral sphere, too, humour serves again and again as a basic element of self-evaluation. It fits things into their rightful places in the scale of being, robbing them of any usurped worth. Arrogant seriousness, when seen through the spectacles of Shakespearean humour, becomes mere pomposity; and false grandeur becomes grandiosity. Yet humour in Shakespeare never evinces . . . a deliberate intention to destroy. It is rather the things themselves, which, upon seeing their images as mirrored by this elemental power of the intellect, recognise so to speak their true inner proportion and return to it. In so doing they regain their appointed place in reality. In the realm of humour, too, epochs meet and intermingle in strange ways. For humour looks before and after; it helps to usher in the vital shapes of the future without renouncing the past.[12]

Freedom of Thought

If, for Shaftesbury, humor is both a method and a state of mind, freedom is the condition under which humor operates most effectively for rational ends. Shaftesbury's passion for moral, civil, and intellectual liberty is one of the dominant characteristics of his life and work. Even his critic, John Brown, speaks admiringly of "that generous Spirit of Freedom which shines throughout the whole" of his writings.[13] Referring to the *Characteristics*, Shaftesbury himself calls the theme of moral and political liberty "the hinge and bottom of the whole work."[14] Freedom of thought and civil liberty not only have utilitarian value for man, but they are defining characteristics of his true humanity, being "necessary and essential to his Manly Dignity and Character." [15]

We have already seen that Shaftesbury argues against appealing to the magistrate, i.e., the power of the state, in religious and philosophical controversies. He suggests that the attempt to use civil force in such instances is motivated by fear of the inadequacy of one's own position; the more force necessary to maintain a religious belief, the more it is to be suspected. And those who try to deprive us of our freedom have already lost their own power of free thought: "Tyranny can never be exercised, but by one, who is already a Slave." [16] One of his main arguments is that the attempt to force people to hold a particular opinion is not likely to succeed, since external power cannot enforce internal feelings where the will is opposed. Furthermore, it is likely to produce a counterreaction which reinforces the belief one is attempting to repress. Martyrdom only arouses greater zeal in believers, and if "stubbornness of the will" is the cause of heresy, violence will only stimulate it further.

At the same time, Shaftesbury is not unaware of the fact that if a government wants to control men's minds it may achieve considerable success by instituting a systematic and *total* control of the intellectual and spiritual spheres. The whole apparatus of the state would have to be concentrated on this process of conditioning the minds of men through a carefully applied system of rewards and punishments. On the other hand, a partial effort to do this, or a "halfway persecution," will have the least success. It is strong enough to arouse resistance, but not strong enough to wipe out the supposed heresy. Shaftesbury could direct his argument mainly at this kind of partial persecution because he was confident that Englishmen would overwhelmingly reject the alternative of totalitarianism or absolute tyranny.

Since for Shaftesbury fanaticism is basically the product of "ill-humour" and fear, persecution is bound to stimulate it:

To be pursued by petty inquisitors; to be threatened with punishment or penal laws; to be marked out as dangerous and suspected; to be railed at in high places with all the studied wit and art of calumny, are indeed sufficient provocations to ill-humour, and may force people to divide who at first had never any such intention. (II, 221) [17]

Thus, in dealing with the type of fanaticism that has dangerous social effects, the state should exercise good humor and seek to allay the people's fears rather than arouse them. This provides the only hope for inducing an attitude of acceptance toward new or different ideas.

Shaftesbury's defense of freedom of thought, like that of freedom of wit, is based on the assumption that truth is more powerful than error. "Truth is the most powerful thing in the world, since even fiction itself must be governed by it, and can only please by its resemblance." (I, 6) One is reminded of southern senators, in our own time, who argue in the name of human freedom for a social system which is, in effect, the denial of freedom. Falsity mimics truth, and exists only as a parasite of truth. Lies paradoxically reaffirm truths. Thus, Shaftesbury is overwhelmingly confident that, where men are allowed free trial and experiment, truth will prevail: "Let but the search go freely on, and the right measure of everything will soon be found." (I, 10) Free trade in goods means a healthy economy, and, analogously, free trade in ideas means a healthy culture. Thought, like wit, is self-correcting; when men reason badly, reason itself is the only remedy.

With an unquestioning faith in reason, Shaftesbury advocates that we follow reason wherever she may lead. Just as he believes that there should be no philosophical sanctuaries above and beyond examination, he believes that religious beliefs—at least as far as they involve genuine philosophical questions—should be freely discussed. As one would expect in an advocate of rational religion, reason represents no threat to religious truth. True theism would only benefit from "the establishment of an entire philosophical liberty," [18] though he means rational dispute and not merely emotional appeal. This defense of religious freedom by the Augustan philosopher is not new, but reflects the arguments of the Latitudinarian divines and the Cambridge Platonists.[19]

Shaftesbury's confidence in the power of truth to prevail may seem overly optimistic, and yet he was not as naïve as might appear. He recognized that men have a great facility for self-deception and are all too easily misled by others. He was well aware of the fact that liberty can be abused, whether through religious fanaticism or philosophical "libertinism," but he believed that the extremes would temper one another. In his own time, he notes that the atheists were already using "modester and more polite" language.[20] It is important to remember, finally, that his optimism about the predominance of truth is conditional on the degree to which men had attained self-mastery and that harmony of the affections which is the prerequisite of sound reasoning and true freedom.

Shaftesbury was too much of a social realist to advocate absolute freedom. He realized that an organized society cannot exist without rules and regulations which are in effect limitations on one's freedom of behavior. While thought, in the strict sense, cannot be forcibly controlled, the *public* expression of opinion can be and, Shaftesbury seems to concede, *must* be regulated to some degree. Thus, he states clearly that the liberty he defends is "the liberty of the *club*," or complete liberty of *private* conversation. (I, 53) In public gatherings certain conventional limitations should be accepted willingly out of respect for common feeling and as a matter of good taste. "The lovers of mankind respect and honour conventions and societies of men." (*Ibid.*) Shaftesbury may have had the case of John Toland in mind when he wrote this. After the bad reception of his book, *Christianity Not Mysterious* (1696), by churchmen and its condemnation by the Church of England, Toland, to the dismay of his friends, insisted on arguing his views openly in coffeehouses and other public places. This would be for Shaftesbury a breach of good taste. Whether he would have recommended intervention by the magistrate in such a case seems doubtful. Yet in a letter to Le Clerc he writes: "It is the profane mocking and scurrilous language that gives the just offence, makes fatal impressions on the vulgar and corrupts men in another manner than by their reason. And . . . it is the only case in which I would wish the magistrate to interpose on our side." [21] This suggests that he believed in the necessity of laws restraining highly offensive, licentious, or libelous language in public. Protecting the good name of citizens would, at least, be another guarantee of individual security and liberty.

In general, Shaftesbury's views on toleration are in accord with those of Locke and Matthew Tindal, whom he expressly praises.[22] Tindal argued that the state had the right to punish both those who committed crimes and those whose principles encouraged crime, which included atheists as well as those who used profane language. However, the civil government should

not attempt to regulate opinions which were not directly connected with morality. This would include speculative opinions,
such as theology, which Tindal believed should be left to the
individual. But Tindal, Locke, and Shaftesbury all agreed with
the prevailing opinion that atheism was a threat to morality
and not simply a theological or philosophical issue. However,
in "The Moralists," Shaftesbury suggests a further distinction
between an absolute atheist and one who merely doubts, i.e., an
agnostic. The former categorically denies Deity, and thus,
seemingly, sets himself up against the interests of society and
against morality itself. He is "punishable" by law, but not the
mere agnostic. (II, 49) In his *Discourse of Freethinking* (1713),
Anthony Collins carried the logic of Shaftesbury's position to a
more consistent conclusion, calling for complete freedom of
expression for all types of religious or irreligious opinion.
Given the fact of changing social and intellectual conditions in
England, there is little reason to doubt that, had Shaftesbury
lived, he would eventually have come to hold the same position. (cf. II, 51)

During his political career, Shaftesbury followed the Whig
party line of upholding civil liberties. It is said that his maiden
speech in the Commons (November, 1695) turned the tide in
favor of a bill providing the right of counsel to one accused
of treason. In later years, though no longer active, he followed
political developments closely. His letters reveal his strong
opposition to such repressive legislation as the Occasional Conformity Bill which was passed, over Whig objections, in 1711.
It provided that anyone who had qualified for state or munici-
pal office by taking the Anglican sacrament, as was required,
but who subsequently participated in Nonconformist services,
was to be punished by ruinous fines. Shaftesbury did not live

to see the passage of the even more odious Schism Act in 1714, but his knowledge of the trend in that direction soured his last years.

Though England had suffered from bloody civil and religious strife in the seventeenth century, Shaftesbury believed that greater intellectual freedom would lessen the likelihood of such violence. In an age still plagued by riot and turmoil, it took courage and faith to call for greater freedom. Shaftesbury found this in his assurance that the power of truth would be predominant, an assurance grounded in his optimistic metaphysics—in his faith that the universe is ultimately good and rational.

PART TWO

CHAPTER NINE

HUMAN NATURE:
The SOCIAL AFFECTIONS

According to Sidgwick, "Shaftesbury is the first moralist who distinctly takes psychological experience as the basis of ethics." [1] It is true that Shaftesbury's philosophical psychology provides him with a model of human nature that is crucial to his ethical theory, though his interest in psychology is largely limited to its bearing on ethical and religious issues. Sidgwick regards the *Characteristics* as a turning point in English moral philosophy, shifting the center of ethical judgment away from revelation or discursive reason toward the realm of the affections. [2] But this is only partly true, for Shaftesbury is no anti-rationalist, and it is clear that both the Cambridge Platonists and the Latitudinarians prepared the way for him. [3] Though he drew heavily on the ancient Stoics, his emphasis on the affections—the emotional sources of judgment—makes it clear that he was not merely restating Stoic doctrine. Shaftesbury describes his task in the "Inquiry Concerning Virtue" thus: "Since it is therefore by affection merely that a creature is esteemed good or ill, natural or unnatural, our business will be to examine which are the good and natural, and which the ill and unnatural affections." (I, 247) In undertaking this study, he is not only interested in examining the individual *qua* individual, but he is concerned with man as a social and political creature, and as a "citizen of the world." Ultimately, he seeks to understand man's "end and constitution in Nature itself." (II, 5)

Shaftesbury entered into this examination of the "territories of the heart" because he believed that the virtues were rooted in the affections. He aimed to establish the *natural* basis of virtue, and to demonstrate that the social impulses were a necessary component of human nature. In so doing he was responding to attacks on human nature coming from two directions: from Hobbes, on the one hand, with his doctrine of "the state of Nature" and his psychological egoism; and from the Calvinists, on the other, with their concept of the total depravity of fallen man. In this struggle to vindicate human nature, Shaftesbury once again aligned himself with the Cambridge Platonists and the Latitudinarians. For the Cambridge scholars, the *imago Dei* had not been utterly destroyed in the Fall; for the Latitudinarians, the natural emotional drives of man tended to lead to acts of love and good will. In contrast, Hobbes denied the natural sociability of man, arguing that our natural affections lead to conflict and war, and that fear and self-interest are the prime considerations that lead men to join in mutual pacts guaranteeing peace and order. Shaftesbury could not accept the dichotomy between the so-called "state of Nature" and human society as we commonly experience it. He argues that if there ever was such a chaotic stage through which men went, it could not have lasted long. Thus, it shouldn't properly be called a "state" since that term denotes a period of relative equilibrium and of some duration. If our forebears ever were in the condition described by Hobbes, it could only be said to be "the rough draft of man, the first effort of Nature, a species in the birth, a kind as yet unformed; not in its natural state, but under violence, and still restless, till it attained its natural perfection." (II, 79) These creatures, even though related to us biologically, could no more be called "men" than could embryos. Hobbes's reductionism makes man something less than man, stripping him of his natural affections and his inherent sociability, and thus, in effect, of his humanity. Moreover, in the Hobbesian state of Nature, language and art could hardly have existed; therefore, the creatures living in it could have had little capacity for reasoning. How they ever emerged from this anarchic condition would remain a mystery. Lacking the natural social impulses, such intelligence as they may have had would hardly explain how they could have had the good sense to enter into mutual covenants requiring trust and loyalty to be effective.

Continuing his attack, Shaftesbury reasons that man either must have existed from eternity or not. If from eternity, there could not have been any primitive state differing decisively from the present condition of man. If man has *not* existed from eternity, he either must have been at the beginning as he is now, or he developed gradually through various stages to his present state. Shaftesbury contends that the latter is the only hypothesis conforming to the state of Nature theory, conceiving of a gradual development of man through various plantlike and animal-like forms to the present. However, as long as this process is regarded as the product of chance rather than of a designing intelligence, no particular stage in it could be considered "the state of Nature" or more "natural" than any other stage unless it were "that in which Nature was perfect, and

her growth complete . . . ," her end being attained. (II, 81)
This would necessarily be a social rather than a presocietal
state. Moreover, Shaftesbury doubts that men could have survived at all in the Hobbesian state of Nature. Without any
social impulses, how could the family or the propagation of
the species be accounted for? He points out that no existing
human groups actually live under such totally anarchical conditions.

Shaftesbury's reference to the possibility of biological evolution is interesting but it is clear that he associates this theory
with his opponents rather than adopting it for himself. He
could accept it only if it were understood to be the means by
which the Supreme Mind operated, and if it were purged of
the element of chance. He uses the hypothesis here only as a
device to attack Hobbes on his own grounds. For the third
Earl, man *as man* always existed in society, though he allows
for the evolution of social forms in human history from family,
to tribe, to nation. Basil Willey considers Shaftesbury's criticism of Hobbes's state of Nature to be important "as one of
the earliest attempts to replace that philosophical abstraction
by a historical and evolutionary view of the origin of society." [4] Yet Shaftesbury takes no more than hesitant steps in
that direction.

In his attempt to expose the inconsistencies in Hobbes's reductionistic theory, Shaftesbury directs his attention to the
suggestion that human beings are at bottom no better than
animals in their behavior—that, for example, they act like
wolves. Yet the state of Nature pictures men as acting even
worse than many animals, including wolves. After all, Shaftesbury points out, wolves are gregarious and they co-operate in
various activities. If animals are capable of sharing a common

life, is there not a presumption in favor of believing that man always had this capacity? It does not bother Shaftesbury that the elementary forms of social life that we observe in animals may be largely instinctive. What Nature accomplishes through automatic instincts in animals, she accomplishes through voluntary reason in man. All is accounted for in terms of the purposive structure of Being.

Though the attack on Hobbism was one of the major aims of the *Characteristics*, Shaftesbury wrote in a letter that he "must confess" Hobbes was "a genius, and even an original among these latter leaders in philosophy." [5] In the *Characteristics*, he concedes that he was a "good sociable man, as savage and unsociable as he would make himself and all mankind appear by his philosophy." (I, 61) Though he taught that there was "nothing which naturally drew us to the love of what was without, or beyond ourselves," his own life was a refutation of his principles. (I, 62) Hobbes's genuine concern for the welfare of man reveals that very natural affection which he denied. If men are in fact motivated solely by narrow self-interest, why would anyone communicate this to others? Would it not be more reasonable in this case to keep it a secret, and preach altruism as a means of gaining self-advantage? The consistent scoundrel, Shaftesbury writes, has "no such passion for truth, or love for mankind"; he is sure to "preach honesty, and go to church." (I, 64) Moral theory itself can be an instrument of exploitation. But instead, Hobbes genuinely conceived of his system as one that would save us from social disorder and the ravages of fanaticism. Unfortunately, both his analysis and his program are faulty, according to Shaftesbury.

The Natural

It is evident that in this discussion of Hobbes's theory, the meaning of the term "natural" is crucial. Unfortunately, one finds in Shaftesbury that same variety of meanings and connotations that Bayle noted in other philosophers of that era, and which, in fact, had long been a characteristic of Western philosophy. "Natural" and "according to Nature" are used to mean different things in different contexts—in places two or three meanings all at once—in a way that sometimes leaves the reader uncertain as to the precise significance. Following are some of the primary senses in which Shaftesbury uses the term "natural":

(1) It may mean the permanent or underlying structure of a creature or thing, as distinguished from its changing, surface characteristics. In this respect "natural" may refer to (A) those characteristics which a living creature has "by Nature," i.e., is born with, as for example, certain instincts. On the other hand, this sense of "natural" takes in (B) those characteristics which develop inevitably in a creature existing under conditions that would be more or less normal for a member of its species. In man, for example, there are certain potentialities which normal conditions inevitably activate—as the need for fellowship. All of these closely related meanings are generally associated by Shaftesbury with traits that are universal to the members of a particular species.

(2) Shaftesbury also uses "natural" in a decidedly different sense on some occasions to signify a practice or trait which becomes habitual or is ingrained by habit. In this usage, he gives recognition to environmental or self-determining factors in the structure of personality. For example, he suggests in one

place that if the practice of inner dialogue is not natural to us, we should make it so by application.

(3) On the other hand, "natural" may be opposed to "artificial," meaning simply what comes into being without human effort or intervention. As such it is associated with spontaneity in human behavior. This sense is closely related to the first meaning above (1), and yet has its own special signification.

(4) One of the primary meanings of "natural" for the English philosopher is the "rational"; indeed, the terms often seem to function as synonyms. The *truly* natural is by definition the *truly* rational. "Natural" truths are those that conform to reason, are objectively valid, and are rooted in the eternal and immutable structure of Nature.

(5) It is only another step to the ultimate, and I think basic, meaning of "natural" in Shaftesbury's philosophy, which is the "good" or the "ideal." Applied to a living creature, it may connote the healthy or mature state in which that creature is realizing its true ends—its characteristic and *highest* capacities. It is in this sense that Shaftesbury bestows upon man's social drives the honorific title of "natural affections."

Usually, Shaftesbury's meaning is clear enough in context, though the fusion of meanings sometimes leads to imprecision. Furthermore, even the above meanings require analysis that is not always forthcoming in his writings. On occasion, he seems to associate the natural with the "average," though presumably he does so only where he believes that the ideal and the actual have a high degree of coincidence. Shaftesbury conceives of Nature as embodying in itself the ideal pattern of things, from which man might deviate, but which would always be the *truly* natural—the best possible in the structure of finite things.

It is in this light that we must interpret such passages as his famous early defense of the natural garden, in which he describes his

passion . . . for things of a natural kind, where neither art nor the conceit or caprice of man has spoiled their genuine order by breaking in upon that primitive state. Even the rude rocks, the mossy caverns, the irregular unwrought grottoes and broken falls of waters, with all the horrid graces of the wilderness itself, as representing Nature more, will be the more engaging, and appear with a magnificence beyond the formal mockery of princely gardens. (II, 125) [6]

In this and related passages Shaftesbury may seem to be adopting a kind of *laissez-faire* philosophy of letting things take their natural course, and of equating control and regulation with "artificiality." In the "Inquiry" he refers to "the natural state of . . . man . . . when unprejudiced by vicious education." (I, 325) And elsewhere he suggests that his theory of human nature might gain support from a study of primitive cultures. In studying them though, we "should search for that simplicity of manners and innocence of behaviour which has been often known among mere savages, ere they were corrupted by our commerce, and, by sad example, instructed in all kinds of treachery and inhumanity." (I, 226 f.) We might learn something from this of the causes of our own corruption and "deviation from nature." But Shaftesbury is no primitivist, as a careful examination of his philosophy makes clear. He is not opposed to education but to "vicious" education; he is not opposed to control and regulation, but only to that kind which prevents a creature from realizing its own inner form—its true and natural ends. Despite the element of Romantic primitivism, Shaftesbury remains for the most part a devotee of Neoclassical formalism. The natural state of a thing is not necessarily its earliest state in time, or its original condition, but rather the state in which it is conforming to its ideal pattern. The graceful movements of a trained dancer, for example, are more "natural" than the crude motions of a peasant taught only "by nature." There is no sentimental hearkening back to an imaginary primitive ideal state of man, as Shaftesbury's comments on the history of Western civilization make clear, for he finds good standards and practices present at various times and places both early and late in the history of man. The concept of the "natural" provides Shaftesbury with a standpoint from which to judge the religious, moral, and aesthetic standards and practices of all times and places.

It is worth noting that Shaftesbury was hesitant to use evidence taken from descriptions of the mores and beliefs of primitive peoples in supporting his theory, because he recognized the difficulty of obtaining accurate and reliable accounts of them. He criticizes Locke for his credulity with respect to the tales of travelers or the often bizarre accounts of writers who had only second- or third-hand information. Shaftesbury sensibly pointed out that our knowledge of primitive cultures is limited by such factors as our imperfect grasp of their language and their unwillingness to disclose all their secrets to strangers—an unwillingness which our barbarous treatment of them has all too often only reinforced.[7]

The Self

In constructing his model of the self, Shaftesbury focusses on the structure of the affections, and their relation to reason, while giving only passing attention to other related technical issues. He briefly treats the problem of the identity and continuity of the self. The self, he notes, can either be conceived as simple or compound. Some materialists, assuming the former, have described the self as constituted by some distinctive type of "matter or particle of matter, supposed to remain with us when all besides is changed, [but] this is by so much the more contemptible, as that matter itself is not really capable of such simplicity." (II, 101) Moreover, since the material stuff that makes up the body is involved in a constant cycle of change, it cannot be the basis of the enduring self. Nor can the self be conceived as a material compound, for if any part were changed, it would no longer be the same. Materialism cannot account for the continuity of the self in the midst of change. To those who find in memory the basis for the identity of the self, Shaftesbury objects that memory can be false. Yet it is the skeptical Philocles who expresses Shaftesbury's own deep conviction when he says: "I know nothing, after all, so real and substantial as myself. Therefore, if there be that thing you call a substance, I take for granted I am one." (II, 103) It is typical of Shaftesbury's treatment of such issues that he considers our belief in the reality and continuity of the self to rest finally upon intuition or even upon "trust." (II, 276) [8]

As one would expect, he criticizes mechanistic analyses of the self. The self is a "system of fancies, perceptions, thoughts . . . not a figure in flesh or wax; not a statue, a piece of clockwork, a set of strings or wires." [9] He calls instead for a functional analysis of man:

If a passenger should turn by chance into a watchmaker's shop, and thinking to inform himself concerning watches, should inquire of what metal, or what matter, each part was composed; what gave the colors, or what made the sounds; without examining what the real use was of such an instrument, or by what movements its end was best attained, and its perfection acquired; 'tis plain that such an examiner as this would come short of any understanding in the real nature of the instrument. Should a philosopher, after the same manner, employing himself in the study of human nature, discover only what effects each passion wrought upon the body; what change of aspect or feature they produced; and in what different manner they affected the limbs and muscles, this might possibly qualify him to give advice to an anatomist or a limner, but not to mankind or to himself; since according to this survey he considered not the real operation or energy of his subject, nor contemplated the man, as real man, and as a human agent, but as a watch or common machine. (I, 190 f.)

The *whole* man must be studied in terms of his characteristic activities and functions as an individual and social agent.

Basically, Shaftesbury conceives of the self as an organized and organizing unity which is governed by a "principle which joins certain parts, and which thinks and acts consonantly for the use and purpose of those parts." (II, 104) This principle is essentially the mind, described as

. . . something which acts upon a body, and has something passive under it, and subject to it; it has not only body or mere matter for its subject, but in some respect even itself too, and what proceeds from it; it superintends and manages its own imaginations, appearances, fancies, correcting, working, and modelling these as it finds good, and adorning and accomplishing the best it can this composite order of body and understanding. (II, 103)

In relation to mind—the active, formative principle—the body or material self is conceived as passive, as representing potentialities which the mind must activate. In the *Philosophical Regimen,* Shaftesbury uses language that is more dualistic, while in the *Characteristics* the monistic approach dominates. But in both, it is mind which is the essential determinant of personality as "the self-knowing, the self-remembering, the self-determining part." [10] The individual mind in relation to the World Mind is conceived by Shaftesbury "as being of like substance (as much as we can understand of substance), alike active upon body, original to motion and order; alike simple, uncompounded, individual; of like energy, effect, and operation. . . ." (II, 106)

However, Shaftesbury takes an important step in regarding the affections rather than the reason as "the springs of action." The mind is delegated the function of controlling or regulating the "body and its affections, passions, appetites, imaginations. . . ." (II, 105) Thus, human behavior is determined by the interaction of reason and desire. The will is a kind of "football" which reason and desire struggle to control, though since desire is the "elder brother," it tends to be the stronger. Reason can only prevail when it turns from attempting to control the will directly to regulating the desires or affections themselves. (I, 123)

Shaftesbury uses the term "affection" in a variety of ways covering the whole range of human desires and impulses. In the broad sense, (1) it means a particular constitutional inclination, a natural disposition, or a tendency toward or away from something. (2) It may refer to emotion or feeling as opposed to reason, and in this sense it is sometimes used by Shaftesbury as synonymous with "passion." (3) Often the term "affection" carries the connotation of basic drive or primary impulse in the present-day anthropological sense. As such the affections are the basic needs and desires of man which motivate his behavior. (4) Finally, "affection" can have the more restricted meaning of love for some object or person.

The relation of "affection" and "passion" is unfortunately

not always clear. "Passion" may simply mean the excess of some affection due to lack of control or some imbalance within the personality. It is in this sense that Shaftesbury can write: "The only poison to reason is passion." (I, 62) Following tradition, he often refers to the passions as disturbances of the soul which conflict with reason and Nature, and which are stimulated by some external factor rather than being essential elements of the soul. Yet this attitude is more apparent in the *Philosophical Regimen* than in *Characteristics*. In Shaftesbury's mature thought he does not abandon his attack on passion as excess of affection, but he shifts his focus to emphasize the vital role that the passions or affections play in human nature. Here again Shaftesbury reveals the influence of the Latitudinarians and the Cambridge Platonists. His approach is paralleled in George Stanhope, translator of Epictetus (1694), who criticized the Stoics for failing to understand that the passions were the "secret Springs" of action, and that man's problem was regulating rather than suppressing them. For Shaftesbury the affections are spontaneous emotions or dispositions generated from within the structure of the personality rather than merely stimulated from without.

The affections, or primary impulses, represent a broad range of types in Shaftesbury's philosophical anthropology. They may be either conscious or unconscious, transient or long lasting. Some are present at birth in all human beings; others appear later in the development of man, though not necessarily in all men. Basically his approach implies a physiomental continuum since there is no sharp distinction made between physiological and psychological drives. The affections are natural potentialities of the human personality, developed or realized in different degrees by different persons.

One of Shaftesbury's basic concepts—and the one that dominates his theory of human nature—is that of the natural harmony or balance of the affections. For each species of living creature there is a set of affections natural to it which motivates it to act in a manner that will be conducive to its welfare, a thesis which Shaftesbury defends by both deductive and inductive reasoning. If there is a purposive order in the universe at large, there must also be an equivalent order in the constitution of man; if there is an appropriate physical order by which an organism functions effectively, there must also be a corresponding order for the functioning of the affections. The affections of each type of creature are fitted by Nature to its functions and capabilities, and those proper to one species may not be appropriate to another. (I, 314) Nature has provided for each species an economy which is "uniform, fixed, and invariable," so that if anything in the affections of a particular creature is contrary to this economy, the creature is "wretched and unnatural." (II, 293) An example would be a bitch that lacked the instinct to nurse her pups. Shaftesbury tries to show that misery and disorder in individual members of a species is traceable to some distortion or imbalance of the affections, for the natural affections are those that work for a creature's survival and happiness, since Nature has perfectly adapted the "affections, appetites, sensations, mutually to each other, as well as to the matter, form, [and] action. . . ." (II, 76)

It follows that a primary concern for any creature would be that its affections be neither excessive nor defective. An affection in excess not only interferes with the working of other impulses, but also tends to be self-defeating. The proper degree of power for any impulse, however, has to be judged in terms of its function in the total economy of the affections of a particular creature belonging to a particular species. Though Shaftesbury is thinking in terms of an ideal harmony of the affections, he does not propose a rigid absolute; an element of relativism enters in the measurement of the intensity of a particular affection. If, for example, the social affections are weak but the self-directed affections are also weak, a satisfactory balance may still be achieved. He draws an analogy between the proper ordering of the affections and the tuning of a stringed instrument. (I, 290) Each type of instrument, to function properly, must have its strings tuned according to the harmonic requirements of that instrument. This implies that for each species there is a true order or harmony. However, Shaftesbury allows that particular members of a class of instruments have to be tuned not only in accord with these general principles but also in terms of their own inner relationships. Thus, by analogy, each human being has his own finer adjustments to make in terms of the particular inner economy of his own affections. The healthy personality is one in which the affections are duly controlled and proportionate.

The harmony of the affections of which Shaftesbury speaks is not to be simply equated with the order of the affections in the average person. It is an ideal conception which may or may not be realized in the average member of a species at a given time and place. Indeed, man, though capable of the highest possibilities in the development of his affections, is also capable of the greatest corruption of the affections. Yet it is Shaftesbury's conviction that the ideal harmony is inherent in the natural structure of the personality, and, given the right conditions, it is realizable in degree.

Shaftesbury divides the affections into three types:

(1) The "natural," "social," or "public affections" which are directed toward the general welfare of a group.

(2) The "self" or "private affections" which are directed toward an individual's own good.

(3) The "unnatural affections" which are directed neither toward private nor public good.

The Social Affections

Shaftesbury places the "social affections" at the very center of his model of man. It is these impulses—taken as a whole—which mark the true humanity of man and distinguish him from other species. To maintain this, Shaftesbury undertook an attack not only on Hobbes, as we have seen, but on the whole tradition of psychological and ethical egoism in philosophy, from Epicurus and Lucretius to Lord Rochester and La Rochefoucauld. These "narrow-minded philosophers," he contends, in attempting to account for all human behavior by "that one principle and foundation of a cool and deliberate selfishness," (I, 78) commit the fallacy of reductionism, reducing something highly complex to something too simple to really explain it. It is, he writes,

a common saying, that interest governs the world. But, I believe, whoever looks narrowly into the affairs of it will find that passion, humour, caprice, zeal, faction, and a thousand other springs, which are counter to self-interest, have as considerable a part in the movements of this machine. There are more wheels and counterpoises in this engine than are easily imagined. 'Tis of too complex a kind to fall under one simple view, or be explained thus briefly in a word or two. The studiers of this mechanism must have a very partial eye to overlook all other motions besides those of the lowest and narrowest compass. 'Tis hard that in the plan or description of this clock-work no wheel nor balance should be allowed on the side of the better and more enlarged affections; that nothing should be understood to be done in kindness or generosity, nothing in pure good-nature or friendship, or through any social or natural affection of any kind; when, perhaps, the mainsprings of this machine will be found to be either these very natural affections themselves, or a compound kind derived from them, and retaining more than one half of their nature. (I, 77 f.)

In a letter he remarks that "circumstances are apt to raise an ill dust with those who have not very strong eyes in friendship. And *interest, interest* comes in ever and anon, and must seem a kind of key to things with which it has nothing to do." [11] Hobbes, Shaftesbury argues, made the error of omitting the social affections in his conception of man's basic nature, substituting instead "only one Master-Passion, Fear, which has, in effect devoured all the rest, and left Room only for that infinite Passion towards Power after Power, Natural (as he affirms) to All Men, and never ceasing but in Death." [12] But this theory is simply not adequate to explain the origin of man's communal life; nor can the social affections be explained as only "a more deliberate or better-regulated self-love." (I, 79) In response to the hedonism of Hobbes, Shaftesbury argues that it is precisely *because* man is so sensitive to pleasure and pain that he needs strong impulses such as "tenderness, love, sociableness, [and] compassion" to direct him toward his proper ends. These social affections, indeed, comprise the very goals of life, rather than merely the means.

Shaftesbury gives no precise list of the social affections, but treats them as a rather fluid group of related impulses including the drive for preservation of the species, gregariousness, sympathy, the various forms of familial affection—parental, filial, conjugal, and sibling love—friendship, patriotism, and love of humanity. While some eighteenth-century writers were to attempt to reduce all such motives to one type or basic form —usually benevolence—Shaftesbury wisely avoids this. As a result, his theory is richer and more fruitful.

The social affections are those that contribute to the preservation or welfare of a group of beings, or of a whole species, and in the ultimate sense they contribute to the good of Nature as a Whole. Thus, for Shaftesbury they are pre-eminently the "natural" affections, as he often calls them. They pertain to our relations with other persons. They unite the individual to a community, and commit him to work for the values of that community, while the "unnatural" affections do exactly the opposite. Shaftesbury not only argues that these social drives are deeply implanted in the nature of man, but that they predominate there; for otherwise man could not have survived and civilized society developed. Man is a social animal: "Out of society and community he never did, nor ever can, subsist." (II, 83) Like Cumberland, the third Earl finds the sociality of man rooted in his psychobiological structure. The primary level of communal life—the family—arises inevitably out of the attempt to satisfy such basic needs as sex, hunger, or shelter. The weakness of the human infant makes his protection a necessity, and Nature, Shaftesbury points out, provides parents with a natural impulse to protect him. Family life, furthermore, teaches us our dependence on others, as well as the coalescence of our private interests and the interests of a larger group.

The dynamic forces set up by the social affections lead logically and naturally to the formation of larger social units —from family, to tribe, to nation—each in its own way "a society for mutual defense and common interest." (II, 83) Yet this process, Shaftesbury insists, cannot be explained solely on materialistic grounds or as a product of narrowly conceived self-interest. Like Grotius and Cumberland, he finds in it evidence of a deep-seated human need for fellowship and communion with other persons. Society is not the product of mere "invention" or "art," but rather it is the inevitable expression of this "herding principle." (I, 75) Shaftesbury contends that nothing is "more apparent than that there is naturally in every man such a degree of social affection as inclines him to seek the familiarity and friendship of his fellows." (I, 315)

Obviously, in a large social unit one can only have direct contact with a small number of other persons; thus, it becomes increasingly difficult in larger communities to perceive the interest of the whole and to retain a sense of loyalty to it. In a large nation with a heterogeneous population, the associative principle may, according to Shaftesbury, "lose itself for want of direction." (I, 75) The paradoxical result is that this combining impulse finds an outlet in the formation of parties, factions, clubs, or societies within the larger community. "Nothing is so delightful as to incorporate," (I, 76) he writes, taking note of that fondness for clubs and organizations that still characterizes both the English and American common life. But even though these organizations may be divisive forces and work against the interest of the larger whole, they are still manifestations of the social impulse. Paradoxically, factionalism is an expression, even when distorted, of the need for fellowship.

Shaftesbury's keen understanding of human nature—and further evidence that he was no simple optimist—is reflected in some related comments he makes on the relation of heroism and tyranny. "The most generous spirits," he writes, "are the

most combining." (I, 75) But if they fail to find an outlet for
their social impulses in the body politic in peacetime, they
may seek it in war, for the sense of fellowship is nowhere "so
strongly felt or vigorously exerted as in mutual conspiracy or
war; in which the highest geniuses are often known the for-
wardest to employ themselves." (*Ibid.*) Thus, in war, which
the egoistic philosophers argued revealed the inherent selfishness of man, Shaftesbury finds further paradoxical and distorted expressions of the social needs. " 'Tis in war that mutual
succour is most given, mutual danger run, and common affection most exerted and employed. For heroism and philanthropy
are almost one and the same." (I, 76) But he acutely and wisely
warns that "by a small misguidance of the affection, a lover
of mankind becomes a ravager; a hero and deliverer becomes
an oppressor and destroyer." (*Ibid.*)

The love of friends is ranked high among the social affections by Shaftesbury. He distinguishes between Christian charity and friendship, as he understands it, which is not

that common benevolence and charity which every Christian is
obliged to show towards all men, and in particular towards his
fellow-Christians, his neighbour, brother, and kindred, of whatever degree; but that peculiar relation which is formed by a consent and harmony of minds; by mutual esteem, and reciprocal
tenderness and affection. . . . (I, 67)

True friendship is based on disinterested affection, and requires that we be ready to sacrifice our interests for those of
a friend "freely and voluntarily." [13] Friendship has intrinsic
value, and should not be conceived as merely instrumental.
Ideally, it is a relationship between free men dedicated to the
public good; in fact, Shaftesbury argues that a necessary con-

dition for true friendship is that it exist in the context of devotion to the welfare of a larger community.

The Augustan philosopher criticizes Christianity for failing to give sufficient emphasis to personal friendship and for making it, along with patriotism and a public spirit, only a voluntary virtue, rather than "an essential part of his charity." (I, 67) It has been made instrumental to salvation, and its intrinsic value has been ignored. To support his judgment, Shaftesbury quotes at length from Bishop Taylor's *Discourse of Friendship* (1657). Taylor concedes that "the word friendship in the sense we commonly mean by it, is not so much as named in the New Testament, and our religion takes no notice of it." (I, 67) Though Shaftesbury finds some examples of true friendship in the Old Testament, following Taylor, he finds them lacking in the New. This hardly seems a fair judgment, for the high value that Shaftesbury placed upon sacrificial love and disinterested friendship was certainly a product in part of the Christian tradition which is rooted in the New Testament. Shaftesbury's lack of objectivity here is borne out by his failure to refer to John 15:13 (which Taylor *did* quote): "Greater love hath no man than this, that a man lay down his life for his friends." Instead, he singles out a much weaker passage which he translates, "Peradventure for a good man some would even dare to die," (Romans 5:7) and which he criticizes for its conditional nature.[14]

In the New Testament the terms *philia* (friendship) and *agape* (sacrificial love) are generally distinguished, the former referring to a lesser and the latter to a higher type of love. However, they are often closely connected and even used as synonyms. Friendship is one of the levels of *agape*, which is Christian love in its fullest and broadest sense, or as Bishop

Taylor himself expressed it: "Christian charity is friendship expanded like the face of the sun." (I, 68) The concept of disinterested affection shared by Taylor and Shaftesbury is actually grounded in the New Testament concept of *agape*. The Christian attempt to widen and deepen the basis of love, to free it from narrow limitations, is entirely in accord with Shaftesbury's own aims. The basis of his objection seems to be that Christianity fails to acknowledge the intrinsic value of friendship because it makes salvation the ultimate goal. Yet the same objection could be leveled against Shaftesbury's own philosophy, even though his conception of salvation differs. He clearly regards the love of nation and of humanity as having priority over the love of friends; furthermore, he repeats Christian doctrine in teaching that all finite loves have their true consummation in the love of God. The paradoxical element in the relationship between particular loves and man's love for God is no less present in the philosophy of Shaftesbury than in the teachings of Jesus.

Another important social affection is patriotism or love of nation. A true national community is held together by a mental conception—by an "idea"—rather than merely by geographical, racial, or physical bonds. A "nation" is not simply a multitude of people held together by force, but a social confederacy bound together by mutual consent and common interests. A true community cannot be based on self-interest alone, but requires of its members dedication to the public welfare, and a "sense of partnership with human kind." (I, 72) Shaftesbury believes that there are very few individuals who are *totally* lacking in any sense of the public good; existing in a social environment would make this almost impossible. Though absolute power tends to destroy genuine community, even tyran-

nical governments can arouse loyalty in their citizens. Shaftesbury wittily and wisely comments that so great is man's desire
for community that even if there is no public official concerned for his welfare, he will invent one in his imagination!
However, true patriotism flourishes best in a free society.

A nation is only a part of a larger world community—humanity as a whole—which is the object of an even higher form
of affection. While personal friendship is a prerequisite for
being truly a "man," an individual realizes his fullest potentialities as a human being only when he is capable of friendship
toward mankind. The favorite theme of Latitudinarian sermons was "universal Charity," and Shaftesbury goes so far as
to suggest that without this universal love, particular friendships would have little depth or significance. Philocles reports
that Theocles has almost convinced him "that to be a friend
to anyone in particular, 'twas necessary to be first a friend to
mankind." (II, 40 f.) If this is taken to refer to the temporal
order of the development of the affections, it seems doubtful,
and is not consistent with Shaftesbury's analysis elsewhere.
But in the context Shaftesbury probably only means to say
that particular friendships require a concurrent devotion to
the welfare of society or of man in general. On the whole,
he seems to assume that there is within the affections some
inner dynamic that leads to a natural progression from narrower to wider spheres of affection. Yet the transition seems
too easy, and one is left with the sense that he has not done
full justice to the inevitable tensions that arise between particular friendships and more general affections.

It is evident that in Shaftesbury's doctrine of man as well
as in his ethics sympathy plays an important role, though there
are more direct references to it in his philosophical notebook

than in his published writings. To sympathize is defined as meaning "to feel together, or be united in one sense or feeling." [15] Shaftesbury rejects the Hobbesian attempt to reduce this to mere self-interest, and like the Latitudinarians he regards sympathy and compassion as part of Nature's providential order, designed to impel us to help our neighbors in time of trouble, and to share with them their sorrows as well as joys. However, this aspect of Shaftesbury's thought clashes with his Stoic principles, setting up an inner tension in his philosophy that is revealed in such passages as the following:

> To compassionate, i.e. to join with in passion. . . . To commiserate, i.e. to join with in misery. . . . This in one order of life is right and good; nothing more harmonious; to be without this, or not to feel this, is unnatural, horrid. . . . But in another order of life, in . . . a higher relation, nothing can be more dissonant than this; nothing more inconsistent with that true affection, which in a mind soundly rational is, as it were, in the place of all. To act by temper simply is, in such a one, the greatest degeneracy; a sinking down into a lower species of nature. . . .[16]

Shaftesbury goes on to quote Epictetus—"when you see one weeping, have sympathy, but do not inwardly lament" (*Ench.* 26)—adding, "in no way sympathize, or feel as they feel, when they take either this or the other event . . . for good or ill. . . . Be true then to thyself." [17] The *Philosophical Regimen* stresses the Stoic doctrine that true serenity requires that one

live disinterested and unconcerned, as being loose from all those ties and little mean regards which make us to depend so much on others. . . . In the whole of life, he who is secure as to the great events and is concerned but for one thing (which if he will himself, he need not miss), he, and he alone, is truly free; and with respect to things within, is becoming, beautiful.[18]

Natural affection for mankind is possible, according to Shaftesbury, only

when thou no longer seekest for anything they seek, when thou no longer wantest anything from them, or canst be worked by anything that may happen to thee from them. In short, it is then only that thou canst truly love them, when thou expectest neither thy good nor thy ill from them.[19]

It is evident that this is more than saying that one must be free of false valuations, though that is an important part of his meaning: "True affection cannot be except where true liberty is." [20] Shaftesbury is restating the Stoic doctrine of *apatheia*—avoiding emotional involvement. This is the "terrible law": "To take Pleasure in nothing. To do nothing with affection. . . . To engage for nothing." [21] Self-mastery, which is a prerequisite for happiness, requires a degree of detachment; the ordering of the inner life demands that we avoid entrapment by external things.

The conflict is clear: on the one hand, Shaftesbury is stressing the importance of the social affections, which imply a considerable degree of emotional involvement; on the other, he is calling for emotional disengagement. But the reader will note that the crucial passages in the foregoing are all taken from Shaftesbury's philosophical notebook, where this contradiction is clearest. In the *Characteristics* Shaftesbury makes a decisive step beyond his Stoic teachers and attempts a dialectical resolution of these opposing currents of his thought. Those who interpret Shaftesbury as basically a Stoic often miss this point.[22] The "men of Latitude" had already prepared the way: they rejected the Stoic distrust of emotion, doubting that charity was possible without emotional involvement in the welfare of others. The passions were the sources of action,

and as such were neutral in themselves; their goodness or evilness was to be determined by the ends they were directed
toward. Compassion is a necessary adjunct of reason; it distinguishes the truly *good* man from the merely *just* man. Thus,
against "Stoical insensibility" these liberal divines placed their
concept of Christian charity which required the risk of engagement as well as the restraint of reason.

In his final thought, Shaftesbury follows the Latitudinarians,
though it is not clear to what extent he was conscious of breaking with his Stoic teachers. Self-mastery and self-possession
remain necessary conditions for happiness and virtue. But Stoic
"insensibility" is limited to its proper role as an instrument in
the art of self-control. It is necessary to retain some distance
between oneself and the suffering of others, for without this
one might be overcome and incapacitated by grief. Emotional
engagement is required though it must be regulated by reason.
Shaftesbury's position might be described in terms of Edward
Bullough's aesthetic concept of "psychical distance." According to this theory, "distance" is to be reduced, but not beyond
the point where all detachment is lost. Shaftesbury makes the
common-sense point that a person who is so involved with
another's grief that he is "broken up" by it is in no position
to help. And he continues to warn that emotional involvement
should not entail accepting the false judgments made by others.
Maintaining one's integrity is essential, for if you can *be*
nothing, you can *do* nothing. What is desirable is not *apatheia*
—complete absence of emotion—but rather a state in which
positive emotions are present but rationally ordered; the full
development of an individual's natural potentialities requires
the presence in the personality of positive affections existing
in balanced proportion. In the final summation of Shaftesbury's

thought it is not *apatheia* but universal and active love that emerges as the highest ideal. Stoic detachment and self-possession are bound to the service of humanity; they exist to make love possible.

Again it is evident that love plays a central role in Shaftesbury's philosophy, and that his thought brings together elements of Stoic, Platonic, and Christian thought in a new synthesis. The Stoic concept of the brotherhood of man is united with Christian *agape:*

To be truly *philanthropos* (a lover of men), [is] neither to scoff, nor hate, nor be impatient with them, nor abominate them, nor overlook them; [but] . . . to pity in a manner and love those that are the greatest miscreants, those that are most furious against thyself in particular, and at the time when they are most furious. . . . [to] become, as it were, a common father of mankind. So as to say, whatever wretch or whatever number of such thou seest, whether of the most prosperous or most dejected, whether of one country or another, whether of the simplest or of those that are thought wise: "These are they whom, though they have no care of themselves; no, none amongst them truly affected or concerned for them; though they are animated against one another, and can least of all endure one that would take this care of them; yet these are they whom I make to be my care and charge; whom I foster and do good to, against their wills, and shall ever do so, as long as they are *men,* and I am of their kind." [23]

Natural affection impels man to give himself in order to find himself, to lose himself in order to be reborn.

CHAPTER TEN

SELF and SOCIETY

The Self-Affections

Having examined Shaftesbury's general views on the nature of man, and having surveyed the social affections which he regards as the essence of man, it remains to treat the self-directed and the unnatural affections, as well as the relevant problem of the relation of self-interest and public interest.

Despite his vigorous attack on psychological egoism, Shaftesbury was fully aware of the fact that the self-directed impulses or drives are necessary aspects of human nature, since every organism naturally strives to act for its own survival and welfare. He defines these "self-affections" as those that "relate to the private interest or separate economy of the creature . . . and constitute whatever we call interestedness or self-love." (I, 317) The basic list includes (1) "love of life," (2) "resentment of injury," (3) "pleasure" (or "luxury"), (4) desire for wealth and material conveniences ("interest"), (5) love of praise ("emulation"), and (6) "love of ease and rest" ("indolence"). (I, 317)

(1) Though rejecting the attempt to reduce all the affections to the drive for self-preservation, Shaftesbury recognizes its importance as one of the primary "private affections." This impulse to preserve one's own life is just as natural as its analogue among the social affections, the desire to preserve the species. Since each part of an organism acts more or less automatically for its own survival, the organism as a whole ought to direct its activities consciously toward the same end. And obviously, the preservation of individuals (at least in sufficient number) is a necessary condition for the higher social end, the survival of the species. To neglect oneself to the point of endangering one's health is, according to Shaftesbury, not only "unnatural" but immoral. Thus, he gives priority among the private affections to the love of life.

However, Shaftesbury has much to say of the dangers of an excessive love of life or of its correlate, an excessive fear of death. He follows his Stoic teachers in believing that there is a point at which the misery of life may outweigh its value; then death becomes a blessing. "To value life, as far as life is good, belongs as much to courage as to discretion; but a wretched life is no wise man's wish." (I, 81) Life itself has to be weighed in the balances, for the social affections have the higher priority, and the values they imply are the ultimate basis for any evaluation of a particular life.

Shaftesbury points out that the overvaluation of life as such or the excessive fear of death may be obstacles to virtue, since morality sometimes demands that we risk our lives for the sake of others. Moreover, these states of mind may make a person act contrary to his own interest, as in the well-known case of someone paralyzed by fear in the presence of danger. Excessive fear "betrays [us] to danger instead of saving [us] from it."

(I, 318) Shaftesbury's approach to this paradox of behavior is basically rationalistic; its cause is traced to passion, which prevents the reason from operating effectively. He does not recognize that a death-impulse can masquerade in the symptoms of fear; but such a psychoanalytic view would contradict his belief in a wisely structured order of living organisms. The excessive fear of death not only "corrupts and poisons all enjoyment," (I, 319) but makes it impossible to have true piety and resignation to the order of Nature.

(2) While fear impels us to avoid danger, "resentment of injury" enables us to "repel injury and resist violence." (I, 319) Shaftesbury thinks that while some superior persons may be able to resist evil without anger (as there may be caution without fear), in ordinary persons some degree of anger seems necessary or unavoidable. Anger serves the ends of Nature by deterring aggression and by providing extra resources of strength in the struggle to protect oneself and one's interests from attack. But, as with all the affections, when excessive this is self-defeating, since it may lead not only to misery but to our own self-destruction. Shaftesbury also comments on the pleasures of revenge which he rates as no better than those "untoward delights of perverseness . . . and an envenomed malignant disposition . . . for this is only a perpetual assuaging of anger perpetually renewed." (I, 321)

(3) By "pleasure" Shaftesbury means basically the pleasures of sense, which would include the pleasures derived from satisfying such basic physiological drives as hunger and sex. He admits that the sexual impulse may be considered social in character in so far as its end is the propagation of the species. However, he justifies its inclusion here on grounds that "whereas all other social affections are joined only with a

mental pleasure, and founded in mere kindness and love, this has more added to it and is joined with a pleasure of sense." (I, 324) Shaftesbury's basic contention is that the drive for sensual pleasure needs to be regulated and limited as do all the other affections, and that in excess it too is self-defeating. He argues that overrefinement or excessive effort in the pursuit of pleasure is actually destructive of pleasure. In its place he recommends temperance and the Stoic and Epicurean principle of concentrating on the moderate enjoyment of simple pleasures. Nature must provide the norm for the life of true satisfaction. And he warns that there is no worse enslavement than to the pleasures of sense, and no passion "which in its excess more necessarily occasions disorder and unhappiness." (I, 326)[1]

(4) The desire for wealth is also one of the desirable self-affections in so far as it is a stimulus to industry which benefits both the individual and society. Yet, in excess it becomes a boundless desire which cannot possibly be satisfied. Like the Stoics and Epicureans, Shaftesbury believes that true happiness not only does not require more than a moderate share of worldly possessions, but is more readily assured if our ambitions are limited.

(5) The love of praise and public recognition is also natural and desirable in its moderate form, though he suggests that there is a higher vantage point from which this is unnecessary for the individual. In a letter to Lord Somers, Shaftesbury writes:

Mere fame is a rattle to please children, and the famousest people in the world are famous fools. But the fame that arises from the consent and harmony of wise and good men is music, and a charm irresistible to a heroic soul. . . . Not to be pleased with such a fame as this, is to have no love for mankind; for where love is greatest, there is always most pleasure in a return.[2]

The basis of renown is the true measure of its quality. The desire for praise can also become an insatiable appetite leading only to misery.

(6) It is interesting that Shaftesbury includes among these basic self-affections the love of ease or the need for rest, and he recognizes that it stands in a special relation to the others, acting as a sort of brake on them. In excess this impulse is also a disease because it leads to inaction, and lack of exercise is as harmful to the mind as to the body. A basic principle in Shaftesbury's theory of the affections is that they must be given sufficient scope for natural expression; if this is not done, if they are repressed or unexercised, the energies that are gathered in them will break out in other and unnatural outlets, or will be turned inward in a destructive fashion. Anxiety and discontent are mental symptoms of unnatural rest—the unhealthy expressions of unutilized energies.

Shaftesbury's argument, then, is that the self-directed impulses are necessary in their appropriate degree for the well-being of the individual, and are not necessarily harmful to our social relationships, though in excess they become vices. Paradoxically, the very affections which are closest to our "interests" can become the greatest threat to our true interest and happiness. Nevertheless, they are a necessary part of the natural order, and Shaftesbury's use of the term "natural affection," particularly for the social affections, is confusing. Both the public and private affections are equally "natural," as over against the "unnatural affections." This usage has two explanations though: first, in his attempt to refute Hobbes, Shaftesbury wants to emphasize the *naturalness* of the social impulses; second, the social affections are most distinctive of man's humanity. Thus, they are the most "natural" in the special sense that they express man's ideal potentialities and are directed toward his largest ends.[3]

The Unnatural Affections

Shaftesbury defines the "unnatural affections" as those which lead to neither the good of the individual nor the species. They are treated far more briefly than the other affections, and there is no analysis in depth, but his recognition of their role in human motivation is important. The first that Shaftesbury lists is "inhuman delight" in witnessing the suffering or destruction of others. When the person suffering is an enemy, Shaftesbury recognizes that this may really be a manifestation of one of the self-directed affections. However, when it is a matter of someone "indifferent" to us, perhaps even unknown, this kind of sadistic pleasure cannot be explained in terms of the self-affections, but is a distinctly different kind of impulse. "To feed as it were on death, and be entertained with dying agonies; this has nothing in it accountable in the way of self-interest or private good, but is wholly and absolutely unnatural." (I, 331)

The second unnatural affection, which Shaftesbury recognizes is very close to the first, is a more generalized "delight in disorder," or sheer destructiveness, which he regrets is usually encouraged in children. The third is "malice, or ill-will" where there is no self-interest involved, and no apparent external provocation. The fourth is "envy" at the prosperity or happiness of another person which in no way interferes with one's own. The fifth of these affections is a deep-seated misanthropy or "hatred of mankind and society." (I, 332)

The sixth takes in the passions aroused by superstition and related customs. And finally, the seventh category is that of sexual perversion.[4] While, strictly speaking, these are the unnatural affections, Shaftesbury notes that those emotions which are generated from the self-affections may also become uncontrollable passions which have some of the characteristics of these unnatural impulses, driving us to "sacrifice everything" for their sake.

Hobbes's egoism led him to doubt the possibility of disinterested pleasure in another person's sorrow. Francis Hutcheson, though an avowed disciple of Shaftesbury, agreed with Hobbes on this point, arguing that "Human Nature seems scarce capable of malicious disinterested Hatred, or a sedate Delight in the Misery of others, when we imagine them no way pernicious to us, or opposite to our Interest." [5] What appears to be "disinterested Malice" is actually grounded in self-interest. He puts a kindlier light on human aberrations than Shaftesbury, writing that "it is not a Delight in the Misery of others, or Malice, which occasions the horrid crimes which fill our Historys; but generally an injudicious, unreasonable Enthusiasm for some kind of limited Virtue." [6] The changing character of eighteenth-century optimism is reflected in this disagreement between Shaftesbury and his follower.[7] The third Earl held to a tougher view of man, and the fact that he recognized that the unnatural affections may play a powerful part in human motivation is proof that his metaphysical optimism did not blind him to the actual potentialities for irrational evil within man. Moreover, his defense of the possibility of disinterested malice seems a logical, perhaps even necessary, implication of his argument for the possibility of disinterested love. While the unnatural affections are not part of the ideal model of human nature, they are part of man's *actual* nature, and human behavior can only be understood in terms of the dynamic interplay of the self-directed, social, and unnatural affections.

Self-Interest and Public Interest

Shaftesbury describes the relationship of private and public interest as "the main problem" of the "Inquiry Concerning Virtue," and the resolution of this issue is clearly of central importance in his philosophy. His discussion of it was a major influence in keeping the question before the minds of British moralists for several generations. His concern with the question must certainly have been reinforced by his knowledge of the bitter and tumultuous factional strife of the seventeenth century, as well as by his own experience in politics. Something of Shaftesbury's character and point of view is revealed in the independent position he took during his brief political career. With the emergence of the Whig and Tory parties a new emphasis was being placed on party organization, the principle of party loyalty being "indeed the only loyalty that was practised by some very important statesmen in the reigns of James, William and Anne." [8] Though his grandfather had founded the Whig party, and the third Earl in general supported Whig principles and policies, he refused to follow the Whig party line on every issue even though sometimes bitterly censured for failing to do so.[9] While recognizing the social function of political parties, it was an essential element of his theory that party loyalty must be superseded by loyalty to the larger community of which one is a member.

In approaching this problem, Shaftesbury had to reckon, of course, with the theory of psychological egoism, as we have already seen. Previously, we considered those arguments of his against egoism which were designed to establish the reality and importance of the social affections in human nature. But Shaftesbury also attacks the doctrine of egoism directly, suggesting that it may be meaningless or perhaps merely trivial. If everything one does is attributed to self-interest, he asks, what meaning does the term "self-interest" have? If there is no real alternative to egoism, and all actions are equally egoistic, then the very term "egoism" loses significance. One could no longer speak of actions as being *more* or *less* self-centered. Shaftesbury pictures the defenders of egoism saying:

"Act as disinterestedly or generously as you please, self still is at the bottom, and nothing else." Now if these gentlemen who delight so much in the play of words, but are cautious how they grapple closely with definitions, would tell us only what self-interest was, and determine happiness and good, there would be an end of this enigmatical wit. For in this we should all agree, that happiness was to be pursued, and in fact was always sought after; but whether found in following Nature, and giving way to common affection, or in suppressing it, and turning every passion towards private advantage, a narrow self-end, or the preservation of mere life, this would be the matter in debate between us. The question would not be, "Who loved himself, or who not," but "who loved and served himself the rightest, and after the truest manner." (I, 80 f.)

Shaftesbury asks that the egoistic philosopher give some content to the concept of self-interest so that it can serve as a principle of differentiation rather than being a kind of meaningless category which includes all behavior.

Shaftesbury's older contemporary, Richard Cumberland, had also written against Hobbes's reductive egoism in his book,

De Legibus Naturae (1672), maintaining that the social impulses were just as much a part of the original nature of man as the self-directed impulses, and that there was no necessary conflict between the two. Shaftesbury may have been influenced by Cumberland, for there are many parallels between their arguments, though he does not mention him by name and there is no direct evidence that he had read his book. Cumberland proposed the interesting theory that the basic affections have their origin as involuntary responses to sense stimuli or as involuntary manifestations of physical processes, but he insisted that they can and should be developed to a truly moral level by conscious effort—by "art." Cumberland contended that there was a direct, organic continuity between these elementary, involuntary impulses and the more complex impulses as consciously developed. He also held that the social inclinations are accompanied by the spontaneous recognition that the good of the whole is greater than that of the part (which it includes), and therefore that the good of the individual is inseparably connected with the good of the community. Cumberland formulated the supreme, ethical "Law of Nature" thus: "The Endeavour . . . of promoting the common Good of the whole System of rational Agents, conduces, . . . to the good of every Part, in which our own Happiness . . . is contained." [10] Not only do the laws of Nature require us to act in accord with this principle, but our happiness depends upon it. The greatest happiness for a rational agent is to be attained through exercising the maximum possible amount of benevolence toward others of his own kind. Like Shaftesbury, he argues that virtue and happiness, vice and misery, have an ultimate coincidence. The essential identity of public and private interest is regarded as evidence of the providential character of this God-created universe. Shaftesbury, however, would have objected to Cumberland's attempt to retain the sanction of retribution while at the same time admitting that virtue was in large part its own reward, and to his support (again none too consistent) of a legislative view of obligation similar to Locke's.[11] Also, unlike Cumberland, Shaftesbury did not reduce all the virtues to benevolence.

One of the most important ways though that Shaftesbury follows Cumberland is in suggesting that any analysis of the "good" must be in terms of particular functioning systems. The universe is conceived as a hierarchy of systems extending, as we have seen, from the self-system to that of the tribe, the nation, the human species as a whole, and, finally, to the cosmic community of all beings. For each level of this hierarchy, the creatures belonging to it have their appropriate affections.

We know that every creature has a private good and interest of his own, which Nature has compelled him to seek, by all the advantages afforded him within the compass of his make. We know that there is in reality a right and wrong state of every creature, and that his right one is by Nature forwarded and by himself affectionately sought. There being therefore in every creature a certain interest or good, there must be also a certain end to which everything in his constitution must naturally refer. (I, 243)

Each creature is naturally impelled to seek its own good unless something from outside of it upsets the normal balance of the affections, making it desire a falsely conceived self-good.

Thus, self-concern is built into the structure of the individual as a necessary and desirable impulsion; and self-interest is defined by the character of the organism and the community or species to which it belongs. However, Shaftesbury must distinguish proper self-regard from pride, i.e., excessive self-love, on the one hand, and self-contempt or self-hatred, on the other. Human beings naturally tend to attribute good qualities to themselves, a characteristic which becomes sheer vanity unless regulated by reason. But to undervalue oneself is as much an error as to overvalue oneself; self-contempt is in itself no virtue. "Self-valuation supposes self-worth; and in a person conscious of real worth, is either no pride, or a just and noble one." (II, 140) Indeed, Shaftesbury insists, " 'tis the height of wisdom, no doubt, to be rightly selfish." (I, 81) Not only is there no necessary conflict between self-love and love of others, but self-love is made a necessary prerequisite of brotherly love: "What friend art thou like to prove to others, if not so to thyself?" [12] Shaftesbury's belief that a measurable degree of self-acceptance or self-affirmation is a necessary element in the healthy personality is confirmed by many contemporary psychoanalysts. But he insists that true self-love is grounded on self-knowledge. "Know but this self only and what self is indeed, and then fear not being too selfish, fear not to say 'no one is dearer to me than myself.' " [13] It must be recognized though that in such passages Shaftesbury uses "self" to mean the "true self," which is the dominant sense in which he uses the term. But he is not consistent, and at times he means by "self" whatever a person actually is at a given moment. Shaftesbury not only considers the self-affections as necessary for the physical and mental health of the individual, but he regards them as essential constituents of virtue.

The affections towards private good become necessary and essential to goodness. For though no creature can be called good or virtuous merely for possessing these affections, yet since it is impossible that the public good or good of the system can be preserved without them, it follows that a creature really wanting in them is in reality wanting in some degree to goodness and natural rectitude, and may thus be esteemed vicious and defective. (I, 288)

A reasonable self-regard is a necessary though not a sufficient condition of moral goodness.

In the imbalance of the private and public affections, Shaftesbury recognizes two basic possibilities: one, that of being "too good," i.e., having an excess of social affection or defect of self-affection; two, that of being too selfish, i.e., having an excess of self-directed impulses. Selfishness or egocentricity is characterized by narrowness of outlook—a failure to see the larger interests that are involved in any system of interrelationships—and it issues in behavior that is directed toward narrower rather than broader interests. It is one source of moral evil: "For what is knavery but narrowness?—myself, that is to say, my purse against the public purse, my family against the public family, . . . my nation against the world . . . my fancy against the Divine decree." [14] It is a "more than ordinary self-concernment or regard to private good, which is inconsistent with the interest of the species or public," and ultimately with one's own true interest. (I, 248) This narrowing of perspective destroys the grounds of community, undermining trust while generating suspicion. Thus, in Shaftesbury's theory, the emotional basis of excessive self-love is found in the excess of the private affections; its cognitive manifestation is in the failure to see the interests of larger communities. There is another significant aspect to this: consistently selfish persons are unable to commit themselves to larger communities of interest. They "possess themselves too well to be in danger of entering warmly into any cause, or engaging deeply with any side or faction." (I, 77) As we saw in the previous chapter, factionalism, instead of being interpreted as a mere expression of self-affection, is a distorted expression of the social affections. The absolutely selfish person would be incapable of even the limited social involvement that a faction would require. Fortunately, there are few who are so consistent, since, in Shaftesbury's view, the natural bent of human nature is against this; absolute selfishness would require a massive suppression of our social impulsions. One of Shaftesbury's explanations of why men will not allow their social affections free play, is that they fear being "outwitted" or so deceived "by Nature, as to be made to serve her purposes rather than their own. They are ashamed to be drawn thus out of themselves, and forced from what they esteem their true interest." (I, 78)

Unselfishness is characterized, then, by largeness of perspective, by an ability both to see the larger interests at stake in any system of interrelationships, and to commit oneself to those interests. The virtuous man is pictured by Shaftesbury as one who constantly seeks to extend his sphere of knowledge and effective activity to wider and wider systems of being, or in Roycean terms, to larger and larger systems of loyalty. This is not, incidentally, merely a quantitative conception—there is a qualitative increase in meaning and value. Altruistic behavior has its ground both in the affectional and intellectual nature of man. It is rooted in our natural impulses toward the good of the species, but it requires intellectual discipline and a development of the cognitive faculty. Shaftesbury goes so far as to say that no rational person can be entirely without some conception of the public interest, though this becomes increasingly difficult as the size of the community expands. The "Inquiry Concerning Virtue" may be viewed as an attempt to explain how and why men fail to see the public interest or to act in its behalf.

Shaftesbury makes it clear that though self-concern is necessary, when an apparent private interest conflicts with the public interest, the latter must prevail. He writes that if one could imagine an impulse toward self-good which was "in its natural degree, conducing to private interest, and at the same time inconsistent with the public good, this may indeed be called still a vicious affection." (I, 247) He is aware of the difficulties we experience in conflicts between private and public interest, and in a letter he remarks that in a conflict between family and public interest the conscientious person is likely to be "hard set, and perhaps ground between the parties. . . ." [15] Devotion to the common good often requires "the greatest hardships and hazards." In fact, "all social love, friendship, gratitude, or whatever else is of this generous kind, does by its nature take place of the self-interesting passions, draws us out of ourselves, and makes us disregardful of our own convenience and safety." (I, 281) While Shaftesbury recognizes the difficulties in adjusting private and public interest, his basic assumption that private interest and public interest must be ultimately identical prevents him from appreciating fully the actual disjunctions between the two. It is at just such points that his theory of the ideal harmony of Nature limits his realism.

Shaftesbury rejects the idea that the interests of the self and those of society stand in necessary opposition. Quite the contrary, the *true* interests of an individual are necessarily in accord with the organic system of which he is a member. As the organs of the body function for the good of the whole organism, so the members of a community ought to act for the welfare of the whole group. Shaftesbury assumes that the kind of relationship involved in each of these cases is essentially the same, with the exception that the organs of the body are operated by physical mechanisms while human beings are rational agents. But if the relationship can be shown to be *not* the same, Shaftesbury's argument is greatly weakened. At any rate, he contends that what is good for a group as a whole is to be assumed good for the individual members of the group. Self-interest is "not only consistent with but inseparable" from public interest. (I, 282)

Shaftesbury attempts to support this further by an extended argument in the "Inquiry Concerning Virtue" for the proposition that virtue is to the advantage and vice the disadvantage of both the individual and society. In his words:

> Now, if by the natural constitution of any rational creature, the same irregularities of appetite which make him ill to others, make him ill also to himself, and if the same regularity of affections which causes him to be good in one sense, causes him to be good also in the other, then is that goodness by which he is thus useful to others a real good and advantage to himself. And thus virtue and interest may be found at last to agree. (I, 243 f.)

Virtue, moreover, is defined as that state in which the affections of a creature are directed toward the "good of his kind, or of that system in which he is included. . . ." (I, 280) The organic continuity between virtue—acting in the public interest—and self-concern is expressed in a letter to Lord Somers:

> I pray strenuously for you . . . that the command of passion so advantageous to you in public, and with others, may be of the same use and happiness to you in private with yourself. . . . That courts and mistresses, and all charming things, may be yours, and not you theirs; nor any powers have the privilege to call you theirs except reason and your own country. For when you are most theirs, you will be most your own.[16]

As we have seen, Shaftesbury was aware of the proximate inconsistencies between self-interest and public interest, though perhaps not as much as one would wish. There is an *ultimate* though not always *proximate* identity between self-interest and public interest. Bishop Butler, though he repeats many of the points that Shaftesbury makes in his discussion of the relation of self-interest and public interest, draws a sharper line between the dictates of conscience and the counsels of self-interest. As Sidgwick has pointed out, this contributed to the developing split between deontological and utilitarian ethics. Shaftesbury's philosophy has importance as a heroic effort to preserve the insights of both positions in a unified system. As a consequence, his ethical theory has a special richness and comprehensiveness, but it also leaves us with some serious questions that Shaftesbury himself fails to answer, and which we will examine briefly here and in more detail in subsequent chapters.

There are several points at which Shaftesbury's "solution" to the problem of private versus public interest seems weak. We have already questioned his claim that the relation between an individual and his community, or an individual and his species, is organic in character, or of the same order as the relation of the organs of the body to the whole organism. Another difficulty is his claim that the interests of a community are necessarily the interests of the members of that community. While he allows for some disjunction here, his basic strategy is to argue that the conflicts that arise between the two are for the most part only apparent: your *true* self-interest is always in accord with the *true* interests of the community. For Shaftesbury this seems to function as an irrefutable truth required by his world view, but when applied to experience, doubts arise. For example, suppose I own a home which has great sentimental value for me, but the state wants this property for a road. Let us assume that this location for a road is clearly in the public interest. Shaftesbury, of course, would say that I should sacrifice my home willingly for the larger interests at stake. Yet in so far as he asks me to make such a sacrifice, he is asking me in effect to abandon a significant interest of mine—the sentimental value—which cannot be replaced. It is not enough to say that I am doing this for a larger good; that may be true, but there is also an absolute loss here. Perhaps Shaftesbury could accede to this, but argue that we should not think in terms of single interests but rather of a *set* of interests. Thus, while I might, in fact, lose in respect to one interest, I would gain in respect to other interests, i.e., those which would be advanced by the general welfare of the state to which the road would be a contributing element. However, we can open the question again by asking if an individual's *set* of interests are necessarily in accord with the total interests of the community. If empirical counterevidence were presented, Shaftesbury could respond by insisting that the question must be put in terms of the *true* interests of the individual and community. These true interests have to be determined finally in the light of Shaftesbury's ideal model of man and the universe, upon which his treatment of this problem ultimately rests.

Shaftesbury's position seems to boil down to this: the problem of moral choice is one of finding a way of acting for the public interest that is at the same time coincident with one's private interest. The man of good will, i.e., one who is moved by social affection, does not act out of sheer impulse or mere self-interest, but consciously seeks that kind of action that is at the same time personally desirable and socially beneficial. The problem is not one of *either* self-interest *or* public interest, but rather of self-interest *and* public interest. Since, in Shaftesbury's system, men have diverse interests and a variety of motivations, it is his conviction that it is always possible to work out effectual and satisfying combinations of private and public interest. In the kind of universe he believed in this is not only the ethical ideal, it is the ideal possibility.

Here again it is apparent that every aspect of Shaftesbury's thought is dominated by his vision of the cosmos as a rational, coherent, effusive, and creative Whole. Neither this vision nor his ideal model of man is derived empirically; each is essentially a product of enthusiasm and creative imagination. Yet he is much concerned to give them empirical support and to demonstrate their relevance to experience. They represent intuitions of an order that is essentially ideal—an order from which experience gains its structure and behavior its *telos*.

In the hierarchy of systems, devotion to the public good can have its only consummation in devotion to the Whole of Being. As Shaftesbury writes,

besides that relation to a species, there is a further relation which every creature has, viz., to the whole of things as administered by that supreme will or law which regulates all things according to the highest good. If it be thus, it follows that a creature who is in that higher degree rational, and can consider the good of the whole, and consider himself as related to the whole, must withal consider himself as under an obligation to the interest and good of the whole, preferably to the interest of his private species: and this is the ground of a new and superior affection.[17]

The Supreme Intelligence has so ordered Nature that when an individual works for the good of the Whole, he is at the same time working for his own interest and happiness. To accept

Shaftesbury's solution to the problem of self-interest and public interest is to accept his ideal model of the universe, a universe in which individuals find their true selves in community, and in which society finds its true realization in individual selves; a universe in which the human community finds its meaning in God, and in which God realizes his meaning in the human community.

CHAPTER ELEVEN

RELIGION and MORALS

Though Shaftesbury's solution to the problem of self-interest and public interest, as indeed his entire ethical system, must be seen in relation to his vision of God and Nature, he does not accept the traditional religious view that makes morality a product of theology. As his view of the relationship of religion and morals is a complicated one, we need to distinguish here between *theology*, understood as a set of consciously formulated beliefs about God and the related forms of worship, and *religious experience*, understood as enthusiasm or ultimate commitment. Like his friend Bayle, Shaftesbury held that morality was independent of theology, taken in the above sense. Both thinkers point to the obvious fact that many persons who profess religious beliefs are not virtuous, and that many who profess disbelief live morally commendable lives. Shaftesbury discusses this problem at length in "The Inquiry Concerning Virtue," trying, as he tells us, to avoid the orthodox error of identifying theology and morals, as well as the error of "the men of wit" who could not see that religion had any significant relevance to morality.

For one thing, he argues that children can develop a sense

of right and wrong before having any clear conception of Deity, and apart from any formulated theology. Furthermore, once this moral sense becomes an established element in one's personality it cannot be *directly* affected by a religious or irreligious belief: "There is no speculative opinion, . . . or belief, which is capable immediately or directly to exclude or destroy it." (I, 260) While Shaftesbury concedes that the sense of right and wrong can be altered by the effect of habit or custom, he argues, like Bayle, that it can only be *indirectly* affected by theological beliefs. The basic mechanism through which this works is that theological doctrines may stimulate or arouse affections which influence our moral judgments. For example, if some inhuman or unnatural practice or quality is associated with a god, whom we are conditioned to love, we may come to regard that practice or quality as good. This does not happen where worship is purely formalized or where the affections themselves are not engaged. But when religious concepts affect our emotional life, they can be indirect influences for good or evil.

Another aspect of Shaftesbury's argument is his insistence that those who profess belief in a God who is good and just must believe in prior and independent principles of good and evil, just and unjust, on grounds of which God is pronounced good. Shaftesbury rejects the theory which finds the source of value in the will of God: "If the mere will, decree, or law of God be said absolutely to constitute right and wrong, then are these latter words of no significancy at all." (I, 264) Thus, again theology and moral consciousness are distinguished.

But if religious doctrines can indirectly have a harmful effect on morals, they can also have a beneficial influence. In fact, he writes,

nothing can more highly contribute to the fixing of right apprehensions, and a sound judgment or sense of right and wrong, than
to believe a God who is ever and on all accounts represented such
as to be actually a true model and example of the most exact justice
and highest goodness and worth. (I, 264 f.)

In this case, the divine example reinforces the social affections.

While positive religion can thus affect the moral sense,
atheism, being basically a lack of positive belief, is less effective.
Shaftesbury follows Bacon and Bayle in regarding false religion or superstition rather than atheism as the greatest danger
to morality. Yet atheism may be damaging to virtue in the
negative sense that it fails to provide the reinforcement of true
theism. For example, Shaftesbury considers it important that
a virtuous man believe in "the happiness of virtue." Atheism
does not necessarily entail rejecting this; even "without an
absolute assent to any hypothesis of theism, the advantages of
virtue may possibly be seen. . . ." (I, 275) However, this is
not the "natural tendency of atheism." (*Ibid.*) Our recognition
of the happiness of virtue basically rests upon our own immediate experience of it, yet it can be reinforced by our beliefs about God and Nature. True theism does exactly this by
teaching the goodness and beauty of the Whole, and by providing us with a divine exemplar of "good affection." This,
of course, is precisely what atheism lacks. Furthermore, since
the atheist, in Shaftesbury's definition, believes in a Nature
characterized by disorder, he logically is led to believe that
"virtue is the natural ill, and vice the natural good" of living
creatures. (I, 277) Such a belief can hardly help but only hurt
our virtuous inclinations.[1]

A final argument that Shaftesbury makes is that theism prepares us to endure with patience and true resignation the
tragedies and hardships of life; atheism, because of its belief

in a universe ruled by chance, fails to do this. Thus, Shaftesbury contends that virtue is perfected by piety: "The perfection and height of virtue must be owing to the belief of a God." (I, 280)

To summarize, Shaftesbury thinks that morality is autonomous in the sense that it is not necessarily dependent upon the presence or absence of theological beliefs. Yet, the latter may affect our moral consciousness indirectly; this allows him to argue further that virtue gains its greatest support and highest inspiration from true theism. But there is a further question here that we have not answered: how does religious experience, as enthusiasm or ultimate commitment, fit into this picture? The distinction drawn between morals and theology does not seem to apply here. In so far as enthusiasm for the good, the true, and the beautiful is the dynamic source of virtue and true religion, both have a common source within the human spirit. *Proximately*, morals and theology do often diverge; but *ultimately*, there can be no real separation between morality and true religion in Shaftesbury's system. True piety necessarily issues in the moral life. This gives an added dimension to his argument that piety perfects virtue; for both are mutually reinforcing and both presuppose a "love of order, harmony, and proportion." (I, 279)

The relationship of morality and religion is explored further in Shaftesbury's extended discussion of the problem of the role of retribution in religion. A considerable controversy had developed on this subject in England in the seventeenth century, and Shaftesbury was one of the agents who carried it over into the eighteenth century, when it continued to be a dominant concern of writers on religion. Earlier in the seventeenth century even a liberal religious writer like Herbert of Cherbury was not only defending the doctrine of future rewards and punishments, but accrediting it as one of the five basic principles of natural religion. Herbert argued that philosophy, religion, law, and the moral conscience itself all concurred in recognizing the necessity for such a principle. Throughout the century conservative writers were joined by religious liberals like Tillotson and Jeremy Taylor in their defense of divine retribution.[2] In response to those who believed that virtue was its own reward, it was commonly argued that this was insufficient motive for the moral life; morality needed to be supported by fear of divine justice. Some preachers feared that sin was so attractive, and the possibility of avoiding the evil consequences here on earth so great, that without the curb of retribution vice would predominate even more than it did.[3] In fact, the belief in the value of hell as a deterrent for immoral behavior was one of the major reasons why the doctrine of hell was so rarely attacked in the seventeenth century.[4] But the position that was to become the predominant one among religious liberals is foreshadowed in Samuel Parker's opinion that "the first Reward of Vertue is its own natural and intrinsick Pleasure," though he too is unwilling to make this the sole basis of the moral life, adding that without the assurance of a future existence there is "no sufficient foundation for Vertue. . . ."[5]

In the meanwhile, a similar controversy was taking place on the Continent. Spinoza found the state of blessedness in virtue itself, and Bayle argued that the fear of future punishments did not in fact serve as an important factor in the actual moral choices of men, thus questioning one of the prime contentions of its defenders. Perhaps the most famous discussion of the issue was that between Bossuet and Fénelon in which the question of the nature of man's love for God was central. In his *Explication des maximes des saints* (1697), Fénelon contended that the highest type of love for God was without any element of self-interest; it was love of God for His own sake. The kind of love of God which is conditioned by the fear of punishment or the hope of reward is only an imperfect copy of this higher, disinterested love. True love of God excludes all thought of heaven, or one's own salvation. Indeed, Fénelon goes so far as to say that even if God were (though an "impossible supposition") to condemn the souls of the saintly to hell, they would continue to love Him. The Roman Church, spurred on by Bossuet, condemned as erroneous the principles that a soul should acquiesce in its own damnation, and that the highest form of love for God involves the conscious exclusion of all thought of one's eternal happiness. Shaftesbury's familiarity with the controversy is revealed in the "Miscellaneous Reflections," where he indicates his sympathy with "the pious, worthy, and ingenious Abbé Fénelon." (II, 214) Leibniz tried unsuccessfully to act as a mediator in the above controversy by getting the two parties to agree "that the desire for salvation was only the unconscious, not the conscious motive which dictates our love of God." [6]

In the year after Fénelon published his *Explication*, the famous preacher, Robert South, added new heat to the discussion in a sermon attacking the doctrine of virtue as its own reward.[7] Since Whichcote's *Sermons* with the Preface by Shaftesbury may have already appeared, South might have had it in mind. At any rate, he notes the currency of the doctrine, and argues that while it might work effectively as a moral motivation for angels, it is beyond the capacities of ordinary men. The first publication of Shaftesbury's "Inquiry" followed in 1699, and provoked an interesting reply by one Robert Day, *Free Thoughts in Defence of a Future State: . . . with occasional remarks on a Book Intituled, An Inquiry Concerning Virtue* (1700). With Shaftesbury's principles in mind, Day argues that if it is rational for a man to be concerned about his prospects in this life, it is equally rational to be concerned about one's prospects in any future form of existence. Admitting that consideration of rewards and punishments contributes to selfishness, Day contends that all deliberate actions of rational men have the prospect of advantage in view. Self-regard is entirely justifiable so long as it is rationally regulated and is not contrary to the public interest. Day repeats the standard argument that the intrinsic value of virtue is insufficient motive for the virtuous life. This is all the more true since virtue does not always have its proper reward or vice its appropriate punishment in this life. Finally, he reasons that if the world order is indeed good and perfect, there must be a future state in which virtue and happiness are perfectly correlated.[8]

The controversy flared again in an exchange between the conservative High Churchman, the Reverend Francis Atterbury, and the aggressive Latitudinarian, the Reverend Benjamin Hoadly. Hoadly wrote *A Letter to the Reverend Dr. Francis Atterbury* in 1706 in answer to a funeral sermon preached by the latter. Using arguments similar to those of Shaftesbury, Hoadly defends the view that the doctrine of retribution is not essential to morality. His main point is that virtue is the imitation of God, and in it man finds his chief happiness regardless of whether it lasts one day or an eternity. In a letter Shaftesbury refers to this dispute between Atterbury and "the good Mr. H——y." [9] After the publication of the

Characteristics in 1711, Shaftesbury came to be recognized as the chief enemy of the doctrine of divine rewards and punishments in a future life, and his position was alternately attacked and defended for another fifty years. In mid-century, John Brown's *Essays on the Characteristics* (1751), reflected the position that many eighteenth-century moderates found to be an acceptable resolution of the problem. Admitting that the disinterested love of God and the example of a Perfect Being may be sufficiently powerful sanctions for morality in a favored few, he argues that the masses require the hope of reward and the fear of punishment. This approach was often combined with an acceptance of a double standard: the traditional doctrine was to be taught to the masses for its pragmatic value, while the "higher" truth was to be reserved for those intellectually capable of grasping it.[10]

Shaftesbury's interest in this issue is revealed clearly in his first published writing, the Preface to Whichcote's sermons. He makes an extended attack on those clergymen who denied that man had any natural social impulses, and who, as a consequence, thought that the only motivation that men could have for acting morally was the "Prospect of some different Good, some Advantage of a different Sort from what attends the Actions themselves." [11] He finds it strange that those who believe in a God capable of disinterested love deny that His creatures have this capacity in any degree, and that those in whose religion "charity is made all in all" nevertheless find no motive for moral behavior beyond the prospect of self-advantage. These divines have "made War . . . on Vertue itself: Having exploded the Principle of Good Nature; all Enjoyment or Satisfaction in Acts of Kindness and Love. . . ." [12] On the other hand, Shaftesbury praises Whichcote, who opposed this trend, teaching that God does not "in a positive way, inflict Punishment; or any Instrument of God punish a Sinner; yet he would punish himself. . . ." [13]

In the "Inquiry Concerning Virtue," Shaftesbury develops his conception of the true sanctions of morality in greater length and more systematically. He asks two types of questions: (1) what actually motivates men to seek to conform to the will of God; and (2) what *should* motivate them ideally? Basically, he finds two types of relationship between man and God: first, where men conform out of fear of the power of God to reward and punish; second, where men seek to emulate God out of love for His perfection. The first type is not moral in the truest and highest sense so long as one does not really desire to do the good and avoid the evil. Responding to sheer force because of fear is not morally praiseworthy in the distinctive sense of *moral*, even though it may be considered justifiable on grounds of rational self-regard. Shaftesbury approaches Kant at this point, but he never carries his thought as far in this direction as the German thinker. The Lockian sanctions of divine reward and punishment are only on a level with the pressures of civil law and public opinion in Shaftesbury's eyes. They may restrain a wrongdoer by appealing to his self-regard, and moralists and legislators may, indeed do, have to make use of them, but conduct based on these motives is not morally commendable. According to D. P. Walker, the application of this doctrine as a criticism of the traditional concepts of heaven and hell was "extremely rare" at that time.[14] True morality for Shaftesbury is not based on mere fear or sheer self-interest; it must be grounded on the love of the good for its own sake, and on the desire to do the right *because* it is right. The "good" is not an empty abstraction, but it is given content by the social affections; it is important to keep this in mind not only for the understanding of Shaftesbury's concept of "good," but also because it helps to explain his conviction that fear of the absolute power of God is not an adequate sanction for morality. Such fear does not bring with it any real transformation of the self, any essential change in the structure of the will and emotions; thus, it leaves an evil man evil, even though he does the "right" thing. When you fear something, you still stand outside and apart from it as opposed to it; thus, the fear of God (if God by definition is good) is a contradiction in terms.

It follows then that the right kind of relationship between man and God is that where we seek to pattern ourselves after God out of love for his goodness. Shaftesbury seems to be saying two kinds of things: one, that the true sanction of morality is the love of goodness for its intrinsic value; and two, that since God epitomizes perfect goodness, we must love and emulate Him. Thus, Shaftesbury maintains the separation of morality and theology, while positing their ultimate unity in the nature of the Divine Being. This distinction is found in his discussion of "conscience" too. Conscience means basically conscious reflection on our own actions in the light of our moral beliefs, but it may be divided into "religious" and "moral" conscience. Religious conscience presupposes the "moral or natural conscience," (I, 305) that is, a sense of right and wrong which operates independently of any particular theology. With the development of a theology, moral qualities are ascribed to Deity, and religious conscience develops. However, Shaftesbury contends that the real strength of the religious conscience is not derived from our fear of the power of God to punish or enforce; it rests instead upon the sense of shame which arises from our consciousness of the discrepancy between our behavior and the divinely epitomized moral ideals. The fear of God only has moral significance when it is joined with this type of moral consciousness.

Though, as we have seen, Shaftesbury strove to avoid anthropomorphism and conceived of God in largely nonpersonal terms, there is a personalistic note in his explanation of how piety can support and perfect morality through the religious conscience. The mere example of a benevolent Being concerned for the good of all, while helpful, is not enough. Perfect theism entails the belief in "the superintendency of a supreme Being, a witness and spectator of human life, . . . conscious of whatsoever is felt or acted in the universe." (I, 268) The sense of the personal presence—of the approval or disapproval of such a Being—would weigh more than the judgments of other men. Here and in his doctrine of the social affections Shaftesbury seems to recognize that morality must rest on something more than the abstract call of duty. It must originate in and be sustained by concrete impulses directed toward other persons; it finds much of its dynamic in our loyalty or commitment to other persons, and by extrapolation, to a Divine Person.

Thus, the hope of rewards and the fear of punishment are not, taken in themselves, true sources of moral behavior. But there is another argument against divine retribution that Shaftesbury often repeats: that it stimulates self-love at the expense of concern for the public welfare. This, he thinks, explains why "narrowness of spirit . . . is peculiarly observable" in religious zealots. (I, 269) Piety itself is made mercenary when God is merely a means to our own pleasure.

Despite the force of his attack on the traditional doctrine,

Shaftesbury allowed that it could, under certain circumstances, provide support for the moral life. However, he wanted to restrict its use to those on lower levels of development, intellectually or emotionally: "Religion still being a discipline and progress of the soul towards perfection, the motive of reward and punishment is primary and of the highest moment with us, till, being capable of more sublime instruction, we are led from this servile state to the generous service of affection and love." (II, 56) Thus, it may be useful in the education of children, or for the control of the masses where more rational arguments fail. The doctrine may, for example, be employed as a temporary check to the passions, giving an individual time to rethink his behavior. However, these are all conditional and limited applications appropriate only to given stages of development. Shaftesbury draws an analogy between the penalties and rewards provided by a civil government and those taught by religion. Both may not only prevent crime, but they may condition people to think of virtuous action as being to their benefit. Shaftesbury thinks a benevolent government will be more successful in this (as will a benevolent Deity) because its example will be more effective in molding character than the fear of force which a tyranny relies on.

However, Shaftesbury warns that if future rewards and punishments are taught, they must be "annexed to real goodness and merit, real villainy and baseness, and not to any accidental qualities or circumstances." (I, 276) There must be an organic connection between the deed and the retributive consequence, a point that Shaftesbury felt the preachers were failing to make. And in so doing they were presenting God's behavior as arbitrary and irrational.

Despite these concessions to the usefulness of the doctrine, the overall impact of Shaftesbury's discussion is a stinging criticism of divine retribution as commonly preached in his time. He charges that it is at best a crutch for the immature, and "in some respects there can be nothing more fatal to virtue. . . ." (I, 275) Belief in a future life combined with retribution has, for example, given an extra intensity to religious persecution, and out of "supernatural charity . . . has raised an antipathy which no temporal interest could ever do; and entailed upon us a mutual hatred to all eternity." (I, 15) One is reminded of the traditional doctrine that one of the pleasures of the elect in heaven would be observing the suffering of the damned, though by the seventeenth century this belief was, happily, already dying out.

A primary principle for Shaftesbury is that virtue is the goal of life, not merely a means to something beyond itself. Virtue can have no reward "but of the same Kind with itself: Nothing can be superadded to it." [15] "All that virtue seeks is to be virtue. . . ." [16] And as he writes to Anthony Collins: "Thank heaven I can do good and find heaven in it. I know nothing else that is heavenly. And if this disposition fits me not for heaven, I desire never to be fitted for it, nor come into the place. I ask no reward from heaven for that which is reward itself." [17] Shaftesbury's point of view presupposes, of course, his doubts about the possibility of personal survival after death. However, he does not make his case dependent on the resolution of the question of whether there is or is not a future life. He focusses instead on the issue of what makes for morality in the essential sense, or what should be the sanctions of moral behavior. And he is confident that, whatever our future condition may be, the same principles that prevail now will continue to operate. The reward of virtue is the same whether there is or is not personal survival. Shaftesbury finds nothing wrong in the hope for a future life based on the desire to continue enjoying the practice of virtue. But since the quality of life is ultimately and essentially unchanging, to enjoy the qualities of virtuous living in the present moment is to enjoy them in the only way possible. For Shaftesbury, the eternal is known in the present moment.

Shaftesbury points out the problems of a theology which teaches a future existence with rewards and punishments; but the solutions he proposes do not succeed in overcoming all the difficulties. His major contention that virtue is to our advantage and vice to our disadvantage still leaves us with serious questions even without considering the question of personal immortality. The relationship of this appeal to man's concern for his own advantage with the doctrine of the disinterested love of virtue and good is a paradox which perhaps can only be resolved dialectically. Some aspects of the question have already been discussed in the chapter on "Self and Society"; others will have to be treated in our subsequent chapter on the relation of virtue and happiness.[18]

The power of Shaftesbury's attack on the traditional doctrine and its importance in transforming men's conception of their destinies is borne out by D. P. Walker's study, *The Decline of Hell*.[19] Coming at a time when very few men dared to challenge orthodox belief, and when those who did were for the most part forced to resort to anonymity, Shaftesbury struck a telling blow at the whole idea of otherworldly rewards and punishments. Whatever the limitations of his point of view—and there is no need to deny them—he made a major contribution by his assault upon a theological structure that had been built unwarrantably on the metaphorical language of the New Testament—a system which made empirical and logical claims to truth that it could not sustain under examination. It was only one of the ways that Shaftesbury forced men to rethink their Christian heritage.

CHAPTER TWELVE

The NATURE of VIRTUE

The most difficult aspect of Shaftesbury's thought to present systematically is his ethical theory. Many share the judgment of D. D. Raphael that there is "in fact no concise or coherently thought-out theory of a moral sense" or of morality in general in Shaftesbury.[1] It cannot be denied that there is truth in this; yet the question is one of degree—the extent to which Shaftesbury failed to construct a coherent ethical system. At the same time, his discussion of ethical issues remains one of those that are more interesting, precisely because of the kind of synthesis he attempted to make and because of the rich and suggestive variety of his insights. It is not surprising that the *Characteristics* served both as a mine of ideas and as a major stimulus to the discussion of moral issues in the eighteenth century.

Though Shaftesbury is best known as the founder of the moral sense school of ethics, and though the analysis of that moral faculty is of key importance in examining his theory, his primary aim was the construction of a theory of the nature of virtue, as the title, "Inquiry Concerning Virtue or Merit," indicates. He concerns himself particularly with the question of what makes for good character or what determines "merit."

We have already seen how this involves him in an analysis of the nature of man and the structure of the affections. As noted in the previous chapter, moral worth cannot be attributed to actions that are motivated solely by fear or self-interest. A creature can be designated "good" or "evil" only "when the good or ill of the system to which he has relation is the immediate object of some passion or affection moving him," because it is "by affection merely that a creature is esteemed good or ill, natural or unnatural. . . ." (I, 247) What is "not done through any affection at all" is nonmoral. What Shaftesbury means by this has to be seen in relation to his discussion of the affections and their different types. He is arguing that these motivating impulses are decisive in determining the moral quality of an individual's behavior. It is not the act in itself that reveals character, but the intentions or inner motives that lie behind it. An unintentional act would be morally neutral, as would an act one was forced to carry out. Real goodness is determined more by one's inner disposition than by exterior influences. Thus, the particular balance of affections present in an individual is the decisive factor in his character, and Shaftesbury's description of the affections is at one and the same time an exposition of the particular vices and virtues that they entail. In the ideal personality—the virtuous man—all the affections co-operate harmoniously in directing the individual to the public good. The truly virtuous man acts out of "natural affection for his kind." But character is corrupted to the extent that any necessary affection is lacking or too weak, or that any impulse is present which operates in contradiction to the general welfare. As for the "unnatural affections," since they are entirely vicious their presence in any degree in personality is destructive of virtue.

It was in connection with this theory that Shaftesbury developed his concept of the "moral sense," which was also conceived as an essential faculty of moral character. He appears to have been the first to use this term, though Henry More wrote of a "sense . . . whereby we discern Moral good and evil." [2] Actually, the expression "moral sense" appears (to my knowledge) only once in the text of the "Inquiry" (I, 262), though it may be found in the marginal headings and index composed by Shaftesbury himself for the 1714 edition of *Characteristics*.[3] Shaftesbury's more characteristic phrase is "the sense of right and wrong," [4] but it is convenient to use the abbreviated expression as we will here. Hutcheson adopted and popularized the term "moral sense," giving it a more systematic exposition, but because of his commitment to Locke's empiricist theory of knowledge, he shifted its meaning significantly.[5]

In his analysis of how a virtuous disposition may be destroyed, Shaftesbury finds three possible ways: it may be overcome by something (1) which "takes away the natural and just sense of right and wrong" (I, 258); or (2) which creates a false sense of right and wrong; or (3) which sets opposing affections against the moral sense. Whether Shaftesbury meant literally that the moral sense could be entirely destroyed is not clear. Fowler interprets him as asserting this, and Shaftesbury does speak of the possibility of losing "all conscience." (I, 307) The moral sense is a potentiality with which all men have been endowed by Nature. Whether or not he thought of it as being an equal endowment, it is clear that he recognized that it was developed in different degree by different men, and that it could be weakened in varying degree also. Given Shaftesbury's model of human nature though, it would appear that the entire absence of a sense of right and wrong in any individual would remove him from the category of human and rational beings. Thus, his basic position is that one who is human and sane cannot be entirely without a moral sense or natural affection. (I, 257)

Shaftesbury uses a variety of arguments to support his position. He contends that some degree of awareness of the public interest, even though small, is present in all sane men living in communities. He finds it difficult to imagine that any rational human being could be entirely without any "pity, love, kindness, or social affection" for his own kind. (I, 259) The faculty of moral judgment is, thus, inseparable from the social affections. But along with these more immediate social responses there are other logical processes of the mind that reinforce them. For example, Shaftesbury argues that a rational creature knows when he injures another person that he himself will as a consequence be "liable to such treatment from every one as if he had in some degree offended all. Thus, offence and injury are always known as punishable by every one; and equal behavior (which is therefore called merit) as rewardable and well-deserving from every one." (I, 259) From these processes the mind forms images of justice, generosity, and other virtues, which in turn become objects of attraction as their opposites become objects of aversion. "Coming therefore to a capacity of seeing and admiring in this new way, it must needs find a beauty and a deformity as well in actions, minds, and tempers, as in figures, sounds, or colours." (I, 260) Shaftesbury continues in a rather cryptic way: "If there be no real amiableness or deformity in moral acts, there is at least an imaginary one of full force. Though perhaps the thing itself should not be allowed in Nature, the imagination or fancy of it must be allowed to be from Nature alone." (*Ibid.*) It is evident from this passage that Shaftesbury does not consider our judgments of the beauty or ugliness of moral objects to arise from purely passive responses to the givenness of experience; rather they are products of the creative imagination. This creative capacity to grasp experience as meaningful form is deeply rooted in human nature, as is the consequent distinction between right and wrong, and our attraction to or repulsion from moral objects. Thus, only the longest and most strenuous efforts could conceivably destroy it, once developed. This is another aspect of the reasoning that leads Shaftesbury to conclude that "no speculative opinion or belief" could directly destroy the moral faculty.

Bonar writes that Shaftesbury "seems to assume the invincibility of goodness . . . ," [6] but while this may be true on the cosmic level it is not on the proximate level of human experience. For Shaftesbury is well aware that the "natural moral sense" can be seriously weakened and distorted. He suggests two basic ways in which this may happen: first, a false sense of right and wrong can be produced by "force of custom and education in opposition to Nature. . . ." (I, 261) Social conditioning, effected through either religious or political means, can overcome men's normal inclinations and make "naturally foul and odious" actions seem honorable and right. Since this kind of conditioning must alter the affections themselves, it is closely connected to the second way that the moral sense can be distorted—through the creation of affections that run contrary to our natural impulses. Yet this second process can be carried out only through the most extraordinary application of "art," i.e., through a method of systematic checks and controls. Shaftesbury is careful though to point out that natural affection, and the moral sense which arises from it, cannot be altered by a simple act of will or determination. We cannot change deeply ingrained habits or the "temper" of our personality by just wishing it. Fundamental changes in the structure of our affections come about only through powerful factors in the environment or through the development of new habits of thought and feeling. There is a suggestion that such changes require a transformation of the personality as a whole. And if we attempt to suppress the moral sense in ourselves, it still "lies sullen, and ready to revolt on the first occasion." (I, 261)

In opposition to Locke, Shaftesbury contends that "the notions and principles of fair, just, and honest . . . are innate." (II, 135) He proposes that if the term "innate" causes trouble we substitute "instinctive," or Whichcote's term, "connatural." Whichcote described virtue as "connatural . . . to the nature of man." [7] Shaftesbury defines innate ideas as those "which Nature teaches, exclusive of art, culture, or discipline." (II, 135) He dismisses the question of when these ideas are first formed in our minds as "of no great importance": "The question is not about the time the *ideas* entered, . . . but whether the constitution of man be such that . . . sooner or later . . . the idea and sense of order, administration, and God, will not infallibly, inevitably, necessarily spring up in him." [8] Innate ideas appear to be original potentialities of the human spirit which develop inevitably under the normal conditions of social living. It is certainly not Shaftesbury's contention that infants are born with a set of consciously apprehended moral principles or concepts. But just as animals are born with instincts which Nature has provided for their well-being, Shaftesbury thinks of men as being born with mental capacities and tendencies which are equally necessary for their welfare. The rational structure of the mind is "programmed" (to use computer terminology) in such a way that under normal conditions it develops the ideas of the good, the beautiful, and the true.

Shaftesbury accused Locke of undermining virtue by calling our moral conceptions "*unnatural,* and without foundation in our minds." [9] Later, he wrote:

As for *innate principles* which you mention, it is, in my opinion, one of the childishest disputes that ever was. Well it is for our friend Mr. Locke, and other modern philosophers of his sire, that they have so poor a spectre as the ghost of Aristotle to fight with . . . since it is not in reality . . . the original Peripatetic hypothesis, but the poor secondary tralatitious system of modern and barbarous schoolmen which is the subject of their continual triumph.[10]

Yet one would wish that Shaftesbury had explained his own position with more clarity. Evidently he intended to say more than that the mind has a structural predisposition to distinguish between right and wrong. The concepts of the good and the beautiful naturally take form in the mind of man. Yet elsewhere he stressed the need for cultivation and discipline in the development of moral and aesthetic taste. Apparently he meant that under ideal conditions the natural structure of the affections would develop according to its true character, but when ideal conditions do not exist, discipline and training are required to counteract evil influences. Another way of putting it would be that we develop our concepts of the good and beautiful intuitively, but the working out of the meaning of these concepts in practice is required for the formation of "taste." It is only in and through experience that such intuitive ideas can mature in one's consciousness. In one interesting passage, Shaftesbury wonders if the real question is "not whether the very philosophical propositions about right and wrong were innate; but whether the passion or affection towards society was such: that is to say, whether it was natural . . . or was taught by art. . . ." [11] This shifting of the question is significant, for it reminds us that for the English philosopher the basic issue remains that of whether or not the social affections are an inherent element of man's nature. If they are, then the moral sense and the concept of the good must inevitably develop out of these spontaneous impulses. It is in this light probably that we should read such passages as the following, referring to our response to moral objects:

> . . . the heart cannot possibly remain neutral; but constantly takes part one way or other. However false or corrupt it be within itself, it finds the difference, as to beauty and comeliness, between . . . one turn of affection, one behaviour, one sentiment and another; and accordingly, in all disinterested cases, must approve in some measure of what is natural and honest, and disapprove what is dishonest and corrupt. (I, 252)

Though Shaftesbury does not use the term "intuition," it is evident that the moral sense operates in part as an intuitive faculty in so far as there is immediate apprehension of the moral qualities of actions or characters.

> No sooner are actions viewed, no sooner the human affections and passions discerned (and they are most of them as soon discerned as felt) than straight an inward eye distinguishes, and sees the fair and shapely, the amiable and desirable, apart from the deformed, the foul, the odious, or the despicable. (II, 137)

The objects of moral judgment, as well as those of aesthetic judgment, are immediately attractive or repulsive; thus, for Shaftesbury, good "taste" is of as much importance in morality as in aesthetics. It is not merely what we call principle, but a taste which governs men. They may think for certain, "this is right, or that wrong": they may believe "this a crime or that a sin; this punishable by man, or that by God": yet if the savour of things lies cross to honesty; if the fancy be florid and the appetite high towards the subaltern beauties and lower order of worldly symmetries and proportions, the conduct will infallibly turn this latter way. (II, 265)

Fowler and others have criticized both Shaftesbury and Hutcheson on grounds that their systems of thought would tend to encourage men to rely on "hasty judgments." It is true that Shaftesbury suggests that men's "first thoughts" are often better than those refined by sophistical speculation (I, 88), but this presupposes an individual whose natural structure of affections has developed under favorable conditions. Shaftesbury repeatedly stresses that a sound taste must be developed by effort and discipline, and this seems to apply to all but the most exceptional persons.[12] It is only when you "fill your self with Good," he writes to a young protégé (and this condition is crucial), that you will be able to discriminate between good and evil "by a sort of instinct." [13] Moreover, he warns him against the danger of following one's first inclinations: "If you follow your sudden Fancy and Bent; if you fix your Eye on that, which most strikes and pleases you at the first Sight; you will most certainly never come to have a good Eye at all." Superficial things, he continues, will tend to make the strongest first impressions; therefore, "make it a solemn Rule to your self, to check your own Eye and Fancy . . . and turn it strongly on that, which it cares not at first to dwell upon." [14] Recognizing the importance of first impressions in the shaping of taste, Shaftesbury cautions against the danger of exposing young people to examples of bad art as well as bad morals. The rational mind, thus, has to exercise a considerable degree of self-discipline to protect its judgments from distortions arising from within the personality as well as from external influences. "If a natural good taste be not already formed in us, why should not we endeavor to form it, and cultivate it till it become natural?" (I, 218) Indeed, "'tis we ourselves create and form our taste." (II, 271) Even though the moral sense is rooted in human nature, moral taste, like aesthetic taste, is not full-formed at birth but must be developed:

Whatever principles or materials of this kind we may possibly bring with us, whatever good faculties, senses, or anticipating sensations and imaginations may be of Nature's growth, and arise properly of themselves, without our art, promotion, or assistance, the general idea which is formed of all this management and the clear notion we attain of what is preferable and principal in all these subjects of choice and estimation will not, as I imagine, by any person be taken for innate. (II, 257)

Moreover, good taste is impossible "without the antecedent labour and pains of criticism." (*Ibid.*) The moral critic must make us aware of the principles of moral order, as the art critic does for the principles of good design.

Though the concepts of the good and the beautiful arise naturally in the individual under the normal conditions of community life, developing their full implications is a further, necessary step in self-development. Thus, Shaftesbury writes that "the great business in this (as in . . . the whole of life) is to correct our taste." [15] This calls for a critical process in which there is a fuller realization of our natural potentialities. This explains the importance for Shaftesbury of "good-breeding":

To philosophize, in a just signification, is but to carry good-breeding a step higher. . . . 'Tis not wit merely, but a temper which must form the well-bred man. In the same manner, 'tis not a head merely, but a heart and resolution which must complete the real philosopher. (II, 255)

Taste is the activity of judgment as a unity of reason and feeling; it is a response of the whole person to a moral or aesthetic object. Thus, it is susceptible to distortion either through intellectual or emotional failure. Shaftesbury's doctrine of taste is not a plea for emotional subjectivism or relativism. Good taste requires both the consistent employment of the intellect and the harmonious exercise of the affections.

Shaftesbury's concept of moral judgment is an attempted synthesis of two elements: one, an intuitive process in which one responds directly to moral objects, being either attracted or repelled by them; and two, a logical or discursive process utilizing such standards as the good of the whole and consistency. In his *Enquiry Concerning the Principles of Morals*, Hume distinguished between two schools of moral philosophy, one which considered the foundation of morals to be discursive reason, the other which considered it to be sentiment or "an immediate feeling and finer internal sense." [16] Unfortunately, he notes, the two conceptions have been employed inconsistently by many philosophers and without comprehension of their distinctness. And "the elegant Lord Shaftesbury, who first gave occasion to remark this distinction, and who, in general, adhered to the principles of the ancients, is not, himself, entirely free from the same confusion." [17] The charge is a serious one, and admittedly well-founded. Yet what Shaftesbury was attempting to do is suggested by a comment Hume himself makes after reviewing the arguments for these opposing theories. "These arguments on each side are so plausible, that I am apt to suspect, they may, the one as well as the other, be solid and satisfactory, and that *reason* and *sentiment* concur in almost all moral determinations and conclusions." [18] Rejecting the hypothesis that the discursive process and the intuitive or immediate response are necessarily discontinuous or contradictory, Shaftesbury tries to construct a synthesis in which the two are continuous, each functioning as an adjunct of the other. Thus, he writes in the notes to *Second Characters:*

> The philosopher and virtuoso alone capable to prove, demonstrate. But the idiot, the vulgar man can feel, recognise. The eye has sense of its own, a practice method peculiar and distinct from common reason or argumentation. Thus the equilibrium found so instantly in some creatures . . . , as well as all their other instincts, which our kind made by nature to rely on reason . . . possesses in a less degree.[19]

Logical and empirical analysis should confirm what immediate feeling makes known—but always with the condition that the affections themselves be ordered and harmonious. The two processes can serve as a check on each other. If immediate feeling misleads, the intellect may initiate a corrective process; and if the intellect errs, our intuitive response may suggest that something is out of gear. What Shaftesbury undertakes is complex and difficult, yet when his moral theory is compared with Hume's—each in the context of his philosophic system taken as a whole—Shaftesbury's seems finally more coherent. Hume's analysis, brilliant though it be, inflicts wounds his philosophy cannot heal. What Shaftesbury lacks in internal precision, he makes up for in a larger cohesiveness of thought. His moral theory, taken in the context of his vision of Nature and man, does have an overall cogency even though one rightfully wishes for greater clarity of detail.

One serious difficulty in Shaftesbury's discussions of the

intuitive element in moral consciousness is that he fails to make clear what exactly we intuit. At times he suggests that we intuit the rightness or wrongness of behavior in particular cases, i.e., we react immediately to the moral quality of the relationships involved. In other places he seems to be saying that we intuit general moral principles from which we may then deduce what is right in particular cases. And finally, there are numerous expressions of the view that we intuit values as ultimate ends of conduct. Intuition, as we use it here in reference to Shaftesbury's thought, means the immediate response of the whole mind to a moral object. It is not, however, a merely passive response; it is an active, creative movement of the imagination; it belongs to the formative powers of the mind. The good and the beautiful are ultimately known by intuition, and this is probably the fundamental sense in which this concept applies in his system. The meaning or content of the concept of good has to be developed by a combination of reason and feeling. The moral life is itself a continual process of realizing the meaning of the good.

In Shaftesbury's ethics, right action is that which is directed toward the common good or the public welfare; this is the primary ethical principle that the intellect uses in determining right behavior. Cumberland had considered "the common good of all" to be the supreme ethical principle to which all other moral rules were subordinate. Along similar lines, Shaftesbury argues that no creature is "absolute or complete" in itself if it exists in interdependence with other creatures but must be viewed as a functional part of a larger system of beings. The good for any creature is determined by the organic system of which it is a part; and the good for any system of beings is in turn determined by the larger system or systems of which it too is an organic part. This hierarchy of value-systems culminates, of course, in the Good of the Whole. An organic value-system is to be identified primarily by the fact that the vital elements composing it contribute by their activities to the welfare of the whole. Thus, it will be made up of creatures of a particular race or species "who have some one common nature, or are provided for by some one order or constitution of things subsisting together, and co-operating towards their conservation and support." (I, 245) Each particular system of beings points beyond itself in so far as it contributes to the welfare of some other functional whole, and thus it is in turn part of a larger system. Particular species of animals have their special forms of interrelation, but all are united, according to Shaftesbury, in all overall "animal-order." This in turn is comprehended in a larger system including vegetables, and so on in ever-widening circles of inclusion to the universal "system of all things." (I, 246) The good or "ill" of anything must always be gauged in terms of the organic system or context of which it is a functioning part. However, it must be remembered that Shaftesbury's contextualism is hierarchical in nature: the goodness or evilness of any particular being has to be measured ultimately in relation to the good of the total system of the universe. In the last analysis, "good" is objective and grounded in Nature. Shaftesbury is proposing that we do two things which he considers necessarily interrelated: first, that we undertake a contextual analysis of the moral elements in proximate systems; second, that we relate this to good or evil as applied to the cosmic system. Perhaps the most serious questions that we might raise would be with respect to the usefulness of this second process; yet for Shaftesbury it was of utmost importance. In applying his theory he suggests that the evil that we encounter in a particular individual or in a particular species is not *wholly* evil if it contributes in some way to the benefit of other individuals or to other species. Yet "evil" may be used in a relative sense of the behavior of an individual that is harmful to other members of his organic system. The rightness and wrongness of behavior is judged in relation to the context in which it occurs, and the larger the context in which we can view it, the more universal is the judgment we make. The most universal judgment would be that in relation to the Whole of reality. However, since a finite mind can evidently not comprehend the Whole of things, this seems to be more a theoretical ideal than an actually achievable stage. Yet Shaftesbury seems to be saying that in moments of enthusiasm we can attain such a vision of the Whole; moral judgment must be sustained by intuitive vision.

Earlier we saw the application of the same type of reasoning to the problem of the status of evil in the universe as a Whole. Shaftesbury's denial that there is any "real ill" in the cosmos leaves us with the question of whether he can at the same time argue consistently for the reality of moral evil. As we pointed out earlier, he combines a denial of ultimate evil with a recognition of the *actuality* of proximate or relative evil. Moral evil belongs in this second category. Yet if a moral error is not *really* evil, but a necessary part of an organically good Whole, is it really blameworthy? Once again it appears that Shaftesbury's metaphysical optimism is a faith that sustains aspiration rather than a set of principles from which one can deduce logical answers to the theoretical questions of the intellect. Shaftesbury is as fervent in his denunciation of moral evil as he is in his defense of the ultimate goodness of the cosmos; he finds no contradiction in the two.

Shaftesbury suggests another type of principle, that of "equity" or "equal affection," which appears to be subsidiary to and derived from the general principle of the common good. It is an essential element in his definition of virtue, which is defined as a "just disposition or proportionable affection of a rational creature towards the moral objects of right and wrong. . . ." (I, 258) An action is wrong when "done through insufficient or unequal affection (as when a son shows no concern for the safety of a father; or where there is need of succour, prefers an indifferent person to him). . . ." (I, 253) On the other hand, "equity" or right applies to an action based on affection that is appropriate to its object or fitting to the occasion. However, the fitness or unfitness of an affection to an object is determined by the context or system in which it occurs, as discussed above. "Equal affection" is socially advantageous; thus, it appears to be a further application of the principle of the common good.

The idea of harmony or right proportion which is so fundamental in Shaftesbury's metaphysics and aesthetics is equally important in his ethical theory, as his concept of equity reveals. The social affections are relational in nature: " 'Tis . . . on certain relations or respective proportions that all natural affection does in some measure depend." (II, 245) The moral sense judges the moral quality of relationships; equity demands that there be right proportion or true harmony between affections and their objects. Thus, harmony is a condition of virtue on every level of being, whether within man in the balance of the affections, or in society in the consonance of private and public interest, or in the universe in the conformity of man and Nature.

Shaftesbury regarded himself as a "realist" with respect to

moral theory, and an opponent of ethical nominalism. What he means by "realism" is the belief that virtue is

> really something in itself, and in the nature of things; not arbitrary or factitious (if I may so speak); not constituted from without, or dependent on custom, fancy, or will; not even on the supreme will itself, which can no way govern it; but being necessarily good is governed by it and ever uniform with it. (II, 53) [20]

Like the Cambridge Platonists, Shaftesbury repeatedly attacks both the Hobbesian view that morality has its ground in a social covenant, and the Calvinistic derivation of morality from the arbitrary will of an absolute Deity. True morality, according to Shaftesbury and the Cambridge men, was based upon eternal and immutable principles of right and wrong discoverable by the human reason. Right and wrong are not merely matters of opinion, or subject to the vagaries of fashion or custom; nor are they determined in their true nature by civil law as such. Shaftesbury argues that absolute moral relativists contradict themselves, for they inevitably make judgments which imply a reliance on standards which they must believe have some degree of objectivity or reliability. (II, 139) Even the hedonists are forced to introduce standards and rules into the process of discriminating among pleasures.

Shaftesbury's position is that the normal man inevitably develops a faculty for discriminating between "right" and "wrong." This faculty logically implies that moral judgments are true or false, and vary in degree of objectivity. Such judgments are impossible without standards or principles to guide them, and in Shaftesbury's cosmology these moral principles must ultimately be rooted in the structure of Nature itself. Moreover, he argues that there is greater agreement among men on moral issues than is evident on the surface. Not only do men agree more than is realized on basic values, but on moral principles as well; it is in the application that differences arise either because of misapprehension of the facts or an imbalance of the affections. "All own the standard, rule, and measure: but in applying it to things disorder arises, ignorance prevails, interest and passion breed disturbance." (II, 138) Shaftesbury tries to meet his opponents in ethical theory head-on, contending that vengefulness and pride both imply the acceptance of objective standards of worth that transcend mere self-concern. Even the wickedest of men have a sense of justice which makes them willing at times to sacrifice all other interests in avenging themselves for what they consider an unjust wrong done to them. Similarly, the proud man who attributes merit or worth to himself, seeing the same qualities that he admires in himself present in greater degree in another person, is "humbled" or "ashamed." "And thus," Shaftesbury concludes, "as long as I find men either angry or revengeful, proud or ashamed, I am safe," (II, 141) for it is evident that they recognize the validity of the distinction between the just and the unjust, and between the worthy and the unworthy. Though errors in application may and will be made, the distinction itself is "universally acknowledged, [and] . . . of nature's impression, naturally conceived. . . ." (II, 141)

We have previously described Shaftesbury's attack on Hobbes's doctrine of human nature, which is a central element of his criticism of Hobbes's ethics. Like Locke, Shaftesbury rejects Hobbes's contention that in "the state of Nature" there is no "right" or "wrong," and that moral obligation exists only where there is a commonwealth and a sovereign able to enforce a particular moral code. Power cannot constitute "right," nor can it be the ground of moral obligation, whether it be the delegated powers of the state or the absolute power of God. As one would expect, Shaftesbury also rejects Hobbes's attempt to define "good" and "evil" in terms of individual desires and aversions, or likes and dislikes. Shaftesbury's argument is that if we can reasonably ask if a particular desire or aversion is "good," the term "good" clearly means something more than desire as such. He contends that it is inconsistent to maintain that moral obligation exists *after* a commonwealth has been formed but not *before*, even if we accept Hobbes's view of the origin of society. If society is in fact based on a mutual covenant in which each person voluntarily surrenders his unlimited liberty to the sovereign, the pledge on which it rests must have been made originally in the state of Nature; "and that which could make a promise obligatory in the state of nature, must make all other acts of humanity as much our real duty and natural part." (I, 73) A man's obligation to keep his word must be based on something more than the mere fact that he has given his word. It must be grounded in moral values and principles that were effectively true prior to the making of the social contract, since without them the agreement made could have no morally effective binding force.[21]

Though Locke's moral theory was in some respects more acceptable to Shaftesbury, he reserved some of his most vehement criticism for it. He charges Locke with being one of those who made virtue a mere "name" or a matter of mere opinion, which Shaftesbury contends is as ridiculous as telling a musician that the laws of musical harmony are matters of individual opinion. Shaftesbury rejects Locke's theory that moral good and evil are decided by our degree of conformity to laws instituted by a lawmaker.[22] According to Locke, there are various levels of law—the "laws" of public opinion, civil laws, and ultimately, divine law sanctioned by rewards and punishments in a future life. The latter is the "true touchstone" of morality, an "eternal, immutable standard." Along with this, Locke believed in a natural, moral law which was discoverable by reason and which would be in effect in the state of Nature, i.e., even before a commonwealth was formed. Shaftesbury's objections center on Locke's denial of innate ideas, his emphasis on the sanction of retribution (both of which we have discussed previously), the legislative theory of morality, and Locke's concept of God, which Shaftesbury charges makes Him an arbitrary agent. In one of his letters, where Shaftesbury allows himself greater freedom in attacking his friend and teacher than elsewhere, he accuses him of making God

. . . free to [do] anything, that is however ill: for if He wills it, it will be made good; virtue may be vice, and vice virtue in its turn, if he pleases. And thus neither right nor wrong, virtue nor vice, are anything in themselves; nor is there any trace or idea of them naturally imprinted on human minds. Experience and our catechism teach us all! [23]

Yet Shaftesbury also shares some of Locke's convictions. At the end of the "Inquiry" Shaftesbury remarks that "if there be no article exceptionable in this scheme of moral arithmetic, the subject treated may be said to have an evidence as great as that which is found in numbers or mathematics." (I, 336) Locke also held that morality was as demonstrable as mathematics, and spoke of the "eternal and unalterable nature of right and wrong." But Shaftesbury regards this aspect of Locke's thought as inconsistent with the voluntarism and authoritarianism expressed elsewhere. Evidently Shaftesbury felt, as later commentators have, that Locke had failed to reconcile natural and revealed moral law adequately. Shaftesbury himself insists that God as well as man must conform to "the eternal measures and immutable independent nature of worth and virtue." (I, 255)

Throughout Shaftesbury's discussion of the nature of virtue, it is evident that he thinks of the process of moral knowledge and judgment as a complex fusion of intellect and emotion. His organic model of the nature of man demands this. Shaftesbury's approach again reflects that of the Latitudinarian divines and the Cambridge Platonists; liberal churchmen had stressed the importance of benevolent feeling as an element of moral virtue.[24] Isaac Barrow, for example, wrote that "the practice of benignity, of courtesy, of clemency at first sight, without any discursive reflection, doth obtain approbation and applause from us; being no less grateful and amiable to the mind than beauty to our eyes, harmony to our ears. . . ."[25] The Cambridge school avoided a wholly "rationalistic" approach to ethics by conceiving (in Cassirer's words) "the fundamental power of the intellect itself as the pure power of love."[26] Henry More, whose *Enchiridion Ethicum* Shaftesbury praised as "a right good Piece of sound Morals,"[27] defined virtue as an intellectual "Power" or "Energy" of the soul by which "the Passions are so subdued, as in every Case to be able to prosecute that which is the most perfect Good."[28] Though the true and the good are discerned by the intellect, their "sweetness and delight" are "relished by the Boniform Faculty,"[29] an "inward Sense" which enables us to take pleasure in what is best, and creates in us an "unquenchable thirst and affection" for it. "The Desires of the Soul fly not to their Object, as it is intelligible, but as it is good or congruous. . . ."[30] Thus, the emotions play a necessary and positive role in the virtuous life.

Shaftesbury may also have been influenced (as mentioned in Chapter X) by Richard Cumberland's theory of the involuntary element in the shaping of moral character. Cumberland theorized that involuntary impulses from within the self lead to behavior which is satisfying. External stimuli also cause certain involuntary responses which reflect our inner impulses too. The consciousness of the satisfactions gained in these processes generates man's conscious efforts to do "good." For Cumberland, as for Shaftesbury, the basic impulses of man provide the content and original ground of our conceptions of right and wrong. The voluntary self develops what is already implicit in the structure of the involuntary self: "art" develops "Nature" but does not supplant it.

Like the Cambridge men, Shaftesbury insists that one must *be* good before one can really *know* good. The knowledge of good is not a merely intellectual process; it involves the affectional life, the "trial or exercise of the heart." (I, 252) For "wisdom is more from the Heart than from the Head. Feel Goodness, and you will see all Things fair and good." [31] The historian Höffding called Shaftesbury "the first philosopher of feeling" in both the good and bad sense.[32] Indeed, it is particularly this aspect of the English philosopher's thought that has been criticized for two centuries. Richard Price accused him of making moral judgment subject to the dictates of blind instinct without the intervention of the intellect.[33] Höffding interpreted him as setting "immediate feeling . . . in opposition to discursive reason." Irving Babbitt charged that he "undermines insidiously decorum, the central doctrine of the classicist, at the very time that he seems to be defending it." [34] Even his commentator, Fowler, criticized Shaftesbury's moral theory on grounds that "almost the whole stress is laid on the benevolent affections and the 'Moral Sense,' while but little is said either of the controlling power of the Reason over the Passions, or of the share which the Reason takes in estimating the character of our acts." [35] Certainly one has ample ground for wishing that Shaftesbury had analyzed in more detail the role of discursive reason in moral judgment, yet these charges seem to be unjustified on the whole both in the light of Shaftesbury's intentions and in relation to what he actually says in the *Characteristics*. He makes it quite clear that the control of the affections and the will is an essential part of the activity as well as the responsibility of reason. However, since the affections are the "springs of action," the rational mind would be immobilized without them. Furthermore, the affections—particularly the social affections—give content to what would otherwise be a merely abstract sense of duty or good. The relation of the affections and the intellect is reciprocal, for an affectional imbalance may distort our reasoning processes, just as false reasoning may misdirect or misguide the application of our impulses. If Shaftesbury had actually done what the above critics suggest, he would have had to admit that children were as capable of virtue as adults, since they have the basic impulses, though lacking in a developed intellectual capacity. But in the *Inquiry* he clearly states that to be "capable of virtue" and of having a moral sense, a person must not only have the natural affections but also reason or "a reflecting faculty." (I, 266) In comparing men and other animals, Shaftesbury states that virtue is not attributed to animals, since they lack the idea of the public good and they are incapable of the "science of what is morally good or ill." (I, 252) While in his moral theory he gives recognition to the positive function of the emotions in the structure of virtue, he never goes as far as Hume, who spoke of reason as the "slave of the passions." Rather he thinks of the powers of discursive reason as standing in reciprocal interdependence with the emotions. Reason plays a key role in establishing the setting within which the affections function; and the affections in turn provide the materials with which the moral reason must operate. Knowledge apart from feeling can only give us empty forms—skeletal abstractions. Shaftesbury seems to be suggesting, though there is no clear doctrine formulated, that the emotions not only provide the materials for knowledge but are in some degree cognitive functions themselves.

In Shaftesbury's conception of "conscience," the complex interweaving of affectional and intellectual processes is illustrated further. He argues that every rational creature necessarily reflects upon his own thoughts, feelings, actions, and character, to some degree. This process of self-inspection is not only generated by one's own inner self-development but is also stimulated by both the criticism and the flattery of others. In the course of it,

there are two things which to a rational creature must be horridly offensive and grievous, viz. "To have the reflection in his mind of any unjust action or behaviour which he knows to be naturally odious and ill-deserving; or of any foolish action or behaviour which he knows to be prejudicial to his own interest or happiness." (I, 305)

The first of these, according to Shaftesbury, is "alone properly called Conscience, whether in a moral or religious sense." (*Ibid.*) Previously, we examined his contention that in itself the fear of God did not imply conscience in the true moral sense. Conscience in the true sense involves an apprehension of what is morally wrong in itself, i.e., apart from other considerations that may be related but are not essential to the distinction between right and wrong. Conscience is the awareness of the moral deformity of one's own behavior, which is accompanied by feelings of shame as well as by regret at having incurred both one's own displeasure and that of others.[36] The second type of self-review referred to above—"conscience from interest"—though also a characteristic of the rational mind, is not moral conscience in the strict sense, but merely an awareness of what affects one's own self-interest. Where there is a "sense of moral deformity," an individual inevitably recognizes that certain actions are in principle wrong and, thus, "deserve" retaliation in kind by God or man. However, even when this moral sense (or moral conscience) is deficient, Shaftesbury argues, the individual must still see in some degree that evil actions may in fact provoke like actions in response, and thus may be contrary to one's interest. This latter is "conscience from interest," which appears, therefore, to be based on a knowledge of fact rather than on an awareness of moral values as such.

Irving Babbitt has charged Shaftesbury with contributing to the errors of the Rousseauian moralists by "his transformation of conscience from an inner check into an expansive emotion."[37] Yet it is clear in the above account that Shaftesbury does conceive of conscience as being an "inner check" or a means of self-regulation. Babbitt's term "expansive emotion" has more relevance to Shaftesbury's concept of enthusiasm than to his concept of conscience. Conscience is a rational, reflective process of moral judgment by which, with the co-operation of the will, an inward process of self-correction may be initiated, that, if it is thoroughgoing enough, will result in changes in one's behavior. There are certain passages, though, which undoubtedly contributed to Babbitt's misunderstanding, as, for example:

A man of thorough good breeding . . . is incapable of doing a rude or brutal action. He never deliberates in this case, or considers of the matter by prudential rules of self-interest and advantage. He acts from his nature, in a manner necessarily, and without reflection. . . . (I, 86)

But it should be clear that Shaftesbury is formulating an ideal here which he does not claim anyone has attained or ever will except in degree. The ideally virtuous man doesn't say, "X is the morally right action, but perhaps it would be to my advantage to do otherwise." When there is true freedom of mind, true self-mastery, and a true harmony of feeling and intellect, then and then only would an individual's immediate response to a moral issue be consistently correct, and his behavior always right. But even the best of men fall far short of this ideal, "and thus vice and virtue are found variously mixed, and alternately prevalent in the several characters of mankind. . . . it is as hard to find a man wholly ill as wholly good. . . ." (I, 257)

This same model of the "truly well-bred man" was also, no doubt, the basis for another related criticism that has sometimes been made of Shaftesbury's ethical theory, that men "may be Virtuous and Sociable without Self-denial . . . ," as expressed by Mandeville.[38] Shaftesbury never contended that virtue was easy, nor should his belief that virtue was "natural" ever be construed in that sense. Imperfect man cannot be virtuous without "self-denial," that is, without conquest of the false self and control of the passions. He wrote of his own struggle to be an "honest man": "Other people may be born to these qualities. It is my misfortune to be such as that I cannot but

esteem thought, exercise, and a continual application to be
necessary in this case for me." [39] While one who is not strongly
tempted may be "more cheaply virtuous," Shaftesbury regards
the person who overcomes great temptations as having the
greater virtue. However, recognizing that this might make evil
affections a necessary condition of moral worth, he denies that
"a propensity to vice can be an ingredient in virtue, or any way
necessary to complete a virtuous character." (I, 256) Shaftesbury would have been wiser if he had followed through with
the logic of his position and admitted that in the world order
evil impulses existed necessarily, but for the purpose of being
conquered. In "The Moralists," he argues more consistently:
"What merit except from hardship? What virtue without a
conflict, and the encounter of such enemies as arise both within
and from abroad?" (II, 110) Men naturally feel a division
within themselves between a better self—the "true and natural
self"—and a worse self. (I, 183) This is the basis of Shaftesbury's method of inward dialogue or "soliloquy," which he
regards as an essential means of self-knowledge and self-
mastery. By imagining that he is "two distinct persons" the
individual may examine himself and his conduct with the hope
of understanding and improvement. (I, 105) This method is
another aspect of Shaftesbury's concept of rational self-reflec-
tion or "conscience." The truly evil person cannot engage in
this "inward colloquy" because he cannot really face himself.

Shaftesbury's attempt to analyze the dynamic interrelationships of emotion and intellect is further illustrated in his concept of vice. Basically, he thinks of vice as a result of the
imbalance or corruption of the affections. Thus, his discussion
of the affections is at the same time a description of the potentialities for vice in human nature. Moral corruption results

from the excess of either the self-directed or social affections, or from the presence of any of the unnatural affections. Shaftesbury's position leads him logically to argue that an error in sense-perception or "a mistake in fact, being no cause or sign of ill affection, can be no cause of vice." (I, 254) He is not denying that such mistakes may be the cause of an error in judgment; rather he is insisting that moral character is not *necessarily* reflected in each perception or assessment of fact. However, errors in moral belief or in basic moral attitudes *are* a cause of wickedness. Such errors are, in turn, associated by Shaftesbury with "unequal affection"—affection that is inappropriate to its object. An example that he gives is the belief that it is preferable to save a cat rather than one's parent. As a moral belief this is wrong, and its cause would be a deficiency of natural affection. Good character, then, cannot be destroyed by particular errors in perception or even by particular errors in moral judgment. (I, 209) What is "right" to do in a given situation "may even to the most discerning part of mankind appear difficult, and of doubtful decision. . . ." (I, 254) Only when there are repeated and "gross mistakes in the assignment or application of the affection[s] . . . is . . . virtue forfeited. And thus we find how far worth and virtue depend on a knowledge of right and wrong, and on a use of reason, sufficient to secure a right application of the affections. . . ." (I, 254 f.)

Shaftesbury implies but fails to develop clearly a distinction between the problem of goodness of character and that of the rightness of an action. His follower, Hutcheson, made a relevant extension of his ideas: an action is "formally good" when it is motivated by good affections, or issues from good will and the love of moral excellence; an action is "materially good" when it is conducive to the good of the system of which it is a part.[40] A given action, therefore, may be "formally" though not "materially" good, and vice versa. Hutcheson insists though that for the virtuous man it is not enough to have good intentions; he must seek to determine the means by which the happiness of mankind can best be attained. To know what is formally good requires an intellectual analysis of the relevant facts in the situation involved. This approach seems basically in line with Shaftesbury's. In the latter's attempt to maintain a dynamic balance between emotion and intellect, he seeks to provide a positive place for the natural affections as the ground and source of virtue, while recognizing that the intellect must develop conscious conceptions of right and wrong, good and evil, and must direct the application of the basic impulses accordingly. A knowledge of the facts would be essential in deciding what means to employ in attaining one's moral goals; but it would be important in another sense too—for one would presumably have to know the character of an object in order to respond with the appropriate affections. But Shaftesbury's emphasis is clearly on the need for right affection rather than for factual knowledge.

Both the moral and aesthetic points of view are, for Shaftesbury, fundamentally "disinterested." Thus, for example, he distinguishes between the emotions of "shame" and "grief" or "fear." Of one who experiences shame, he writes: "The disorder he feels is from a sense of what is shameful and odious in itself, not of what is hurtful or dangerous in its consequences." (II, 139) Grief and fear are involved with considerations of self-interest; they do not generate shame, which is essentially different from them. To be ashamed of a particular action one has done is to recognize it as in principle evil; it is not merely to fear its consequences or its effect upon one's own interests. Shame may be accompanied by such considerations, but they are not necessary constituents of it. The same type of analysis is made of anger such as is aroused by an injury inflicted upon one by some other person. Shaftesbury argues that such anger implies a sense of the distinction between justice and injustice. He points out that the angry man who seeks revenge may knowingly do so at the expense of his own interests or to the extent of sacrificing his "very being to it." (II, 140) Both shame and vengefulness prove that there is a disinterested moral sense which transcends considerations of self-interest. Yet, as Sidgwick has pointed out, when Shaftesbury undertakes to answer the question, "Why be virtuous?" he often appeals to self-interest. Indeed, a primary purpose of the "Inquiry" is to establish that virtue alone brings true happiness. The moral man seeks virtue for its own sake, yet knows the path of virtue is the path of happiness. Can one reconcile this concept of the disinterested love of virtue with the intellectual recognition that virtue is ultimately to one's own *true* interest? This problem and those related to it will be dealt with in the following chapter.

CHAPTER THIRTEEN

VIRTUE and HAPPINESS

Though Shaftesbury believes that our "chief interest" is to know wherein our true "happiness" lies, he rejects the theory that either happiness or good are to be defined as "what is pleasing." "For if that which pleases us be our good because it pleases us, anything may be our interest or good. . . . No one can learn what real good is. Nor can any one upon this foot be said to understand his interest." (I, 200) Or, as he writes in "The Moralists":

When will and pleasure are synonymous; when everything which pleases us is called pleasure, and we never choose or prefer but as we please; 'tis trifling to say "Pleasure is our good." For this has as little meaning as to say, "We choose what we think eligible"; and "We are pleased with what delights or pleases us." The question is "whether we are rightly pleased, and choose as we should do?" (II, 29)

The hedonistic identification of "pleasure" and "good" reduces itself, upon analysis, to a tautology with little ethical meaning. This seems more of an anticipation of G. E. Moore's "naturalistic fallacy" than A. N. Prior recognizes.[1] Shaftesbury undoubtedly had Locke in mind as well as the traditional hedonists, for Locke had stated that "good and evil . . . are nothing but pleasure or pain, or that which occasions or procures pleasure or pain to us." [2] Those who identify pleasure and good must, however, tell us "which or what sort" of pleasures they are talking about, for otherwise, Shaftesbury reasons, they provide us with no stable grounds for choice. If we take as our guide the pleasant feelings of the moment, we soon find that they constantly change and reverse themselves in the most contradictory manner. No orderly pattern of life could be based upon them. Nor does the identification of "evil" with "pain" help. What is pleasant or painful at one moment may be the reverse at another moment; what is pain at one moment may by its mere cessation produce pleasure in the next moment. Almost every type of sensation has been considered pleasurable by someone or other at some time: "Is not malice and cruelty of the highest relish with some natures?" (II, 30) Therefore, Shaftesbury argues that

either all pleasure is good, or only some. If all, then every kind of sensuality must be precious and desirable. If some only, then we are to seek what kind, and discover, if we can, what it is which distinguishes between one pleasure and another, and makes one indifferent, sorry, mean; another valuable and worthy. And by this stamp, this character, if there be any such, we must define good. . . . (II, 31)

The appeal to the "immediate feeling" of pleasure is not a reliable ground for moral choice. Children have senses as susceptible to pleasure as adults, and animals, sometimes, even keener sensibilities, yet in neither case do we regard their pleasures as necessarily "good." Though Shaftesbury places considerable reliance on the testimony of "immediate feeling" in his discussion of the value of the social affections, here he makes it clear that immediate feeling as such cannot be made the defining quality or sufficient condition of the idea of good. He sees the error of trying to ground morality on the slippery morass of subjective feeling. Everyone, he notes, values his own enjoyment, but the true value of a pleasant experience can only be assessed by an objective analysis of the context in which it occurs. A pleasant feeling can be said to be "good" in the true sense only when it has been validated in relation to its individual and social setting. Like his Stoic masters, Shaftesbury concludes that "pleasure is no rule of good . . ." (I, 200); it is pleasure rather that must be judged by the standard of the good.

Sidgwick writes that

in the greater part of his argument Shaftesbury interprets the "good" of the individual hedonistically, as equivalent to pleasure, satisfaction, delight, enjoyment. But it is to be observed that the conception of "Good" with which he begins is not definitely hedonistic; "interest or good" is at first taken to mean the "right state of a creature," that "is by nature forwarded and by himself affectionately sought"; and in one passage he seems to conceive of a "planetary system" as having an end or good. Still, when the application of the term is narrowed to human beings, he slides— almost unconsciously—into a purely hedonistic interpretation of it. Indeed, he defines Philosophy itself as "the study of happiness." [3]

But this is misleading, for as our analysis above revealed, Shaftesbury did not identify pleasure and the good. If hedonism is defined as the belief that pleasure is the only intrinsic value, Shaftesbury was clearly not a hedonist. The fact that he regarded the good of man as coincident with his ultimate happiness does not make him a hedonist in the strict sense. Though hedonists have commonly failed to distinguish between "pleasure" and "happiness," and, like Mill, have all too often used these concepts with a confusing variety of connotations, Shaftesbury does differentiate between them. He generally associates "pleasure" with particular pleasant feelings or sensations which may be caused by either physical or mental stimuli. "Happiness" connotes a general state of well-being which is primarily mental, but ideally includes physical well-being too. "Happiness" is not merely a succession of pleasant feelings; it is an order of being in which the whole is more than the sum of its parts. As Shaftesbury's conception of man and Nature requires, it is a state of well-being characterized by harmony within the individual as well as harmony between the individual and his physical, biological, and spiritual environment.

It is true, though, that Shaftesbury does not rigorously maintain this distinction between pleasure and happiness at every point in his language. As a graceful stylist, he does not use words only with logical considerations in mind, but he seeks to persuade by the grace of his rhetoric as well as by his logic. Moreover, his glowing accounts of the pleasures of the social affections and the displeasures of the unnatural affections might lend themselves to a hedonistic interpretation. Yet, despite this, his position on this issue is on the whole clear and consistent. It is essentially a form of eudaemonism for, like Aristotle, he regards the highest good as a state of well-being (or happiness) in which the individual is actively realizing his potentialities as a rational or spiritual being, i.e., his distinctively human possibilities. Thus, for Shaftesbury, though happiness is constituted by particular pleasant feelings, it is not attained by any random group or succession of such feelings, but only by those sets of feelings which contribute to a harmony within as well as a harmony without.

Shaftesbury thinks of the hedonists—the "men of pleasure"—as proponents of "mere pleasure" as distinguished from "real enjoyment." "Mere pleasure" means for him primarily the more immediate sensual pleasures, while "real enjoyment" is primarily composed of the deeper and longer-lasting satisfactions of the mind. He argues that the hedonists, in attempting to include mental satisfactions under the term "pleasure," are guilty of "a collusion and a plain receding from the common notion of the word." (II, 32) Rather unfairly, he charges "modern epicures" with being unable to appreciate "purely mental" satisfactions, despite their professions to the contrary. At any rate, he takes the position of the Stoics, and for that matter, of Epicurus, that the satisfactions of the mind are superior to those of the body. As evidence of the priority of mind over body, he points to the fact that for the sake of a mental conception, or an idea of what is right, men can endure the greatest physical torments. Furthermore, preoccupation with a mental problem may make sensual pleasure impossible at a given time. Elsewhere though Shaftesbury admits that sensual pleasures can also have an adverse effect on the enjoyments of the mind, since "the eagerness and irritation of mere pleasure is as disturbing as the importunity and vexation of pain." (I, 33) However, Shaftesbury never advocates an ascetic denial of physical pleasures but recommends temperance. Such pleasures may contribute to the total sum of one's happiness but they must be enjoyed as accompaniments of the more fundamental social and mental satisfactions.

Both Shaftesbury and Hutcheson distinguish between pleasure or satisfaction on a qualitative rather than a merely quantitative basis. They can do this consistently because they are not committed to the principle that pleasure is the only intrinsic value. Shaftesbury regards a number of values as having intrinsic worth. He provides no list, but among them would be not only the basic triad of beauty, truth, and good, but others such as love, justice, and virtue. Thus, the quality of a pleasure has to be measured by the context in which it is experienced, and in relation to a constellation of intrinsic values. Though Shaftesbury does not pose the question, his treatment of values implies that a particular value need not be considered as exclusively instrumental or intrinsic, but may be of a mixed nature. There is good reason to interpret his philosophy as implying further that all intrinsic values are at the same time instrumental values to some degree.[4]

Again, though Shaftesbury does not explicitly formulate it, he seems to have recognized the hedonistic paradox. At any rate, he clearly teaches that to pursue pleasure as one's sole end, either for this life or the next, will not lead to true enjoyment. (I, 218) Furthermore, his doctrine seems to be that happiness is an intrinsic element or accompaniment of the virtuous life, but that to attain it one must not, indeed in the strict sense cannot, seek it directly.

The problem of determining what the true good is cannot be separated in Shaftesbury's thought from the problem of determining what true happiness consists of. Thus, Philocles asks to know "what that good is, or where, which can afford contentment and satisfaction always alike, without variation or diminution." (II, 35) Theocles's response is significant: though he does not profess to answer the question in full, he offers to show Philocles where that good may be found within his own experience, i.e., in love and friendship, which are sources of continual satisfaction and "increasing joy." Here then, he says, is "that fixed and constant good you sought." (I, 36)

Like the Stoics, Shaftesbury believes that the conditions for our true happiness and good lie within ourselves and within our own power. Thus, he also follows them in stressing the importance of "opinion" in attaining the good life: "The affections of love and hatred, liking and dislike, on which the happiness or prosperity of the person so much depends, being influenced and governed by opinion, the highest good or happiness must depend on right opinion and the highest misery be derived from wrong." (II, 277) We must, therefore, "regulate fancy and rectify opinion, on which all depends." (II, 278) Shaftesbury accepts the Stoic principle that our assent or judgment plays a crucial role in determining how the excitations of sense affect our will and, therefore, our behavior. Our opinion of what is "good" has a vital effect on our chances for happiness.

In his analysis of that which is our evil or our good, Shaftesbury writes: "That which being present can never leave the mind at rest, but must of necessity cause aversion, is its ill. . . . In the same manner, that which being absent can never leave the mind at rest, or without disturbance and regret, is of necessity its good." (II, 276 f.) Thus, the "good" is a necessity of man's nature if he is to attain true satisfaction. It follows that what we do not really need for contentment is *not* our true good. Shaftesbury repeats the Stoic argument that if we can be happy without the so-called "goods" which depend on external factors, i.e., material possessions as well as fame and worldly power, then our true good does not consist in them. It lies rather in the development of our inward potentialities. He does not, however, advocate that we abandon all worldly possessions or ambitions; rather he asks that we see them in the proper perspective. He is aware that our real problem is assigning priorities to these inward and outward values, to intrinsic and extrinsic goods, in order to guide our actual decisions. He knows that every choice of values means giving something up for the sake of something else, "since everything in this world goes by exchange. Nothing is had for nothing." (II, 151) Shaftesbury's conception of happiness allows him to consider a man in a sense "happy" even though experiencing discomfort or unpleasant sensations. *True* happiness is a product of deeper levels of satisfaction. Thus, the virtuous man may undergo hardship and self-denial, and yet be essentially "happy" at the same time.

The highest good is not the "tumultuous joy" of unregulated passions but a "constant, fixed, and regular joy, which carries tranquillity along with it, and which has no rejolt. . . ." [5] Shaftesbury concludes that

> if I join the opinion of good to the possessions of the mind, if it be in the affections themselves that I place my highest joy, and in those objects, whatever they are, of inward worth and beauty (such as honesty, faith, integrity, friendship, honour), 'tis evident I can never possibly, in this respect, rejoice amiss or indulge myself too far in the enjoyment. (II, 279)

Since true happiness is conditional upon the inner state of one's mind, the activities of conscience become a major source of inner pleasure or displeasure. "Moral conscience," as we saw, is a process of self-review in which our unjust actions arouse shame and regret, and our just actions, by contrast, give satisfaction. And if it be supposed that being without conscience would be an advantage, Shaftesbury responds that this would be to lack "natural affection," the primary source of happiness, and thus to be the most miserable of all creatures!

He argues further that those who have no clear notion of

right and wrong, or whose moral beliefs are inconsistent, will also be unhappy as a result. They will be caught by self-contradictory emotions for they lack "any fixed principle at all, any real standard or measure" by which they can regulate their "esteem or . . . approbation." (I, 307) The resulting contradictions in their behavior will be a source of misery. In fact, Shaftesbury proposes the paradox that if one is going to be immoral one had better be a complete scoundrel rather than a halfway one, for there is more chance of happiness then. "True interest is wholly on one side or the other. All between is inconsistency, irresolution, remorse, vexation . . . a perpetual discord. . . ." (I, 87) So the man who considers himself justified to do even *one* thing that he clearly knows is morally wrong, will be caught in a never-ending indecision as to why he should not do further wrong.

The heart of Shaftesbury's argument in the "Inquiry" is designed to establish that (1) "to have the natural [i.e., social] affections . . . is to have the chief means and power of self-enjoyment; and that to want them is certain misery and ill" (I, 293); (2) to have the self-directed impulses in excess is to be miserable; and (3) "to have the unnatural affections is to be miserable in the highest degree." (*Ibid.*) Since the evidence for the second proposition has been dealt with in Chapter X, I will discuss the first and third propositions here, but in reverse order.

Shaftesbury denies that the unnatural affections can give *true* satisfactions. The pleasure that may accompany them is analogous to that we feel when some great pain is alleviated. "So the fiercest and most raging torments of the mind do, by certain moments of relief, afford the greatest of mental enjoyments to those who know little of the truer kind." (I, 334) But obviously the worth of such pleasure must be devalued in proportion to the pain preceding it, on which it depends. Furthermore, the unnatural affections not only deprive us of the pleasures of knowing we merit the love of others, but by arousing the hatred of others they lead us to fear and distrust them:

> . . . everything around must appear ghastly and horrid; everything hostile and, as it were, bent against a private and single being, who is thus divided from everything, and at defiance and war with the rest of Nature.
> 'Tis thus, at last, that a mind becomes a wilderness, where all is laid waste, everything fair and goodly removed, and nothing extant beside what is savage and deformed. (I, 335)

Shaftesbury, who did so much to still the fires of the other-worldly hell, creates in its place a secular counterpart—a nightmare of isolation and of the estrangement of man from man, foreshadowing one of the characteristic themes of modern literature. What Hobbes defined as the "state of Nature," Shaftesbury describes as that unnatural condition into which man is plunged when he denies his true nature.

Shaftesbury's prime interest is to convince us that strong social affections are the source of the "highest happiness." Having already established that the mental pleasures are superior to the physical, he goes on to connect them with the social affections. "The mental enjoyments are either actually the very natural affections themselves in their immediate operation, or . . . are no other than their effects." (I, 294) He contends that the social affections and the related mental satisfactions manifestly provide "a more intense, clear, and undisturbed pleasure" than the sensual pleasures. (I, 295) In an argument that anticipates J. S. Mill, Shaftesbury contends that the superiority of the social-mental pleasures to the private-sensual pleasures is borne out by the fact that those who have experienced both equally will "ever" prefer the former. Another argument that Shaftesbury employs is that the sensual pleasures decline in intensity when separated from the social affections upon which they are actually dependent. For example, the physical satisfactions of sexual love are greater or less depending on the sociomental context in which they occur. Even prostitutes "know very well how necessary it is that everyone whom they entertain with their beauty should believe there are satisfactions reciprocal, and that pleasures are no less given than received." (I, 310) Sensual pleasures cannot bring any significant contentment when they are isolated from all "natural affection." Indeed, all pleasures are greater when communicated and shared with others.

Man's pre-eminently social nature renders him of all creatures least able to bear enforced solitude. The pleasure of sharing satisfactions with others is so great that it pervades all types of life, whether virtuous or vicious. "So insinuating are these pleasures of sympathy, and so widely diffused through our whole lives, that there is hardly such a thing as satisfaction or contentment of which they make not an essential part." (I, 298) Everyone to some extent desires to have someone with whom he can share "his good," or someone whose welfare he can be concerned with: "'Tis to this soothing hope and expectation of friendship that almost all our actions have some reference." (I, 299) Indeed, Shaftesbury suggests that if a man had no friends, he would invent them. The consciousness of the esteem of others is such an essential form of satisfaction for normal beings that it is almost impossible for a rational man to live without having it in some degree, even if it is a fiction of his imagination. But these social joys are not merely of instrumental value—they have intrinsic value. "To love, and to be kind; to have social or natural affection, complacency, and good-will, is to feel immediate satisfaction and genuine content. 'Tis in itself original joy, depending on no preceding pain or uneasiness, and producing nothing beside satisfaction merely." (I, 334) The social affections prove to be the only constant source of pleasure and enduring satisfaction.

But the degree and duration of this satisfaction is conditioned by the breadth of the affection involved, or its *wholeness*. Thus, Shaftesbury distinguishes between "entire affection" and "partial affection." If one's social impulses are directed toward only a part of the system to which one belongs, one is bound to fall into inconsistencies and self-contradictions that will limit the ultimate satisfaction-value of the affection. On the other hand, "entire affection," which is directed toward the whole of the system or species, transcends these inconsistencies through commitment to a higher unity. It not only provides the ideal object for our outgoing social energies, thus giving them their highest fulfillment, but it "carries with it a consciousness of merited love and approbation from all society, from all intelligent creatures, and from whatever is original to all other intelligence." (I, 301)

It is clear that Shaftesbury thinks of the highest good as being attained by an active movement of the human spirit rather than by a passive response. Moreover, the joys of active goodness, or of the realization of good affection, are greater than those of purely intellectual or theoretical contemplation. Though Shaftesbury rates the pleasures of the theoretical intellect very high, and finds them grounded in the love of that harmony which underlies all Nature, he considers them to be yet "far surpassed by virtuous motion, and the exercise of benignity and goodness. . . ." (I, 296) In virtuous action, the love of harmony attains its concrete realization; the potential becomes actual—abstract form is given its sufficient content.

Since the substance of virtue is the social affections, and since the social affections are the source of our greatest joy, it follows that virtue is the true source of happiness. And since vice is the product of the imbalance or destruction of social affection, it is the ultimate source of misery. As Shaftesbury concludes the "Inquiry": "Virtue, which of all excellencies and beauties is the chief and most amiable . . . is that by which alone man can be happy, and without which he must be miserable. And thus virtue is the good, and vice the ill of every one." (I, 338)

An examination of Shaftesbury's arguments for the happiness of virtue reveals that he follows two patterns—the one deductive and the other inductive. He argues on the one hand that a "sound theist" who believes in a Supreme Mind, ruling all for the best, must deduce from this that virtue is "naturally good and advantageous for man." (I, 277) On the other hand, Shaftesbury appeals to our experience of the social impulses to convince us that his conclusion is correct. Indeed, he reasons that " 'tis in a manner impossible to have any great opinion of the happiness of virtue without conceiving high thoughts of the satisfaction resulting from the generous admiration and love of it; and nothing beside the experience of such a love is likely to make this satisfaction credited." (I, 275) This duality of argument runs throughout the whole of Shaftesbury's ethics, and it is interesting that Locke exhibits the same tendency. Locke suggests in one place that one might deduce moral principles from the concept of the nature of God and man; on the other hand, he seeks to derive moral ideas from experience.

Taking Shaftesbury's ethical theory as a whole, it would be difficult to say on which of these he places the greater weight. Evidently, he sees no contradiction in the two approaches but regards them as complementary. While his model of God and man is of central importance in his ethics, he recognizes that his argument, to be finally convincing, must coincide with the directly apprehended forms of consciousness.

However, Shaftesbury's appeal to experience is not to a merely passive response of the mind to the materials of sensation. Intelligent thought requires that the mind act creatively upon its materials rather than merely respond to them. Without such a creative and synthetic movement of thought, experience would be a meaningless flux. In this respect Shaftesbury is a kind of pre-Kantian advocate of *a priori* principles, but such principles have no meaning apart from experience. Again there is a dual process implied: on the one hand, intelligible form is imposed upon experience, and on the other, experience impresses upon us the patterns of meaningful form. The mind that is capable of grasping intelligible form is the mind that is at one and the same time active, free, and "open."

While Shaftesbury's ethical system when viewed as a whole has a strong element of utilitarianism in it, it is clear from our analysis of it that it is far from the hedonistic and quantitative utilitarianism of Bentham. It is closer to John Stuart Mill, and shares some of the areas of vagueness and imprecision of Mill's philosophy, yet on the whole it is more consistent, given Shaftesbury's concept of Nature and man. Shaftesbury's utilitarianism might be described as "ideal utilitarianism," or perhaps better as "ideal theistic utilitarianism," for he does not advocate the greatest increase of pleasure as such, but the maximization of the good. The true happiness that virtue alone can bring is not "mere pleasure," but rather the fulfillment of the laws of our inner being. One must not strive directly for pleasure or happiness, but rather for the good as embodied in a set of values.

The "right" action is always that alternative which leads to the greater good. The content of "good" is defined in terms of the social affections and the self-affections, though sometimes the term actually seems to function in his system as a kind of unanalyzable and indefinable concept. Shaftesbury's attempt to bring together an ethical system combining intuitionism with a metaphysical theory encompassing a doctrine of natural law pervading man and Nature is impressive despite its weakness in precision of detail.

As mentioned earlier, a key element of his theory is the belief that there is a constellation of intrinsic values, the experience or realization of which gives immediate satisfaction. Thus, he writes that men have a natural sense or "imagination" of the beautiful and good, and that they must seek that which embodies these qualities not merely for their instrumental value but "as excellent in themselves, necessarily attractive of my admiration, and directly and immediately causing my happiness and giving me satisfaction." (II, 278) This appeal to immediate satisfaction is the final appeal which Shaftesbury makes to his reader, since apart from this all of his other arguments would seem insufficient to convince the skeptic.

From Bishop Butler on, a perennial criticism of Shaftesbury has been that he failed to resolve with clarity the problem of obligation. Butler thought that Shaftesbury had erred in stressing moral taste at the expense of the sense of duty, and in granting insufficient strength to the authority of conscience. But Shaftesbury understood that duty for duty's sake was an empty abstraction when isolated from those values that are experienced in the human community. He realized that apart from the direct experience of the satisfaction found in realizing those values the sense of obligation was finally empty. Sidgwick points out that Shaftesbury often appeals to our self-interest. However, it must not be forgotten that Shaftesbury understood this as an appeal to man's *true* interests, which could only be attained through the realization of his potentialities as a rational and spiritual being. Altruism, for Shaftesbury, is a sacrifice of the lesser for the greater good. It is in this context that one must understand his advocacy of self-sacrifice. The giving of self to that which is more than self is in one sense *selfless* and in another *selfish*. It is selfless in that it may require hardship and suffering, and, in a deeper sense, in that it always entails risk—the risk of loss of self. An altruistic act is an act of "self-exposure" at the same time that it is an act of self-affirmation. Moral behavior is in the highest sense the giving of oneself to the good of a larger system in which one's own *true* good is realized. The paradox here is perhaps what led one writer to suppose that Shaftesbury did not approve of heroic self-sacrifice.[6] This is true only in the sense that he insisted, as Mill did later, that an act of self-sacrifice must be for the sake of *good*, and not for its own sake. The paradox of the disinterested giving of self in Shaftesbury's ethics is substantially that expressed in the words of Jesus: "Except you die, you cannot be born again."

Shaftesbury realized that to have the highest moral significance the sense of obligation could not simply be imposed upon us from without. Nor does one become "good" simply by willing it. Even the strongest efforts of will, if not accompanied by a transformation in the structure of the affections, cannot produce truly moral behavior. For Shaftesbury, obligation is in the last analysis neither wholly autonomous nor heteronomous, but in Tillich's sense it is "theonomous," i.e., grounded in a unity that transcends both heteronomy and autonomy. The rational self finds the unity of its own being in the power of God, and its fulfillment in the good that is both God and beyond God.

While moral character, as we have seen, entails a rational and cognitive element, Shaftesbury is unwilling to ground it solely on intellectual or logical functions of the mind. Moral "affection" is required—those outgoing energies within the individual that stimulate action and direct one toward the good. But moral affection must mature in cognition and must be controlled by reason. "Virtue itself" is described by Shaftesbury as "no other than a noble enthusiasm justly directed and regulated. . . ." (II, 176) Enthusiasm is a dialectical conception generated by forces both within and without. Moral form is in one respect impressed upon us from without, or *given:* "There are certain moral species or appearances so striking and of such force over our natures, that when they present themselves they bear down all contrary opinion . . . all opposite passion, sensation or mere bodily affection." (II, 176) But in another respect moral form must be found or achieved *within* the self. Enthusiasm is the inner movement of the human spirit which carries it beyond itself in the vision of the Good. Only the mind so "taken up in vision" is capable of that affection or energy which is the substance of the moral life—the life in harmony with Nature and with God.

CHAPTER FOURTEEN

CREATIVE FORM: BEAUTY

Cassirer describes Shaftesbury as "the first great aesthetician that England produced," [1] and points out that "aesthetics . . . occupies the central position of the whole intellectual structure" of the third Earl's philosophy.[2] The truth of the latter has already been amply evident in these pages. Shaftesbury's profound interest in literature and the other arts played an important part in the shaping of his thought, and he considered Locke's lack of concern for the arts as one of his serious failings. Indeed, Shaftesbury may be viewed as trying to construct a theory more adequate to the arts than the new empiricism. In doing so he drew heavily, of course, on the Neoplatonic tradition, though the Cambridge Platonists themselves had never developed a systematic aesthetic theory, as Shaftesbury attempted to do. Unfortunately, death prevented him from completing his projected book, *Second Characters*, in which he planned to develop his concepts in even fuller detail. No complete study of Shaftesbury's aesthetic theory will be attempted in these pages, but a brief analysis will be made of some of those concepts which bear particularly on his religious and moral philosophy.[3] In the *Characteristics*, at least, his aesthetic speculations serve primarily moral and religious ends, though at the same time he affirms the intrinsic value of beauty and of aesthetic contemplation. His major concern is to show the relationship between moral and aesthetic experience, and between creative form in morality and in the arts.

Shaftesbury not only regards truth, beauty, and goodness as the basic intrinsic values, but he accepts the Neoplatonic conception of their ultimate identity, which provides the unifying ground for all the forms of the human spirit. Thus, he writes that "the most natural beauty in the world is honesty and moral truth. For all beauty is truth." (I, 94) Harmony and proportion are the classic attributes which link this triad of values: "What is beautiful is harmonious and proportionable; what is harmonious and proportionable is true; and what is at once both beautiful and true is, of consequence, agreeable and good." (II, 268 f.) Shaftesbury's concept of the ultimate harmony of Nature leads him necessarily to assert the substantial unity of the true, the beautiful, and the good. Nature is a teleological continuum in which all things contribute (when viewed in the largest sense) to the good and the beautiful. The harmonious and the proportionate are also the fruitful or the useful in the highest sense: "And the same shapes and proportions . . . make beauty afford advantage by adapting to activity and use. . . . Thus beauty and truth are plainly joined with the notion of utility and convenience. . . ." (II, 267) The physical harmony of the body, Shaftesbury notes, is linked both with attractiveness and health, just as emotional harmony is a prerequisite of virtue. However, "utility," as Shaftesbury uses the term, is not limited to a material or economic connotation, but is broadly conceived to comprehend all that is useful in achieving the larger ends of human life. And so it is not merely the *appearance* of beauty that counts but the beauty that lies within. External beauty really serves the purpose of leading us to the inner beauties which are "the most real and essential," and which not only afford the greatest pleasure but are of the highest advantage.

The aesthetic character of Shaftesbury's thought is nowhere clearer than in this emphasis on harmony and proportion which is a ground-motif of his metaphysical and ethical theory as well as of his aesthetics. "The study and love of symmetry and order . . ." (II, 267) is not only the basis of our appreciation of beauty; it is also the source of philosophical and scientific inquiry. In it he finds the basis of the disinterested pleasure that the study of mathematics affords. The mind delights in those "inward numbers" that designate the ultimately proportionate relationships of all that participates in Being itself. This "natural joy" in the contemplation of harmony and proportion is not limited by Shaftesbury to the so-called fine arts; he finds it evident throughout the whole range of human activities and pleasures, whether it be in toys or sports, in dress or gardens. For Shaftesbury, harmony is not a merely mechanical symmetry of parts in a whole, but it is organization which manifests an inner formative force. He is saved from conceiving of harmony as a merely static balance of forces by thinking of it dialectically as the product of a complex interplay of tensions. This is clearly seen in his conception of the inner harmony of the affections as well as in his concept of the ultimate harmony of Nature. Though he praises symmetry, it is not understood as a simple balance of uniform elements; his description of the beauties of the natural world reveals a genuine appreciation for irregular or asymmetrical design. (II, 125) There are, however,

conflicting currents in his thought, for while to a considerable
extent he remains a Neoclassicist in taste and theory, the seeds
of the Romantic reaction are already obviously germinating.
Though, for example, he has little use for medieval and Renaissance art, and he attacks the newly fashionable Oriental art as
"worse than Gothic," [4] he is at the same time an advocate of
the natural as opposed to the formal garden. His rhapsodic
account of the beauty of mountains and deserts, caves and
grottoes, contributed to the revolution in attitudes toward natural scenery then occurring, as Marjorie Nicolson points out.[5]
It was just at this point that his Neoclassical attachment to harmony and proportion came into tension with his view of a
dynamic and exuberant Nature, though if Nature shatters proportions and symmetries, it must in Shaftesbury's universe do
so to attain still higher or more essential levels of form.

In Platonic fashion, Shaftesbury traces the stages in the evolution of aesthetic taste in the individual. In the appreciation of
beauty one moves from the particular to the general, from the
material to the spiritual, from the outer to the inner. The
child's enjoyment of regular forms and simple sounds becomes
the adult's pleasure in the complex symmetries of architecture
or music; from the beauty of the individual person one moves
to an appreciation of the beauty of social forms and spiritual
relationships. The stages in the development of aesthetic taste
are analogous to the evolution of moral taste, for both involve
a progression to larger contexts as well as to qualitatively
deeper levels of value. Both have their highest culmination in
the vision of the beauty and perfection of Nature and God.

The close relationship of the sense of beauty and the moral
sense has already been evident in our discussion of Shaftesbury's ethics. While Hutcheson sought to distinguish between

these two senses, Shaftesbury offers no clear way to differentiate between them, and slides often imperceptibly from one to the other. The same kind of mental process is involved in the operations of both the moral and aesthetic senses: the only possible distinction being in their objects—the one being directed toward the good, the other toward the beautiful. But, as we have noted, the good, the true, and the beautiful are ultimately one, so that they tend to merge in the higher reaches of thought, and the processes by which they are apprehended also tend to be basically the same. An action is "right" if it is appropriate to the context in which it occurs. The appreciation of its appropriateness is not only "moral" in so far as it involves a recognition of its rightness, but it is "aesthetic" in so far as it includes an element of sheer satisfaction in its proportionateness. Moral form is also aesthetic form, and the true enjoyment of the one entails the enjoyment of the other. Thus, in Shaftesbury's language, certain words such as "beautiful," "fair," "ugly," or "deformed," have at one and the same time both aesthetic and moral connotations.

It is for this reason that Shaftesbury can write that "the science of virtuosi and that of virtue itself become, in a manner, one and the same." (I, 217) The virtuoso is one who appreciates or creates aesthetic form. Since in Shaftesbury's theory aesthetic and moral form are continuous, virtuosoship is one of the best modes of preparation for the moral life, better, he remarks, than mere pedantry or empty scholarship. The true virtuoso understands the principles of harmony that underlie both good art and true character. "The moral artist who . . . is thus knowing in the inward form and structure of his fellow-creature, will hardly, I presume, be found unknowing in himself, or at a loss in those numbers which make the harmony of a mind. For knavery is mere dissonance and disproportion." (I, 136) However, Shaftesbury explains that this does not apply to the artist who merely copies external forms, but to the one who represents "the graces and perfections of minds," (I, 135) i.e., who knows the laws of inward form. In the contemplation of the beautiful the mind advances its own true worth and interest. While Shaftesbury's argument here has a certain logical coherence, experience makes us realize that the problem of the relation of an artist's character and his work is a much more complex one than he recognized. There is far too much evidence that particular flaws in character or behavior do not necessarily destroy artistic capacity.

Beauty, as we have seen earlier, is one of Shaftesbury's "innate ideas," i.e., one of those ideas that men are "really born to and could hardly by any means avoid." (II, 178) It depends upon the sense of harmony and proportion which Shaftesbury considers "con-natural"—one of the strongest capacities of the mind. We intuitively recognize a difference between the harmonious and the discordant, between that which has been purposely designed and that which is accidental, between, for example, the regularity of an architectural construction and a "heap of stones": "This difference is immediately perceived by a plain internal sensation. . . ." (II, 63) Shaftesbury points to the pleasure that children have in simple, symmetrical figures such as cubes or balls, and to the fact that adults seem to prefer regular to irregular forms. As mentioned earlier, he believes that this pleasure in aesthetic proportion finds expression on every level of human life, if not in greater, then in lesser things, if not in the fine arts, then in the arts associated with daily living. Beauty, like good, is known intuitively by an "inward eye." His explanation is that we naturally approve of balance and symmetry in design because the inner structure of the mind responds sympathetically to that which is most like itself.

Such an approach would seem to suggest that good taste in aesthetic matters is easily acquired. However, as we saw in our discussion of moral taste, Shaftesbury insists again and again that taste must be cultivated and refined. We must develop our natural aesthetic potentialities; if we do so, and if we are emotionally well-balanced, we will respond favorably to the better things. However, he does not suppose that our aesthetic capabilities can be realized without being influenced by our environment or without involving an expenditure of effort. A good illustration of his approach is found in his discussion of the grace of bodily movements. He notes a "great difference in this respect between such persons as have been taught by nature only, and such as by reflection and the assistance of art have learnt to form those motions which on experience are found the easiest and most natural." (I, 124 f.) While some in the first category have "still something of a natural grace," these capacities are perfected only in those who have had the benefit of a favorable environment and good training. Thus, the "natural" for Shaftesbury is here as elsewhere not simply the primitive or the elementary stage of human growth but the realization of its ideal potentialities. He warns that first impressions cannot always be trusted. They *can* be trusted only when one is in the right frame of mind and when one has a cultivated taste; then and then only is the intuitive response likely to be the correct one. It is only because taste can be badly corrupted that a relatively uncultivated taste may sometimes be better. But Shaftesbury's main point is to call for the development of an art of seeing and hearing, since aesthetic appreciation must not be left to mere "fancy." The artist as well as the critic has an obligation to "polish the age" and "refine the public ear."

Aesthetic, like moral, taste is not conceived by Shaftesbury as merely relativistic or subjective, nor is it a purely emotional response. In so far as he is a Neoclassicist, he is committed to the existence of objectively conceived rules of art that are universally applicable: "The art itself is severe, the rules rigid." (I, 219) On the other hand, he is aware of the emotional and intuitive elements in the structure of taste. Thus, aesthetic, as well as moral, taste is a response of the total self involving us both intellectually and emotionally. Good taste not only requires intellectual development but also emotional harmony. Our immediate aesthetic responses must be checked against or correlated with intellectual rules and standards. Shaftesbury does not tell us exactly what to do if they conflict; he only tells us what the general conditions are that are necessary for the operation of good taste.

Shaftesbury's concept of beauty and creativity, which is central to his aesthetic system and bears on his entire philosophy, requires further analysis. In distinguishing between "three degrees or orders of beauty," he obviously is drawing on Neoplatonic sources either directly or through the Cambridge Platonists. The first degree of beauty is found in those forms, called "dead forms," which are products of man or Nature but have themselves "no forming power, no action, or intelligence." (II, 132) The beauty of such forms is not the product of their material nature, for "there is no principle of beauty in body." (II, 131) The second degree of beauty is that of the "forming forms . . . which have intelligence, action, and operation." (II, 132) This is a higher level of beauty because it includes both form, the product of mind, and mind itself. The third order of beauty is that of the Supreme Mind "which fashions even minds themselves, contains in itself all the beauties fashioned by those minds, and is consequently the principle, source, and fountain of all beauty." (II, 133) The underlying principle here is that "the beautifying, not the beautified, is the really beautiful." (II, 131) Plotinus had expressed the same idea in these words: "Beauty is that which irradiates symmetry rather than symmetry itself and is that which truly calls out our love." [6] The source of beauty is traced by Shaftesbury to mind; rationality is essential to beauty, or in Brett's words, beauty is "the sensuous representation of rational ideas." [7] Shaftesbury's conclusion is: " 'Tis mind alone which forms. All which is void of mind is horrid, and matter formless is deformity itself." (II, 132)

It is evident from the above that "form" has different levels of meaning for Shaftesbury. It is, on one level, "pattern" or "design," on another, "purposeful order," and ultimately it is the inner essence of reality manifest to us. Aesthetic appreciation is more than the grasping of an external unity, it is the apprehension by the mind of the inner organizing forces of an organic system: " 'Tis not the form rejoices, but that which is beneath the form." (II, 142) Thus, the sensations in themselves do not give us access to the realm of form, which is why animals are incapable of aesthetic appreciation. Shaftesbury's approach is similar to that of Cicero, one of his favorite authors, who taught that the comprehension of the beautiful is based on the presence in the mind of an "ideal image." For the English philosopher too, beauty is an expression of mind, and the appreciation of beauty is the discovery of mind by mind.

In distinguishing between the beautiful and the merely pleasing, Shaftesbury applied his concept of "disinterested pleasure," which Cassirer considers to be his "most important individual contribution to aesthetics." [8] The idea, which proved to be of particular influence on German philosophers later in the century, was not entirely original, for Shaftesbury could have found it in Sir Thomas More as well as in Plato. However, he applied it more extensively not only in his aesthetics, but, as we have seen, in his ethics and theology also. In the true appreciation of the beautiful, our minds transcend all desire for the possession, use, or mastery of the object of our contemplation. In a striking passage he wrote that to enjoy the beauty of the sea was decidedly different from attempting to control it: "The bridegroom-Doge, who in his stately Bucentaur floats on the bosom of his Thetis, has less possession than the poor shepherd, who from a hanging rock or point of some high promontory, stretched at his ease, forgets his feeding flocks, while he admires her beauty." (II, 127) Shaftesbury makes an element of disinterestedness a necessary condition for both aesthetic contemplation and artistic creation.

As we have seen, Shaftesbury traces the sense of beauty to the creative forces in man's mind and ultimately to the supreme creative principle in Nature. Creation is an active, formative process of mind, not merely a passive response to sense-stimuli. The artist is a genuine creator, not a mere imitator of natural appearances; nor can the creative process be explained in terms of the psychology of association. The artist is an "imitator" in the sense that he re-presents the materials of experience. Artistic imitation is really an imitation of the creative process of Nature itself. As he writes in Second Characters: "All is invention (the first part of painting), creation, divining, a sort of prophesying and inspiration, the poetical ecstatic and rapture.

Things that were never seen; no nor that ever were: yet feigned."[9] Thus, Shaftesbury rates the exact naturalistic representation of objects as inferior in aesthetic value to the idealization of forms and to the communication thereby of moral truths. The artist composes out of the elements of his natural experience an artistic whole that is complete in itself and not identifiable in every detail with particular natural objects. Since Shaftesbury does not conceive of the mind as a blank tablet receiving impressions of sense, he understands the creative process both in art and philosophy to require an interpretive ordering of the materials of sensation. He does not try to deny the "reality" of the material work of art or to bypass the senses, for his concept of the aesthetic includes both, though in a higher unity. The creative artist

is indeed a second *Maker;* a just Prometheus under Jove. Like that sovereign artist of universal plastic nature, he forms a whole, coherent and proportioned in itself, with due subjection and subordinacy of constituent parts. . . . The moral artist . . . can thus imitate the Creator. . . . (I, 136)

Man's inspired creativity reveals the divinity within.

Shaftesbury's concept of the creative genius was also destined to have great influence on Romantic aesthetic theory in Germany. For the English philosopher, the artistic genius was not simply one who had a superior faculty of sensation or who had particularly developed his powers of discursive reason. Inspiration or enthusiasm was a necessary condition of artistic creativity: the genius was one through whom the formative forces of Nature itself were released and given expression. Shaftesbury did not consider this approach to contradict his adherence to the rules of art; the rules were necessary guides whether in art or in morality. Nevertheless, neither great art (as, indeed, such critics as Boileau and Rapin were well aware) nor the highest morality could be attained merely by a pedantic adherence to such rules. There is always a *je ne sais quoi* in the highest achievements; there is always the power of enthusiasm itself which defies reductive analysis. However, it is a gross misinterpretation to say, as Louis Bredvold does, that for Shaftesbury "man is the measure of all things" because beauty is in the artist and not in the art.[10] True creative power, for Shaftesbury, is always in accord with the objective structure of reality and expresses universal values. The artist is at one and the same time a true creator and a true discoverer. A dual law operates in the creative imagination, in art as well as in ethics and religion, for it both "makes" and "finds" the forms of Nature's inner being. In the creative genius the opposition of autonomy and heteronomy is dialectically resolved as the level of true theonomy is at last attained.

In Shaftesbury's aesthetics as in the rest of his philosophy, enthusiasm provides the dynamic force. The free, contemplative, and selfless devotion to the true, the good, and the beautiful provides human life with its goals and its justification. Through this alone man realizes his true self and attains true joy. Shaftesbury's ideal of "harmony with Nature" is only another form of the same principle. In aesthetic experience man appreciates the unity of law and order which is present throughout the whole creation: beauty is the "language of forms" spoken by the universe. Through the experience of beauty man transcends the separation of subject and object, and is at last at one with Nature and with Nature's God.

CHAPTER FIFTEEN

CONCLUDING REMARKS

Montesquieu described Shaftesbury as one of *"les quatres grands poètes,"* along with Plato, Malebranche, and Montaigne,[1] and it is as a "poet" that he must finally be judged. Shaftesbury understood the philosopher's need for inspiration in the highest reaches of thought. Philocles, the skeptic, can only become a convinced theist when he is able to share Theocles's vision of Nature and man—when he can share his enthusiasm. Enthusiasm, as we have tried to demonstrate in this study, is not only the culmination of Shaftesbury's philosophy, but is the dynamic element that gives it life and sets his thought apart from that of the Deists and rationalists of the Augustan age. Not that he was any less devoted to reason than they, but he understood (more, perhaps, than he was fully aware of) that reason must continually seek to transcend itself, that the processes of discursive reason are not and never can be complete in themselves. They are completed only in intuitive vision—in those moments when man is "lifted out of himself" and catches sight of the higher beauty and truth. This is not for Shaftesbury an irrational or antirational act. His entire philosophy may be viewed as an attempt to refute the claim that, in Hocking's words, "no rational enthusiasms are possible." [2] Enthusiasm is the fulfillment of our highest potentialities as rational beings—the extension of the powers of reason to their highest limits. However, "reason" is understood here in its broadest sense: it includes but is more than the processes of the discursive intellect. It comprehends that whole realm of common concepts that arise out of the shared life and experience of the human community. The symbol-making, form-creating capacity of man, which is the basis of language and art, is also part of the rational nature of man. Enthusiasm, like Tillich's description of "faith," is "reason in ecstasy," but it is ecstasy that is "fulfilled, not denied, rationality." [3] Shaftesbury carefully distinguished between his idea of religious commitment and what he regarded as the false enthusiasm of the evangelical sects. Denying supernatural revelation, he proposed rational tests for claims of inspiration; religious zeal unchecked by reason and by "common sense" not only subjects men to mental delusions but produces social disorder. Shaftesbury was not unaware of the dangers in his own type of enthusiasm though. In one place he warned that since we know more clearly what is evil than what is good,

we are to work rather by the weaning than the engaging passions; since if we give way chiefly to inclination, by loving, applauding, and admiring what is great and good, we may possibly, it seems, in some high objects of that kind, be so amused and ecstasied as to lose ourselves and miss our proper mark for want of a steady and settled aim. (II, 280 f.)

It may seem strange to have linked Shaftesbury, an advocate of rational theology, with a modern theologian like Tillich, who is identified with the critical reaction against liberal theology, for which Shaftesbury's philosophy is one of the basic historical sources. But besides the connection already established between their respective concepts of enthusiasm and faith, there is an even deeper link in their common emphasis on the necessity of commitment. Tillich defines faith as "the state of being ultimately concerned"; [4] similarly, Shaftesbury's concept of enthusiasm calls for a total commitment to those higher values which define the character of human life—which make it what it is and what it ought to be. (I, 87) The giving of self to that which is more than self is the only true mode of self-realization. This stress on commitment anticipates the central concern of modern religious thought, and in particular of existentialism, which seems at first sight so distant in tone and approach from the Augustan philosopher.

Actually, theologians like Tillich, Reinhold Niebuhr, and others have a greater debt to the Enlightenment than is commonly acknowledged in theological circles today. So-called "post-liberal theology" owes much to the very tradition of liberalism that it has sought to re-examine and in part to replace. These theologians take for granted a body of biblical criticism that has taken them far beyond the simple biblical literalism that was still rife in the seventeenth century. It must not be forgotten that Shaftesbury and the Deists played an important role in stimulating and in some respects even forcing the critical study of religious scriptures. Their impetus contributed to the growing body of studies in the following centuries, historical, psychological, anthropological, and sociological, which have in turn vitally affected the methods and content of contemporary theology. We owe to the Enlightenment such basic presuppositions as the rights of freedom of thought and of freely examining religious beliefs. The seventeenth century, for all its seminal vitality, still clung to much of the furniture of medieval religious doctrine, as for example, the belief in an actual hell of eternal torment for the wicked, and the argument for God based on miracles. We have shown that Shaftesbury delivered a powerful blow to the whole theology of retribution and contributed to the important shift in man's conception of God, stressing His love rather than His justice or power. The abandonment of the argument based on miracles was paralleled by attacks on the other classical proofs of Deity. Shaftesbury's own favorite argument—the teleological—which Hume was to attack so strongly, still survives, though generally it dons the garb of evolution, as in Teilhard de Chardin. But the primary criticisms of the arguments for God generated by the Enlightenment lead directly to Tillich's abandonment of the attempt to prove the "existence" of God by rational argument, and instead to demonstrate the dynamic significance of faith in human experience.

All this is not to deny the many differences that lie between Shaftesbury's thought and modern existential theology; they are so obvious that they need not be spelled out here. One, however, that is particularly interesting is the absence of any concept of symbolism in Shaftesbury. His understanding of poetic truth, his doctrines of creative imagination and enthusiasm, all would suggest that a genuine theory of symbols would not only have been consistent with his thought but would have provided a valuable means for the development of the implications of his ideas. However, like the Deists, he tended to dismiss religious myths as mere legends or products of unregulated fancy. No doubt the abuses of the allegorical method in the Middle Ages militated against the positive use of symbolic interpretation, but the lack of such a method made it impossi-

ble for Shaftesbury and the Deists really to grasp the significance of much of traditional theology.[5]

John Brown criticized Shaftesbury's conception of disinterested love for God as "not calculated for Use," and fit only
for "a Mind taken up in Vision." [6] Yet Shaftesbury wrote
precisely in order to make it possible for other minds to share
his vision of Nature and God, to see Reality as an aesthetic
Whole—the harmonious product of a Supreme Artist. Thus,
he does not rest his case on logical argument alone, and his
appeal to experience is not to a mere accumulation of sense-
data; Shaftesbury seeks to develop our aesthetic capacity as a
means of arriving at higher truths—the ability to see things
in their connections as parts of organic unities. His approach
to Nature and to God is finally aesthetic and intuitive rather
than analytical or logical—"a mere dream; but . . . truly rational, and divine. . . ." [7] It is the poetry of thought and aspiration that gives his work its final form.

The universe no longer seems as orderly as it did to those
who lived in the age of Newton, and yet we still seek order
and believe that it is there to be found. The type of optimism
that Shaftesbury preached has been seriously challenged, and
yet many who reject it accept some modified form of it,
though sometimes without being fully conscious of the fact.
I have tried to show in this study that Shaftesbury was not a
simple optimist, that he was well aware of the depths of potential evil in man, and that he did not seek to deny the reality
of proximate evil. Yet his "solution" to the problem of evil
is acceptable only as an enthusiastic *faith*, not as a logical argument. Shaftesbury's formulation of the basic faith of the Enlightenment is neither as naïve as its critics have sometimes
regarded it, nor as convincingly reasonable as its proponents

thought. It is a faith that still underlies in large part the liberal, democratic culture of the Western world, despite the intensive re-examination of it that has been going on for over a hundred years. Which of its axioms are we prepared to abandon? and what will the consequences be? These are the questions that modern man must ask. But in asking them we must still hope, as Shaftesbury did 250 years ago, for a new birth of freedom which will

bring not Europe only but Asia (which is now concerned), and in a manner the whole world, under one community; or at least to such a correspondence and intercourse of good offices and mutual succour as may render it a more humane world than it was ever known, and carry the interest of human kind to a greater height than ever.[8]

In the last analysis, Shaftesbury's philosophic faith has to be assessed by what it means for the making and remaking of man. According to Shaftesbury, man is truly himself only when he acts creatively, as a co-creator with Deity. And the creative life is supremely the life of love in which man finds his true freedom and true being. In Shaftesbury's words:

We are made to contemplate and love God intirely, and with a free and voluntary Love.[9]

The highest principle, which is the Love of God, is best attained not by dark Speculations and Monkish Philosophy, but by moral Practice, and Love of Mankind, and a Study of their Interests.[10]

NOTES

NOTES: PREFACE

1. "The Augustan Age of England," *The Bee*, No. 8, Nov. 24, 1759.
2. Johann G. von Herder, *Briefe zu Beförderung der Humanität*, Letter 33 (1794), in *Sämmtliche Werke*, ed. B. Suphan (Berlin: Weidmann, 1877–1913), XVII, 158. My translation.
3. G. W. von Leibniz, "Remarks on the . . . *Characteristics*," in *Philosophical Papers and Letters*, ed. Leroy Loemker (Chicago: Univ. of Chicago Press, 1956), II, 1030. The *Theodicy* was published in 1710.
4. *An Enquiry Concerning the Principles of Morals*, Sect. 1; *A Treatise of Human Nature*, Bk. I, part iv, Sect. 6.
5. A complete edition of Shaftesbury in French appeared in 1769, though some of his writings had appeared in translation earlier. Diderot published his free translation of the "Inquiry Concerning Virtue" in 1745. The complete German translation of the *Characteristics* was issued in 1776–79.
6. Article on "Génie." Denis Diderot, *Oeuvres Complètes de Diderot*, eds. J. Assézat et M. Tourneux, 20 vols. (Paris: Garnier Frères, 1875–77), XV, 39. My translation.
7. *History of English Thought in the Eighteenth Century* (New York and London: G. P. Putnam's Sons, 1902), II, 18 (1st ed., 1876).
8. *Shaftesbury and Hutcheson* (New York: G. P. Putnam's Sons, 1883).
9. London: Hutchinson's University Library, 1951.
10. *Transactions of the American Philosophical Society*, Vol. XLI, Part II (Philadelphia: The American Philosophical Society, 1951). This study is neither well-organized nor clearly written. Where his interpretation of Shaftesbury can be understood, it often seems doubtful. On the other hand, Aldridge has dug up some interest-

ing background information on Shaftesbury which is found here and in some of his articles.

11. Trans. by F. Koelln and J. Pettegrove (Princeton: Princeton Univ. Press, 1951).

12. Trans. by James P. Pettegrove (Edinburgh: Thomas Nelson & Sons, Ltd., 1953).

13. *ELH: Journal of English Literary History*, XX (1953), 267–299.

14. *Philosophical Quarterly*, XI (April, 1961), 97–113.

15. Anthony, Earl of Shaftesbury, *Characteristics of Men, Manners, Opinions, Times*, ed. John M. Robertson, Vols. I–II (New York: The Bobbs-Merrill Co., Inc., 1964). I have provided a new introduction, and a new, greatly enlarged index for this reprinting of Robertson's text, which appeared originally in two volumes (London: Grant Richards). Volume and page numbers are the same for both editions. Except where indicated, my references to the *Characteristics* will be given in the text in parentheses with volume and page, or in the footnotes as *Char.*

16. For more detailed information on Shaftesbury's life see "A Sketch of the Life of the Third Earl of Shaftesbury, by His Son, the Fourth Earl," in *Anthony, Earl of Shaftesbury, the Life, Unpublished Letters, and Philosophical Regimen*, ed. Benjamin Rand (London: Swan Sonnenschein & Co., Ltd., 1900). Referred to hereafter as *Life, Letters*. See also Thomas Fowler, *op. cit.* and R. L. Brett, *op. cit.*

17. See A. O. Aldridge, "Two Versions of Shaftesbury's *Inquiry Concerning Virtue*," *The Huntington Library Quarterly*, XIII (1949–1950), 207–214. Shaftesbury's comment on this edition may be found in *Life, Letters*, p. 405.

18. See *Life, Letters*, p. 336.

19. E. T. Mitchell writes that the *Inquiry* is youthful and "does not represent his more mature thought." See Edwin T. Mitchell, *A System of Ethics* (New York: Scribner's Sons, 1950), p. 468. This seems doubtful if, as I presume, Mitchell is referring to the *Inquiry* as it appeared in the 1711 or 1714 editions. A. O. Aldridge, who has compared the 1699 and 1711 versions, writes that the *Inquiry* was "methodically polished, revised, and carefully reorganized over a ten-year period . . ." ("Two Versions of Shaftesbury's *Inquiry* . . . ," *op. cit.*, p. 208). Later, he adds that " . . . the outlines and fundamental principles of the 1699 version are essentially the same as those of 1711 . . ." (p. 212). I have found little evidence of significant development in Shaftesbury's thought from the earlier to the later writings. For one thing, the time span involved is only about 15 years. The *Inquiry* is representative of Shaftesbury's mature thought, though, of course, in his other writings he supplemented and enlarged the basic philosophy of religion and ethics that is formulated there.

20. *Life, Letters*, p. xxix.

21. Cambridge: Cambridge Univ. Press. Hereafter referred to as *Second Characters*.

22. Cited above. Shaftesbury probably never intended that his philosophical notebooks be published. See *Char.* I, 109. For this reason when I quote from the notebooks I will follow my reference with the abbreviation (PR), standing for the "Philosophical Regimen," the title Rand gave to these notes.
23. For a comment on his character see Thomas Fowler, *op. cit.*, pp. 34 ff.
24. *Ibid.*, p. 61.
25. *Essays on the Characteristics*, 3rd ed. (London, 1752), p. 9 (1st ed., 1751).
26. Quoted by A. O. Aldridge, *Shaftesbury and the Deist Manifesto*, p. 297.
27. *Bibliothèque Choisie*, ed. Jean Le Clerc (Amsterdam, 1710), XXI, 188.
28. *The Moral Sense* (London: Oxford Univ. Press, 1947), p. 17.
29. *The Idea of Value* (Cambridge: Cambridge Univ. Press, 1929), pp. 185, 188.
30. Robert Marsh has pointed this out in "Shaftesbury's Theory of Poetry: The Importance of the 'Inward Colloquy,' " *ELH*, XXVIII (1961), 54–69. See *Char.* I, 105 f., 130–134; II, 6 f.

NOTES: CHAPTER I

1. E.g., Thomas Fowler, *op. cit.*, pp. 98 f.
2. *The Philosophy of the Enlightenment*, p. 313.
3. *Life, Letters*, p. 353.
4. *Ibid.*, p. 469.
5. *Several Letters Written by a Noble Lord to a Young Man at the University*, pp. 42 f.; also p. 20. Hereafter referred to as *Letters to a Young Man*.
6. Quoted in R. L. Brett, *op. cit.*, p. 59.
7. It is surprising to find that there is no reference to Shaftesbury in Caroline Goad's *Horace in the English Literature of the Eighteenth Century* (New Haven: Yale Univ. Press, 1918).
8. Another passage which sounds Plotinian—II, 69—is attributed in Shaftesbury's own index in the 1714 edition to Maximus Tyrius, a predecessor of Plotinus.
9. "Shaftesbury as Stoic," *PMLA*, XXXVIII (1923), 642–684.
10. *Shaftesbury and the Deist Manifesto*.
11. *The Platonic Renaissance in England*.
12. *Life, Letters*, p. 359.
13. *Ibid.*, p. 416.
14. *Letters to a Young Man*, pp. 4 f.
15. Out of a sense of gratitude for Locke, Shaftesbury concealed his differences with him during Locke's life, though after Locke's death he expressed himself strongly in some of his letters. (See *Life, Letters*, pp. 344–347, 403–405, and 414–417.) In general, Shaftesbury praises Locke's political, economic, and educational

theories. (See *Life, Letters,* pp. 331–332, 403–405.) His criticisms of Locke's religious and moral ideas will be dealt with later.

16. *Life, Letters,* p. 269 (PR).
17. *Ibid.,* p. 268 (PR).
18. R. L. Brett, *op. cit.,* p. 97.
19. *Letters to a Young Man,* p. 22.
20. *Infra,* Ch. XIII.
21. *The Platonic Renaissance,* p. 160.
22. *Second Characters,* p. 8.
23. *Infra,* Ch. IX.
24. *Life, Letters,* p. 367.
25. See Leo Courtines, *Bayle's Relations with England and the English* (New York: Columbia Univ. Press, 1938), p. 123. Shaftesbury intervened in Bayle's behalf in 1706, saving him from spending his last days in jail.
26. *Life, Letters,* pp. 373 f. This tribute is matched by some high words of praise written by Bayle about Shaftesbury. See Leo Courtines, *op. cit.,* pp. 128 f.
27. *Life, Letters,* p. 338.

NOTES: CHAPTER II

1. *Life, Letters,* p. 399.
2. *The Eighteenth Century Background* (London: Chatto and Windus, 1953), pp. 62–64.
3. See the chapter on "The Aesthetics of the Infinite" in *Mountain Gloom and Mountain Glory* (Ithaca, N. Y.: Cornell Univ. Press, 1959).
4. *A History of Philosophy,* trans. by J. H. Tufts (New York: The Macmillan Company, 1901), p. 488.
5. *Life, Letters,* p. 336.
6. *Ibid.,* p. 394. Letter dated Dec. 10, 1708. Rand describes a printed copy of "The Sociable Enthusiast" in the London Record Office that is "full of corrections and additions in the handwriting of the third Earl . . . nearly as printed in the *Characteristics*" (*Life, Letters,* p. 336, n. 2). I interpret this corrected version to be the one printed in 1709 and 1711. Some small revisions were presumably then made by Shaftesbury for the 1714 edition.
7. It bears the date Sept., 1707.
8. For a fuller account see Ronald A. Knox, *Enthusiasm* (Oxford: The Clarendon Press, 1951), ch. xv, though there are some curious lapses in the book. (See below, note 28.) The Wesleys encountered some of the survivors of the movement twenty years later (Knox, p. 361; also p. 371).
9. Three of the prophets arrived in London in September, 1706, according to Aldridge (*Shaftesbury and the Deist Manifesto,* p. 315). D. P. Walker writes that "quite a number" were in Eng-

land by 1706. See *The Decline of Hell: Seventeenth-Century Discussions of Eternal Torment* (Chicago: Univ. of Chicago Press, 1964), p. 254.

10. *The New Pretenders to Prophecy Examined* in George Hickes *et al., The Spirit of Enthusiasm Exorcised* (London, 1709), pp. 499 f. It should be added that the prophets were also accused of advocating antinomianism.

11. One of them was Nicholas Fatio, "an eminent mathematician" and "member of the Royal Society" (D. P. Walker, *op. cit.*, pp. 254 f.).

12. Aldridge, *Shaftesbury and the Deist Manifesto*, p. 316.

13. See the Introduction to Robertson's 1900 edition (I, xxiv).

14. *Op. cit.*, p. 297. Its date of composition is mistakenly given as 1708.

15. *Life, Letters*, p. 504.

16. *A Treatise Concerning Enthusiasm As It is an Effect of Nature . . .*, 2nd ed. (London, 1656) (1st ed., 1655).

17. My references are to the edition published in *A Collection of Several Philosophical Writings of Dr. Henry More* (London, 1712).

18. *Letters to a Young Man*, p. 43. Shaftesbury was no doubt thinking of More's belief in miracles performed by supernatural spiritual agencies.

19. Cf. Joseph Addison, *The Spectator*, No. 412.

20. E.g., *The Advancement and Reformation of Modern Poetry* (London, 1701). In later years, Dennis praised Shaftesbury's "good sense," and described him as "most ingenious and most judicious." *The Critical Works of John Dennis*, ed. Edward N. Hooker, 2 vols. (Baltimore: The Johns Hopkins Press, 1939), II, 255 and 257.

21. *The Advancement and Reformation of Modern Poetry*, p. 26.

22. *Ibid.*, p. 29.

23. *Ibid.*, p. 33; also p. 46.

24. Marjorie Nicolson, *op. cit.*, p. 282.

25. *Ibid.*, p. 294. For references to "sublime" see the new Index in the 1964 reprinting of *Characteristics* (New York: The Bobbs-Merrill Co., Inc.).

26. See *Second Characters*, p. 163. But such references as *Char.* II, 124, may be taken to imply this association.

27. *Enthusiamus Triumphatus*, p. 2.

28. *Enthusiasm*, p. 8. Knox not only shows little comprehension of Shaftesbury's views but also misdates and mistitles the "Letter Concerning Enthusiasm." He is apparently not familiar with "The Moralist" or Shaftesbury's other writings. He is unaware of the earlier studies of enthusiasm by Meric Casaubon and Henry More, and he thinks that Bishop Hickes started the vogue of the word in his sermon of 1680, "The Spirit of Enthusiasm Exorcised."

29. Also *Life, Letters*, p. 449.

30. *Enthusiasmus Triumphatus*, p. 14. One is reminded of Santayana's famous definition: "Poetry is called religion when it intervenes in life, and religion, when it merely supervenes upon life, is seen to be nothing but poetry."

31. *The True Intellectual System of the Universe* (London, 1678), Bk. I, Ch. iii, Sect. xix, pp. 134 f.
32. See Marjorie Nicolson, *op. cit.*, p. 299.
33. *Enthusiasmus Triumphatus*, p. 12.
34. *Ibid.*, p. 45.
35. There are some interesting similarities between Shaftesbury's philosophy of love and that of Marsilio Ficino, though there are no direct references to the Italian thinker in Shaftesbury. The Cambridge Platonists may have transmitted some of his doctrines. On the other hand, if Shaftesbury was familiar with Ficino's Latin translations of and commentaries on Plato and Plotinus, he would have found some of the ideas expressed there. The *De Amore*, which contains Ficino's theory of love, was included in all editions of the translation of Plato. However, when the English philosopher quotes from Plato it is from the Greek text.
36. *Essays on Man*, Ep. III, ll. 7–8.
37. Since the types of love belong to the "social affections," they will be discussed further in Ch. IX.
38. *Life, Letters*, p. 5 (PR).
39. *Infra*, Ch. IV.
40. *Enthusiasmus Triumphatus*, p. 54.
41. *Life, Letters*, p. 33 (PR).

NOTES: CHAPTER III

1. Other aspects of his theory will be developed in later chapters as I treat specific problems in his philosophy of religion and ethics.
2. *Enthusiasmus Triumphatus*, p. 20.
3. *The Platonic Renaissance in England*, p. 162.
4. *The Philosophy of the Enlightenment*, p. 314.
5. *Life, Letters*, p. 380.
6. *Essay Concerning Human Understanding*, Bk. II, Ch. xi, Sect. 2.
7. *Ibid.*
8. Ch. 9.
9. *Second Characters*, p. 139.
10. In the remainder of this chapter I will discuss how this is true of religion. Its application to morals will be treated in Ch. XII.
11. Quoted in Cassirer, *The Platonic Renaissance in England*, p. 164.
12. There is the implication here that such divine "sanction" remains to be proven, which would make this point academic.
13. *Life, Letters*, p. 38 (PR).
14. *Ibid.*, p. 39 (PR).

NOTES: CHAPTER IV

1. *The Platonic Renaissance,* p. 192.
2. Alfred North Whitehead, *Science and the Modern World* (New York: The New American Library, 1948), p. 56.
3. Pascal did not, I think, intend it as a rational proof of the existence of God, but rather as a device to lead the individual into a state of mind wherein belief would be possible.
4. Shaftesbury's solution to the problem of evil, which is an essential part of his statement of the teleological argument, is taken up later in Ch. V.
5. For further explanation see Chaps. IX and XIII.
6. As argued, for example, in John Ray, *Wisdom of God Manifested in the Works of the Creation* (1691).
7. *Life, Letters,* p. 15 (PR).
8. *Ibid.,* p. 307.
9. As it was only in the form of a rough draft, Shaftesbury was professedly angry at Toland. Yet the fact that he asked Desmaizeaux to translate it in 1701, and to show the translation to Bayle, indicates that he was not entirely dissatisfied with it. The fourth Earl claims that his father never had "any great opinion" of Toland but one cannot be sure of the accuracy of this, since Toland was out of favor with the Shaftesbury family after the third Earl's death. Toland himself claimed to have "cultivated a most intimate acquaintance" with Shaftesbury. See *Letters From the Right Honourable the Late Earl of Shaftesbury to Robert Molesworth, Esq.,* ed. John Toland (London, 1721), Preface, p. v. Referred to hereafter as *Letters . . . to Robert Molesworth.*
10. *Life, Letters,* p. 460 (1712). Collins had also been a close friend of Locke.
11. By Robert Jenkins in *Remarks on some Books lately published,* quoted by John Edwards, *Some new discoveries of the uncertainty, deficiency, and corruption of human knowledge and learning* (London, 1714), p. 200.
12. *Life, Letters,* p. 403.
13. *The Seventeenth Century Background* (New York: Doubleday and Co., Inc., 1953), p. 277.
14. *Select Discourses* (Cambridge: Cambridge Univ. Press, 1859), Disc. i, Sect. 1, p. 1.
15. Denis Diderot, *Oeuvres Complètes, op. cit.,* I, 15. From the "Discours Préliminaire" to the *Essai sur le Mérite.*
16. *The Philosophy of the Enlightenment,* p. 84.
17. *Ibid.,* p. 85.
18. *The Third Earl of Shaftesbury,* p. 66.
19. *History of English Thought in the Eighteenth Century,* II, 17.
20. My italics.
21. *The Journal of Philosophy,* XLVIII, No. 19 (1951), 591.

NOTES: CHAPTER V

1. Thomas Fowler, *op. cit.*
2. *The Eighteenth Century Background*, p. 35. Willey documents these changes in ch. ii.
3. *Select Discourses*, Disc. x, pp. 463 f.
4. *The Advancement and Reformation of Modern Poetry*, pp. xvi–xvii.
5. Ch. IX.
6. *Life, Letters*, pp. 70 f. (PR).
7. *Ibid.*, p. 73.
8. *Ibid.*
9. See Ernest Tuveson, *Millennium and Utopia* (Berkeley: Univ. of California Press, 1949).
10. Arthur O. Lovejoy, *The Great Chain of Being* (New York: Harper & Row, 1960), p. 242.
11. *Essay on Man*, Ep. I, 11.
12. *Original Letters of Locke, Algernon Sidney, and Anthony Lord Shaftesbury*, ed. T. Forster (London, 1830), p. 271. Hereafter referred to as *Original Letters*.
13. *Life, Letters*, p. 30 (PR).
14. *Ibid.*, p. 43 (PR).
15. Ch. XIII.
16. *History of English Thought in the Eighteenth Century*, II, 32.
17. *Life, Letters*, pp. 256 f. (PR).

NOTES: CHAPTER VI

1. *Life, Letters*, p. 415.
2. *Ibid.*, p. 416.
3. *Ibid.*, p. 31 (PR).
4. Almost all of the few references to this problem are in the *Philosophical Regimen*. See *Life, Letters*, pp. 90 ff. (PR).
5. *Second Characters*, p. 167.
6. *Life, Letters*, p. 340.
7. *Ibid.*, p. 137. (PR).
8. *Ibid.*, p. 261 (PR).
9. *Ibid.*, p. 149 (PR).
10. *Ibid.*, p. 265 (PR).
11. Interestingly, defenders of pre-existence like More and F. M. Van Helmont denied that we have any memory of previous existences. See D. P. Walker, *The Decline of Hell*, p. 148.
12. *Life, Letters*, p. 90 (PR).
13. *Supra*, Ch. V.
14. D. P. Walker, *op. cit.*, Ch. viii.
15. *Life, Letters*, p. 263 (PR).

16. Ch. XI.
17. *Life, Letters,* p. 263 (PR).
18. *Ibid.,* p. 124 (PR).
19. *Ibid.,* p. 263 (PR).
20. *Ibid.,* p. 344.
21. *Religio Medici,* Part II, Sect. 12.
22. *Life, Letters,* pp. 345–347.

NOTES: CHAPTER VII

1. Bernard Mandeville, *The Fable of the Bees,* ed. F. B. Kaye, 2 vols. (Oxford: The Clarendon Press, 1924), II, 357.
2. Quoted in Thomas Fowler, *op. cit.,* p. 148.
3. Quoted in Charles Elson, *Wieland and Shaftesbury* (New York: Columbia Univ. Press, 1913), p. 75, n. 98.
4. Benjamin Whichcote, *Select Sermons of Dr. Whichcot,* ed. William Wishart (Edinburgh, 1742), p. xxxiii.
5. *History of English Thought in the Eighteenth Century,* II, 20.
6. *Life, Letters,* p. 276.
7. *Ibid.,* p. 420.
8. Thomas Fowler, *op. cit.,* p. 38.
9. From *The Religion of Protestants a Safe Way to Salvation* (1638).
10. *Letters to a Young Man,* p. 43.
11. *Select Sermons of Dr. Whichcot,* Preface, p. xxvii.
12 *Life, Letters,* p. 394. The other piece referred to is the "Letter Concerning Enthusiasm."
13. *Life, Letters,* p. 338.
14. William Warburton, *Letters from a Late Eminent Prelate to One of His Friends,* 2nd ed. (New York, 1809), p. 26; letter dated Jan. 1749/1750.
15. Samuel Parker, cited in A. O. Aldridge, *Shaftesbury and the Deist Manifesto,* p. 320.
16. 3rd ed., 2 vols. (London, 1757), I, Letter 5, pp. 48 f. (1st ed., 1754).
17. Joseph Warton, *An Essay on the Genius and Writings of Pope* (London, 1782), II, 100, n. 2.
18. *Life, Letters,* p. 420
19. For example, the Blasphemy Act of 1697–1698 provides that any person of Christian background who in writing or speaking denies any person of the Trinity, or the truth of Christianity, or the divine authority of Scripture, should be subject to certain legal disabilities and, for repeated offenses, be imprisoned.
20. *Life, Letters,* p. 355.
21. *Ibid.,* p. 400.
22. Quoted in Thomas Fowler, *op. cit.,* p. 38.
23. Quoted in A. O. Aldridge, "Henry Needler's Knowledge of Shaftesbury," *Modern Language Notes,* LXII (1947), 266.
24. *Life, Letters,* p. xxvii.

25. *Select Sermons,* p. xxviii.
26. *Life, Letters,* p. 434; also p. 432.
27. *Select Sermons,* pp. xxxi ff.
28. *Letters to a Young Man,* p. 43.
29. *Ibid.,* p. 34; also *Life, Letters,* p. 421.
30. In 1717, as Bishop of Bangor, he was to precipitate the famous Bangorian controversy
31. *History of English Thought in the Eighteenth Century,* II, 19.
32. *Life, Letters,* p. 29 (PR).
33. *Ibid.,* p. 403. Tindal also wrote *A Defence of the Rights of the Christian Church* (1709). In 1710 the Commons condemned these books and ordered them to be burnt.
34. *Select Sermons,* p. xxv.
35. *Ibid.,* p. xxiv.
36. *The Art of Lawgiving* (1659) in *The Oceana and Other Works of James Harrington, Esq.* (London, 1747), Bk. III, Ch. ii, p. 448.
37. *Letters to a Young Man,* p. 36.

NOTES: CHAPTER VIII

1. Quoted by James Clifford, *The New York Times Book Review,* Aug. 17, 1958, 2.
2. *Essays of John Dryden,* ed. W. P. Ker, 2 vols. (Oxford: The Clarendon Press, 1926), II, 260.
3. At end of Vol. III.
4. Quoted in A. O. Aldridge, *Shaftesbury and the Deist Manifesto,* p. 373, from Benjamin Ibbott, *A Course of Sermons . . .* (1727). (Delivered in 1713-1714.)
5. *Essays on the Characteristics,* p. 6.
6. *The Third Earl of Shaftesbury,* p. 184.
7. *Ibid.,* pp. 184 f.
8. Quoted in Ennemond Casati, "Hérauts et Commentateurs de Shaftesbury en France," *Revue de Litterature Comparée,* XIV (1934), 623. Cf. Leibniz, *Philosophical Papers and Letters,* ed. Leroy Loemker, II, 1023.
9. *Bibliothèque Choisie,* ed. Jean Le Clerc (Amsterdam, 1709), XIX, 429.
10. *Life, Letters,* p. 504.
11. *Tripos; in Three Discourses,* Disc. I, Ch. ix, Sect. 13.
12. *The Platonic Renaissance in England,* p. 179.
13. *Essays on the Characteristics,* p. 2.
14. *Life, Letters,* p. 449.
15. *Letters to a Young Man,* p. 9.
16. *Ibid.,* p. 19.
17. A striking parallel to contemporary "McCarthyism"!
18. *Life, Letters,* p. 353.
19. Cf. Henry More, *Enthusiasmus Triumphatus,* p. 16.

20. *Life, Letters*, p. 353.
21. *Ibid.* (1706).
22. *Supra*, Ch. VII.

NOTES: CHAPTER IX

1. Henry Sidgwick, *Outlines of the History of Ethics* (London: Macmillan and Co., Ltd., 1949), p. 190.
2. *Ibid.*, p. 184.
3. Cf. J. A. Passmore, *Ralph Cudworth* (Cambridge: Cambridge Univ. Press, 1951), pp. 99 f.
4. *The Eighteenth Century Background*, p. 68.
5. *Life, Letters*, p. 414.
6. The importance of this is suggested by Lovejoy's statement that "the first great revolt against the neo-classical aesthetics was not in literature at all, but in gardening. . . ." A. O. Lovejoy, *Essays in the History of Ideas* (New York: G. P. Putnam's Sons, 1960), p. 240. The dialogue of Philocles and Theocles in "The Moralists" is set, significantly, in the country.
7. *Life, Letters*, pp. 403 f.; Shaftesbury was not satisfied that Locke's concept of the state of Nature avoided the difficulties of Hobbes's theory. (See *Life, Letters*, p. 415.)
8. *Supra*, Ch. I.
9. *Life, Letters*, p. 150 (PR).
10. *Ibid.*
11. *Ibid.*, p. 443.
12. *Select Sermons*, p. xxvi.
13. *Life, Letters*, p. 5 (PR).
14. Though both passages refer in context to Christ's sacrifice, they have a larger significance.
15. *Life, Letters*, p. 17 (PR).
16. *Ibid.*, pp. 158 f. (PR)
17. *Ibid.*, pp. 159 f. (PR).
18. *Ibid.*, p. 180 (PR).
19. *Ibid.*, p. 2 (PR).
20. *Ibid.*, p. 3 (PR).
21. *Ibid.*, p. 145 (PR).
22. E.g., Esther Tiffany, "Shaftesbury as Stoic," *op. cit.*
23. *Life, Letters*, pp. 1 f. (PR). Cf. *Char.* I, 27 f.

NOTES: CHAPTER X

1. A fuller discussion of pleasure and its relationship to happiness follows in Ch. XIII.
2. *Life, Letters*, p. 340.
3. Cf. Henry Sidgwick, *op. cit.*, p. 187, n. 1.

4. Shaftesbury refers to these without elaboration. In his revision of the *Inquiry* for the 1711 edition, he cut out some references to sexual practices and shortened his treatment of sexual indulgence. See A. O. Aldridge, "Two Versions of Shaftesbury's *Inquiry Concerning Virtue*," *op. cit.*

5. Francis Hutcheson, *An Inquiry Concerning the Original of our Ideas of Virtue or Moral Good*, in *British Moralists*, ed. L. A. Selby-Bigge (New York: The Bobbs-Merrill Co., Inc., 1964), I, 88.

6. *Ibid.*, I, 125.

7. Lester Crocker fails to recognize this difference between Shaftesbury and Hutcheson. *An Age of Crisis* (Baltimore: The Johns Hopkins Press, 1959), p. 332.

8. George M. Trevelyan, *History of England*, 3 vols. (Garden City, N. Y.: Doubleday and Co., Inc., 1952), II, 260.

9. *Life, Letters*, p. 300.

10. *A Treatise of the Laws of Nature*, trans. by John Maxwell (London, 1727), p. 16.

11. *Ibid.*, p. 233.

12. *Life, Letters*, p. 107 (PR).

13. *Ibid.*, p. 133; the quotation is from Epictetus, *Disc.* iii, 4, 10.

14. *Life, Letters*, p. 103 (PR).

15. *Letters . . . to Robert Molesworth*, p. vii.

16. *Life, Letters*, p. 341.

17. *Ibid.*, p. 4 (PR).

NOTES: CHAPTER XI

1. See Ch. VIII for a discussion of the question of whether atheism should be restricted by law.

2. Though Tillotson's uneasiness about the doctrine is revealed in his sermon of 1690, in which he argues that God would not be breaking His word if He did not actually carry out his threat of *eternal* punishment for the wicked.

3. For examples of preaching on rewards and punishment, see Francis Atterbury, *Sermons and Discourses* (London, 1740).

4. For a detailed study of changes in the conception of hell and of related doctrines, see D. P. Walker, *The Decline of Hell: Seventeenth-Century Discussions of Eternal Torment*. Walker points out the important role that Origen's ideas had in stimulating criticism of the traditional doctrines, and it is significant that Shaftesbury rates Origen as the best of the Church Fathers (*Letters to a Young Man*, p. 28).

5. *A Demonstration of the Divine Authority of the Law of Nature and of the Christian Religion* (London, 1681), p. 64.

6. Ronald Knox, *Enthusiasm*, p. 339.

7. "The Recompense of the Reward," (Sept., 1698) in *Sermons Preached Upon Several Occasions* (London, 1845) I, 345–355.

8. Fuller discussion of Day's argument may be found in A. O. Aldridge, *Shaftesbury and the Deist Manifesto*, pp. 305–307, and his article, "Shaftesbury's Earliest Critic," *Modern Philology*, XLIV (1946), 10–22.
9. *Letters to a Young Man*, p. 37; also p. 44.
10. For an example of this in Berkeley, see D. P. Walker, *op. cit.*, pp. 176 f.
11. *Select Sermons*, p. xxviii.
12. *Ibid.*, p. xxx.
13. *Ibid.*, p. xxxi.
14. *The Decline of Hell*, p. 41.
15. *Letters to a Young Man*, p. 19.
16. *Life, Letters*, p. 75 (PR).
17. *Ibid.*, p. 347.
18. See Ch. XIII.
19. *Op. cit.*

NOTES: CHAPTER XII

1. *The Moral Sense*, pp. 16 f.
2. *Divine Dialogues* (London, 1713), pp. 146 f. In his article, "The Origins of the Moral Sense," published in *The Huntington Library Quarterly*, XI (1948), 241–259, Ernest Tuveson points to some interesting similarities between the arguments used in Shaftesbury's "Inquiry" and three pamphlets by Thomas Burnet, two published in 1697 and one in 1699. He suggests that Shaftesbury may have been influenced by Burnet. See also Tuveson's chapter on "The Origin of the 'Moral Sense'" in *The Imagination as a Means of Grace* (Berkeley: Univ. of California Press, 1960), ch. ii. While Burnet uses the term "Natural Conscience" rather than "moral sense," he believes, like Shaftesbury, that man has a natuural ability to discriminate between right and wrong, that this discrimination can be immediate—without any process of discursive reasoning. His criticisms of Locke are also similar to those made by Shaftesbury. Tuveson questions the dating of the original publication of the *Inquiry* as 1699, suggesting it may have been later. However, A. O. Aldridge, in "Two Versions of Shaftesbury's *Inquiry Concerning Virtue*," *op. cit.*, pp. 207 214, reports having examined a copy of the 1699 edition in the British Museum and presents other evidence that the "Inquiry" was circulated in manuscript form before that. The fourth Earl claims that his father wrote a rough draft of it when he was twenty (i.e., 1690–1691; *Life, Letters*, p. xxiii). In that case, it is at least possible that Burnet was influenced by Shaftesbury rather than the reverse. It should be added that Shaftesbury refers directly to Burnet's *Archeologiae philosophicae sive doctrina antiqua de rerum originibus* (1692) and categorizes him as one of the "most learned

and eminent divines of our own church," (*Char.* I, 231) though this particular book was violently attacked by many churchmen.

3. II, 41–46, 53 f.; also see "Moral Sense" in "Index," Vol. III.
4. See *Char.* I, 251–267.
5. I do not know why Tuveson says that Hutcheson's contribution was "to invent the phrase 'moral sense' " (*The Imagination as a Means of Grace*, p. 54).
6. James Bonar, *Moral Sense* (New York: The Macmillan Company, 1930), p. 43.
7. Cited in F. J. Powicke, *The Cambridge Platonists* (London: J. M. Dent and Sons, Ltd., 1926), p. 62.
8. *Life, Letters*, p. 403; Locke made a slight concession to such a view as Shaftesbury holds. See *An Essay Concerning Human Understanding*, ed. A. C. Fraser (New York: Dover Publications, Inc., 1959), I, 72, n. 1.
9. *Life, Letters*, p. 403.
10. *Ibid.*, p. 414.
11. *Ibid.*, p. 415.
12. Edward Hooker distorts Shaftesbury's views by attributing to him the belief that taste is "a faculty sprung full-blown from the brow of gentility, without pain or labor. . . ." (*The Critical Works of John Dennis*, II, lxxviii).
13. *Letters to a Young Man*, p. 35.
14. *Ibid.*, p. 27.
15. *Second Characters*, p. 114.
16. Sect. 1.
17. *Ibid.*
18. *Ibid.*
19. *Second Characters*, pp. 177 f.
20. J. A. Passmore suggests that Shaftesbury's use of the term "factitious" in this sense is evidence that he was familiar with the ms. of Cudworth's *Eternal and Immutable Morality*. (See *Ralph Cudworth*, p. 98.)
21. See Arthur N. Prior, *Logic and the Basis of Ethics* (Oxford: Oxford Univ. Press, 1949), p. 22. Prior restates Shaftesbury's argument thus: "We cannot, in short, infer 'We ought to do X' from 'We have promised to do X,' unless we also grant the ethical proposition 'We ought to keep promises,' and for this latter, no non-ethical substitutes, such as 'We have promised to keep our promises,' will do."
22. *Life, Letters*, p. 416.
23. *Ibid.*, p. 404; cf. pp. 414–416.
24. See R. S. Crane, "Suggestions Toward a Genealogy of the Man of Feeling," *ELH*, I (1934), 205–230.
25. Quoted by R. S. Crane in a review of an article by W. E. Alderman, *Philological Quarterly*, XI (1932), 206.
26. *The Platonic Renaissance in England*, p. 124.
27. *Letters to a Young Man*, p. 43.

28. *Enchiridion Ethicum,* trans. by Edward Southwell, facsimile of ed. of 1690 (New York: The Facsimile Text Society, 1930), pp. ix–x.
29. *Ibid.,* pp. 28–31.
30. *Ibid.,* pp. 6 f.
31. *Letters to a Young Man,* p. 32; cf. *Char.* I, 180.
32. Harald Höffding, *A History of Modern Philosophy,* trans. by B. E. Meyer, 2 vols. (New York: The Humanities Press, 1950), I, 393.
33. Another eighteenth-century critic, Bolingbroke, charged the advocates of "moral sense" with being "enthusiasts in ethics" who deny the need for reason in discovering the laws of Nature, and believe that we can instinctively perceive the difference between good and evil "without the trouble of observation and reflection." *The Works of Henry St. John, Lord Viscount Bolingbroke,* 5 vols. (London, 1754), V, Fragment 6, p. 86.
34. *Rousseau and Romanticism* (Boston: Houghton Mifflin Co., 1919), p. 45.
35. Thomas Fowler, *op. cit.,* p. 71. More recently, Ernest Tuveson has stated that "Shaftesbury seems to eliminate the reason altogether. . . ." ("The Origins of the Moral Sense," *op. cit.,* p. 258).
36. I can't wholly agree with Bernard Peach that Shaftesbury does not differentiate between "conscience" and the "moral sense." Conscience would, of course, be distinguished by having a narrower sphere of application—particularly one's own thoughts and behavior. But there is also the implication that conscience is a somewhat more complex reflective process that presupposes the moral sense. See his article on Shaftesbury, *Encyclopedia of Morals,* ed. Vergilius Ferm (New York: Philosophical Library, 1956), pp. 107–114.
37. *Rousseau and Romanticism,* p. 45.
38. Bernard Mandeville, *The Fable of the Bees, op. cit.,* I, 233.
39. *Life, Letters,* p. 296.
40. Francis Hutcheson, *A System of Moral Philosophy,* 2 vols. (London, 1755), I, 252.

NOTES: CHAPTER XIII

1. *Logic and the Basis of Ethics,* pp. 95–98. Prior does not quote these passages but another one (*Char.* I, 264) where Shaftesbury employs similar reasoning in criticizing the identification of "right" with the "mere will" of God.
2. *Essay Concerning Human Understanding,* II, xxviii, 5.
3. *Outlines of the History of Ethics,* p. 185, n. 1.
4. Of this more will be said subsequently.
5. *Life, Letters,* p. 116 (PR).
6. M. F. Libby, "Influence of the Idea of Aesthetic Proportion on the Ethics of Shaftesbury," *American Journal of Psychology,* XII (1901), 458–491.

NOTES: CHAPTER XIV

1. *The Platonic Renaissance*, p. 166.
2. *The Philosophy of the Enlightenment*, p. 152.
3. Shaftesbury's theory of art and artistic creation has been discussed at length by R. L. Brett, Cassirer, Ernest Tuveson, Marjorie Nicolson, and Jerome Stolnitz, in the works cited in this and other chapters. See the bibliography for details.
4. *Second Characters*, p. 105.
5. *Mountain Gloom and Mountain Glory*, ch. vii.
6. *Plotinus: On the One and Good*, trans. by S. Mackenna and B. S. Page (London: Faber and Faber, Ltd., 1930), V, 189.
7. *The Third Earl of Shaftesbury*, p. 143.
8. *The Philosophy of the Enlightenment*, p. 326; also Jerome Stolnitz, "On the Origins of 'Aesthetic Disinterestedness,'" *The Journal of Aesthetics and Art Criticism*, XX (Winter, 1961), 131–143.
9. *Second Characters*, p. 119.
10. "The Tendency Toward Platonism in Neo-Classical Esthetics," *ELH*, I (1934), 91–119.

NOTES: CHAPTER XV

1. *Pensées Diverses*, in *Oeuvres Complètes*, 7 vols. (Paris: Garnier Frères, 1879), VII, 171.
2. W. E. Hocking, quoted in *The Journal of Philosophy*, XLVIII (May 10, 1951), 325.
3. Paul Tillich, *Dynamics of Faith* (New York: Harper and Brothers, 1957), pp. 76 f.
4. *Op. cit.*, p. 1.
5. When Shaftesbury does refer to allegorical interpretation, it is likely to be in the course of an attempt to discredit the Scriptures, as, for example, in *Char.* II, 231, where he refers to Thomas Burnet's *Archeologicae philosophicae* in which an "allegorical" interpretation of the Fall was presented. Its publication in 1692 caused Burnet to lose his post as Clerk to the King. Ernest Tuveson writes that "although Burnet calls his interpretation 'allegorical,' he actually abandons the great allegorical tradition. . . . The story is a parable, and nothing more. . . . Burnet, unlike most writers of generations before him, found allegory in general unsatisfactory and uninteresting except historically." (*Millennium and Utopia*, pp. 175 f.)
6. *Essays on the Characteristics*, p. 211.
7. *Second Characters*, p. 52.
8. *Life, Letters*, p. 417 (1709).
9. *Letters to a Young Man*, p. 12.
10. *Ibid.*, p. 8.

SELECTED BIBLIOGRAPHY

I WRITINGS OF SHAFTESBURY

Select Sermons of Dr. [Benjamin] Whichcot. Ed. with Preface by Shaftesbury. 1698. (Later edition ed. William Wishart. Edinburgh, 1742.)

Characteristics of Men, Manners, Opinions, Times. 3 vols. London, 1711.

Characteristics . . . . 3 vols. 2nd ed. revised. London, 1714.

Characteristics . . . . Other editions: 1723; 1727; 1732; 1733; 1737–1738; 1743–1745; 4 vols. Glasgow, 1758; Birmingham, 1773; 1790; ed. William M. Hatch. 1 vol. only. 1870.

Characteristics . . . . Ed. John M. Robertson. 2 vols. London: Grant Richards, 1900.

Characteristics . . . . Ed. John M. Robertson. 2 vols. in one. New York: The Bobbs-Merrill Co., Inc., 1964. With a new Introduction by Stanley Grean and an expanded Index.

The *Characteristics* includes the following treatises listed here with their date of first publication:

I. "A Letter Concerning Enthusiasm," 1708.
II. "Sensus Communis; An Essay on the Freedom of Wit and Humour," 1709.
III. "Soliloquy, or Advice to an Author," 1710.
IV. "An Inquiry Concerning Virtue or Merit," 1699; revised, 1711.
V. "The Moralists, A Philosophical Rhapsody," 1709.
VI. "Miscellaneous Reflections on the Preceding Treatises, etc.," 1711.

The following are printed in some editions of the *Characteristics* although Shaftesbury originally intended them to be part of another work which he did not complete. The latter has been partially reconstructed and published as *Second Characters* (see below).

"A Notion of the Historical Draught or Tablature of the Judgement of Hercules," 1712 (French), 1713 (English). Included in the 1714 edition of *Characteristics*.

"A Letter Concerning the Art, or Science of Design." First published in the 1732 edition of *Characteristics*.

Several Letters Written by a Noble Lord to a Young Man at the University. London, 1716.

Letters from the Right Honourable the Late Earl of Shaftesbury to Robert Molesworth, Esq. Ed. John Toland. London, 1721.

Original Letters of Locke, Algernon Sidney, and Anthony Lord Shaftesbury. Ed. T. Forster. London, 1830.

The Life, Unpublished Letters, and Philosophical Regimen of Anthony, Earl of Shaftesbury. Ed. Benjamin Rand. London: Swan Sonnenschein & Co., Ltd., 1900.

Second Characters, or the Language of Forms. Ed. Benjamin Rand. Cambridge: Cambridge University Press, 1914.

Second Characters includes:

I. "A Letter Concerning Design" (see above).
II. "The Judgment of Hercules" (see above).
III. "The Picture of Cebes" (translated from the Greek).
IV. "Plastics" (uncompleted notes).

II WRITINGS RELATED TO OR ABOUT SHAFTESBURY

A *From the Seventeenth and Eighteenth Centuries*

Balguy, John. *A Letter to a Deist Concerning the Beauty and Excellency of Moral Virtue* . . . . London, 1726.

Berkeley, George. *Alciphron; or, The Minute Philosopher*. Ed. T. E. Jessop. Vol. III, 1950, of *The Works of George Berkeley, Bishop of Cloyne*. Eds. A. A. Luce and T. E. Jessop. 9 vols. London: Thomas Nelson and Sons, Ltd., 1948–1957.

Blount, Charles. *The Miscellaneous Works of Charles Blount, Esq*. London, 1695. Includes *The Oracles of Reason* by Blount *et al.*, and *Anima Mundi* by Blount.

Brown, John. *Essays on the Characteristics*. 3rd ed. London, 1752.

Bulkley, Charles. *A Vindication of My Lord Shaftesbury on the Subjects of Morality and Religion*. London, 1752.

Butler, Joseph. *The Works of Bishop Butler*. Ed. J. H. Bernard. 2 vols. London: Macmillan and Co., Ltd., 1900.
Casaubon, Meric. *A Treatise Concerning Enthusiasm As It is an Effect of Nature* . . . . 2nd ed. London, 1656.
Collins, Anthony. *A Discourse of Freethinking* . . . . London, 1713.
Cumberland, Richard. *A Treatise of the Laws of Nature*. Tr. John Maxwell. London, 1727.
Dennis, John. *The Critical Works of John Dennis*. Ed. Edward N. Hooker. 2 vols. Baltimore: The Johns Hopkins Press, 1939.
————. *The Advancement and Reformation of Modern Poetry*. London, 1701.
————. *Vice and Luxury Publick Mischiefs: or Remarks on a Book Intituled, The Fable of the Bees* . . . . London, 1724.
Fiddes, Richard. *A General Treatise of Morality* . . . . 2nd ed. London, 1726.
Harrington, James. *The Oceana and Other Works of James Harrington*, 3rd ed. London, 1747.
Histoire des Ouvrages des Savans. Review of "Letter Concerning Enthusiasm," December, 1708, Article ix.
Hutcheson, Francis. *A System of Moral Philosophy*. 2 vols. London, 1755.
Journal des Sçavans (Paris). Review of "Letter Concerning Enthusiasm," March 25, 1709, pp. 450–458; review of "An Essay on the Freedom of Wit and Humour," March 31, 1710, pp. 354–355, and April 21, 1710, pp. 446–450.
Le Clerc, Jean. Reviews of Shaftesbury's writings, *Bibliothèque Choisie* (Amsterdam), XIX (1709), pp. 427–438; XXI (1710), pp. 177–197; XXIII (1711), pp. 89–168.
Leibniz, G. W. von. *Philosophical Papers and Letters*. Ed. Leroy E. Loemker. 2 vols. Chicago: University of Chicago Press, 1956.
Leland, John. *A View of the Principal Deistical Writers* . . . . 2 vols. 3rd ed. London, 1757.
Leslie, Charles. *A Short and Easy Method with the Deists*. New York: The Protestant Episcopal Press, 1830.
Locke, John. *An Essay Concerning Human Understanding*. Ed. A. C. Fraser. 2 vols. New York: Dover Publications, Inc., 1959.
Mandeville, Bernard. *The Fable of the Bees*. Ed. F. B. Kaye. 2 vols. Oxford: The Clarendon Press, 1924.
More, Henry. *Enthusiasmus Triumphatus; or, a Brief Discourse of the Nature, Causes, Kinds, and Cure of Enthusiasm*. London, 1712. Published in *A Collection of Several Philosophical Writings of Dr. Henry More*. London, 1712.
————. *Enchiridion Ethicum*. New York: The Facsimile Text Society, 1930. Facsimile edition of translation of 1690 by Edward Southwell entitled *An Account of Virtue*.

Norris, John. *The Theory and Regulation of Love.* 2nd ed. London, 1694.

Nouvelles de la République des Lettres. Review of "An Essay on the Freedom of Wit and Humour," March, 1710; review of *Letters . . . to a Young Man at the University,* November-December, 1716.

Reflections upon a Letter Concerning Enthusiasm. . . . London, 1709. Anonymous.

Selby-Bigge, L. A. (ed.). *British Moralists.* Vols. I–II. New York: The Bobbs-Merrill Co., Inc., 1964.

Taylor, Jeremy. *A Discourse of Friendship.* Cedar Rapids, Iowa: Privately printed, 1913.

Tindal, Matthew. *Christianity as old as the Creation: or the Gospel a Republication of the Religion of Nature.* London, 1730.

Toland, John. *Christianity Not Mysterious.* . . . London, 1696.

Traherne, Thomas. *Christian Ethicks.* New York: Kings Crown Press, 1942.

Warburton, William. *The Divine Legation of Moses Demonstrated.* Vol. I. London, 1766.

B　*From the Nineteenth and Twentieth Centuries*

Albee, Ernest. "The Relation of Shaftesbury and Hutcheson to Utilitarianism," *Philosophical Review,* V (1896), 24–35.

———. Review of *Second Characters* (ed. Rand), *Philosophical Review,* XXV (1916), 182–187.

———. Review of *The Life, Unpublished Letters, and Philosophical Regimen of . . . Shaftesbury* (ed. Rand), *Philosophical Review,* XII (1903), 451–452.

Alderman, William E. "Shaftesbury and the Doctrine of Benevolence in the Eighteenth Century," *Transactions of the Wisconsin Academy of Sciences, Arts, and Letters,* XXVI (1931), 137–159.

———. "Shaftesbury and the Doctrine of Moral Sense in the Eighteenth Century," *Publications of the Modern Language Association,* XLVI (1931), 1087–1094.

———. "Bibliographical Evidence of the Vogue of Shaftesbury in the Eighteenth Century," *Transactions of the Wisconsin Academy of Sciences, Arts, and Letters,* XXI (1926), 57–70.

———. "Shaftesbury and the Doctrine of Optimism," *Transactions of the Wisconsin Academy of Sciences, Arts, and Letters,* XXVIII (1933), 297–305.

———. "The Significance of Shaftesbury in English Speculation," *Publications of the Modern Language Association,* XXXVIII (1923), 175–195.

——. "The Style of Shaftesbury," *Modern Language Notes*, XXXVIII (1923), 209–215.

Aldridge, Alfred O. *Shaftesbury and the Deist Manifesto. Transactions of the American Philosophical Society*, Vol. XLI, Part II. Philadelphia: The American Philosophical Society, 1951.

——. "Shaftesbury and Bolingbroke," *Philological Quarterly*, XXXI (1952), 1–16.

——. "Henry Needler's Knowledge of Shaftesbury," *Modern Language Notes*, LXII (1947), 264–267.

——. "Shaftesbury's Earliest Critic," *Modern Philology*, XLIV (1946), 10–22.

——. "Lord Shaftesbury's Literary Theories," *Philological Quarterly*, XXIV (1945), 46–64.

——. "Shaftesbury and the Test of Truth," *Publications of the Modern Language Association*, LX (1945), 129–156.

——. "Shaftesbury, Christianity, and Friendship," *Anglican Theological Review*, XXXII (1950), 121–136.

——. "Two Versions of Shaftesbury's *Inquiry Concerning Virtue*," *Huntington Library Quarterly*, XIII (1949–1950), 207–214.

Bilsky, Manuel. Review of Brett, *The Third Earl of Shaftesbury*, *Ethics*, LXII (1952), 230–231.

Bonar, James. *Moral Sense*. New York: The Macmillan Company, 1930.

Bredvold, Louis. "The Tendency Toward Platonism in Neoclassical Esthetics," *Journal of English Literary History*, I (1934), 91–119.

Brett, R. L. *The Third Earl of Shaftesbury*. London: Hutchinson's University Library, 1951.

——. Review of A. O. Aldridge, *Shaftesbury and the Deist Manifesto*, *The Review of English Studies*, IV (1953), 78–79.

Casati, Ennemond. "Hérauts et Commentateurs de Shaftesbury en France," *Revue de Littérature Comparée*, XIV (1934), 615–645.

——. "Quelques Correspondants Français de Shaftesbury," *Revue de Littérature Comparée*, XI (1931), 219–236.

Cassirer, Ernst. *The Philosophy of the Enlightenment*. Trs. F. Koelln and J. Pettegrove. Princeton: Princeton University Press, 1951.

——. *The Platonic Renaissance in England*. Tr. James P. Pettegrove. Edinburgh: Thomas Nelson and Sons, Ltd., 1953.

Colie, Rosalie L. *Light and Enlightenment: A Study of the Cambridge Platonists and the Dutch Arminians*. Cambridge: Cambridge University Press, 1957.

Courtines, Leo P. *Bayle's Relations with England and the English*. New York: Columbia University Press, 1938.

Crane, R. S. "Suggestions Toward a Genealogy of the Man of Feeling," *ELH*, I (1934), 205–230.

Crane, R. S. Reviews of two articles by W. E. Alderman on Shaftesbury, *Philological Quarterly*, XI (1932), 204–206.

Fowler, Thomas. *Shaftesbury and Hutcheson.* New York: G. P. Putnam's Sons, 1883.

Grean, Stanley. "Self-Interest and Public Interest in Shaftesbury's Philosophy," *Journal of the History of Philosophy*, II (April, 1964), 37–45.

Knox, Ronald A. *Enthusiasm: A Chapter in the History of Religion with Special Reference to the Seventeenth and Eighteenth Centuries.* Oxford: The Clarendon Press, 1951.

Leroy, André-Louis. Review of Brett, *The Third Earl of Shaftesbury*, *Revue Philosophique*, CXLIII (1953), 270–271.

Lovejoy, Arthur O. *Essays in the History of Ideas.* New York: Capricorn Books, G. P. Putnam's Sons, 1960.

———. *The Great Chain of Being.* New York: Harper Torchbooks, Harper and Brothers, 1960.

———. "Optimism and Romanticism," *Publications of the Modern Language Association*, XLII (1927), 921–945.

Lovejoy, Arthur O. and Boas, George. *Primitivism and Related Ideas in Antiquity.* Vol. I or *A Documentary History of Primitivism and Related Ideas.* Ed. A. O. Lovejoy, G. Chinard, G. Boas and R. S. Crane. Baltimore: The Johns Hopkins Press, 1935.

MacDonald, Margaret. Review of Brett, *The Third Earl of Shaftesbury*, *Mind*, LXII (1953), 417–418.

Marsh, Robert. *Four Dialectical Theories of Poetry.* Chicago: University of Chicago Press, 1965.

———. "Shaftesbury's Theory of Poetry: The Importance of the 'Inward Colloquy,'" *ELH*, XXVIII (March 1961), 54–69.

Moore, C. A. "Shaftesbury and the Ethical Poets in England, 1700–1760," *Publications of the Modern Language Association*, XXXI (1916), 264–325.

Nicolson, Marjorie. *Mountain Gloom and Mountain Glory: The Development of the Aesthetics of the Infinite.* Ithaca, N. Y.: Cornell University Press, 1959.

Passmore, John A. *Ralph Cudworth.* Cambridge: Cambridge University Press, 1951.

Peach, Bernard. Article, "Shaftesbury," *Encyclopedia of Morals.* Ed. Vergilius Ferm. New York: Philosophical Library, 1956. pp. 107–114.

———. "Shaftesbury's Moral 'Arithmeticks,'" *The Personalist*, XXXIX (1958), 19–27.

Powicke, Frederick J. *The Cambridge Platonists.* London: J. M. Dent and Sons, Ltd., 1926.

Raphael, David D. *The Moral Sense.* London: Oxford University Press, 1947.

Schlegel, Dorothy B. *Shaftesbury and the French Deists.* Chapel Hill, N. C.: University of North Carolina Press, 1956.

Sidgwick, Henry. *Outlines of the History of Ethics.* London: Macmillan and Co., Ltd., 1949.

Smith, James Ward. "The British Moralists and the Fallacy of Psychologism," *Journal of the History of Ideas,* XI (1950), 159–178.

Stephen, Leslie. *History of English Thought in the Eighteenth Century.* 2 vols. New York and London: G. P. Putnam's Sons, 1902.

Stolnitz, Jerome. "On the Significance of Lord Shaftesbury in Modern Aesthetic Theory," *Philosophical Quarterly,* XI (April 1961), 97–113.

———. "On the Origins of 'Aesthetic Disinterestedness,'" *The Journal of Aesthetics and Art Criticism,* XX (Winter 1961), 131–143.

Tiffany, Esther. "Shaftesbury as Stoic," *Publications of the Modern Language Association,* XXXVIII (1923), 642–684.

Tulloch, John. *Rational Theology and Christian Philosophy in England in the Seventeenth Century.* 2 vols. 2nd ed. Edinburgh: W. Blackwood, 1874.

Tuveson, Ernest. *Millennium and Utopia: a Study in the Background of the Idea of Progress.* Berkeley: University of California Press, 1949.

———. *The Imagination as a Means of Grace: Locke and the Aesthetics of Romanticism.* Berkeley: University of California Press, 1960.

———. "The Origins of the Moral Sense," *Huntington Library Quarterly,* XI (1947–1948), 241–259.

———. "The Importance of Shaftesbury," *ELH,* XX (1953), 267–299.

Walker, D. P. *The Decline of Hell: Seventeenth-Century Discussions of Eternal Torment.* Chicago: University of Chicago Press, 1964.

Whitaker, S. F. "Pierre Coste et Shaftesbury," *Revue de Littérature Comparée,* XXV (1951), 241–253.

Willey, Basil. *The Eighteenth Century Background.* London: Chatto and Windus, 1953.

———. *The Seventeenth Century Background.* New York: Anchor Books, Doubleday and Co., Inc., 1953.

———. *The English Moralists.* London: Methuen and Co., Ltd., 1965.

INDEX